the
MASKS
of
PLAY

*B*RIAN SUTTON-SMITH, PH.D.
*D*IANA KELLY-BYRNE, PH.D.

D1414527

LEISURE PRESS

NEW YORK

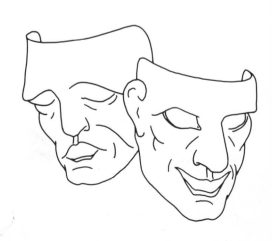

ACKNOWLEDGMENTS

We wish to thank Jeanne Cannizzo, James F. Christie, Robert Fagen and Roberta J. Park for their help and advice in selecting the articles for this issue of the Conference Proceedings of The Association for the Anthropological Study of Play. The Conference was held in London, Ontario in March of 1982.

A publication of
Leisure Press
597 Fifth Avenue; New York, N.Y. 10017

Library of Congress Catalog Number: 83-80745

ISBN: 0-88011-208-5

Cover and book design: Robin Terra
Mask illustration: John Jett
Production: Kate Back
Typesetting: Lewis Publishing

CONTENTS

part *one*

FESTIVAL PLAY

part **two**

ADULT RECREATION AND GAMES

part **three**

CHILD'S PLAY

part *four*

ANIMAL PLAY

part *five*

THEORY OF HUMAN PLAY

part *six*

CONCLUSION

PREFACE

The Association for the Anthropological Study of Play has throughout its eight year history brought together a diverse group of scholars to report their research on the nature of play. Some have focussed on play in festivals, others on adult play, child play, play in literature, play in history, play amongst non-literate tribes, play in humor, speech play, animal play, metaphoric play, play in sports, play and ritual, ritual and sports, games, play in recreation and leisure, play in work.

Throughout all this innovative activity, the term play has been applied to many phenomena, to many kinds of research, kinds of scholarship and kinds of theory. In this present volume we will use the sample of papers available to us from the Eighth Conference of the Society which was held in London, Ontario, in March of 1982 to pursue the issue of what play really is. To this end we have titled this book *THE MASKS OF PLAY* to stand for the elusive nature of the quarry and the various ways it both defies definition and passes itself off under other guises. We must ask the question whether play is masked by the culture for specific reasons or whether in its own nature it always bears this readiness for disguise.

part *one*

FESTIVAL PLAY

INTRODUCTION

In this group of six papers we deal with festive occasions around the world, from Mexico, India, Africa, Toronto, Minnesota, Berkeley, and the Sinai Peninsula. Perhaps it is absurd to attempt to find what these festive occasions have in common, yet it is difficult to resist the modern intuition that they are all in some ways "playful." At least they are all different from the other kinds of events such as economic, political, or familial, that take place in those societies.

The first two papers cover four different societies, the Tarahumara of Mexico, the Santal of East India, the Bo of Sierra Leone and the Mende of the Sierra Leone. These four groups have festivals that are different from the others to be described because their societies are all largely traditional rather than modern. Usually, in traditional societies, membership and participation in festivals or other customary behaviours is expected of all those of the proper age and sex. Choice is not the most important consideration as to whether one attends or not. In the modern festivals however, choice is an essential part of participation. It is because these are defined as leisure events that most people are there. The Canadian Toronto Caribana is an in-between case, because here groups from the West Indies are introducing the spirit of their own homeland festivals into the Canadian way of life. In the Minnesota festivals of the towns of Foley and Glenwood, and in the historical description of changing student responses to athletics in the University of California, we reacquaint ourselves with a kind of festival of which most of us have some direct knowledge. In the last paper, however — an account of how the hippies conducted themselves with nakedness and fornication at an oasis on the Aqaba Gulf with perplexing consequences for their hosts, the Mzeian Bedouin — we are dealing with behavior which has some "festive" character for the hippies, but which could hardly be called a festival either for them or for the Bedouin. Still, it is instructive as an example of how in modern times, festivals which were once traditional, common and fixed in location and season, have become so differentiated by individual choice, that one must often point to behavior that is "festive" rather than to festivals as such. Yet there is still a remarkable continuity between the beer drinking carousing of the Tarahumara high in the Sierra Madres, the annual festival of sexual license amongst the Santal of East India and the motives that have brought the hippies to the Gulf of Aqaba.

chapter 1

THE SOCIAL STRUCTURING OF EXPRESSIVE ACTIVITIES IN TWO CULTURES

Finnegan Alford
Cameron University, Oklahoma

The tradition in anthropology has been to explain expressive or play behaviors with reference to their positive functions (either for the culture, society, or individual). Expressive behavior, however, is not necessarily functional (on any of these levels). In fact, much expressive or play behavior can be quite dysfunctional, both for the society and for the individual. In order to avert this dysfunctional potential, societies channel or structure expressive behavior. This structuring may take the form of restricting the time, place, and/or persons who may engage in any particular form of expressive behavior.

This paper considers the central or most popular expressive activity in two pre-industrial, pre-literate societies: the beer or tesguino complex among the Tarahumara Indians of Mexico, and an annual festival of sexual license, the Sohrae, among the Santal of eastern India. Each of these expressive activities is interpreted in terms of the social structuring of expressive license; i.e., how is such expressive activity structured or channeled in order to avoid its dysfunctional potential and to enhance societal and individual benefits.

This paper is a preliminary report based upon a larger study in progress of the social structuring of expressive license and behavior in a sample of sixty world-wide societies (Naroll's Probability Sample File).

The Tarahumara Indians' beer parties have been studied by Kennedy (1978) and Bennett and Zingg (1935). These Indians live high in the Western Sierra Madres in Chihuahua, Mexico. They live on narrow shelves of land, up and down steep canyons, with one to six homesteads per shelf. The Tarahumara cultivate corn, beans and squash, and tend flocks of goats. The household is the minimal social unit, and besides the tesguino (or beer) network, it is the most important social unit. The focus of these studies is the Inapuchi community, least affected by modernization.

One of the outstanding features of this society is the remoteness and isolation they experience. These individuals may go days or even weeks without interacting with Tarahumara beyond their households. Kennedy (1978) characterizes the Tarahumara as a shy, stoic, withdrawn, but dignified people.

At the center of the tesguino or beer complex is the mild, nourishing maize beer whose origin predates Spanish contact. Kennedy (Ibid.) states: "Beer and beer parties are basic to the social life of the community. . . They are highly valued as one of the few means of communal gathering, recreation and social intercourse." In fact, "the tesguino complex/network constitutes the underlying community structure throughout the Tarahumara region" (Kennedy, 1978, p. 125).

Individuals always drink in groups, and never alone. Beer is consumed in large quantities on two kinds of occasions: at work bees and at ritual occasions. An important aspect of their economic system is the cooperative tradition whereby members of the groups of households in the canyons have reciprocal obligations to supply labor when tasks are difficult or when they are too tedious to do alone. Tesguino is considered sufficient pay for labor and the long difficult trips made from homestead to homestead. What constitutes a beer party/work bee? Weeding is a good example. The host makes the tesguino. When it is ready, in about a week, he invites people from the surrounding ranchos for the party. The emphasis in the invitation is on the sociability of the occasion rather than the work. While men do the outside work, women talk, play, drink beer, and prepare food. Kennedy describes: "weeding time is a period of great euphoria." People "laugh drunkenly as they work" (Kennedy, 1978, p. 63). Often, they have a round of such weeding parties moving from rancho to rancho, leaving the children at home. At harvest, they again hold a series of beer parties.

Tesguino is also an integral part of almost all rituals. Each religious fiesta is followed by a large tesguinada which may last up to 48 hours. In fact, "all of the ritual activities of the Inapuchi community take place at tesguinadas which rotate from rancho to rancho" (Ibid., p. 116). "The tesguinada is the fundamental social gathering" (Ibid.).

The Tarahumaras say that to make tesguino one must have a purpose and rarely do they make it without some practical rationalization. This results in tesguinadas at least once a week. Overall, when making rounds of beer parties, people try consciously not to schedule parties at the same time, because this wastes beer and energy. During winter there are fewer tesguinadas; time is spent resting, and engaging in less social leisure activities.

Who attends these beer parties? Only adults of both sexes attend and participate in the drinking. The tesguino network constitutes the most significant social group aside from the household. These networks are sets of people defined by reciprocal tesguinada invitations. They form a real, meaningful community for each person or household unit. Network personnel vary by proximity. Thus, a tesguino network consists of most of the surrounding ranchos with some groups overlapping. The average number of households involved in a tesguino network is seventeen. But these are very flexible networks because people frequently move up and down the canyons, establishing different sets of neighbors, during the year, as well as over the years. Not all people are involved in these networks. Participation at beer parties is by specific invitation only. When a person is considered to be too violent or disruptive, he/she is not invited. This is a very effective form of social control, because all significant social activities outside the household are carried out in the context of the tesguinada.

The tesguinada, then, is a relatively short period of intense social interaction. The usual peaceful silence of the homestead is broken by drunken playing of violins, shouting, singing, joking and sexual horseplay, fighting, and illicit sex. At a tesguinada a person plays out roles which are usually dormant. For example, men give sermons, make deals for animals or corn, hold religious ceremonies and foot races, search for mates, or at the least, have varied sexual adventures. In fact, it appears to provide almost the only opportunity for releasing aggressive and sexual feelings. An impressive range of expressive activities occurs at these parties: sex, mock fighting, games and races, ribald joking, music, singing, dancing and feasting.

When participants are queried, they express a conscious desire to get drunk. It is a peak experience for them. Some say they are happiest when they are drunk. Informants claim their aim is to achieve "a beautiful intoxication" (Bennett and Zingg, p. 161). Drunken people are said to "weep with delight because they are so perfectly happy." The individuals become a good-natured jolly, silly group out for a good time, and familiarity becomes almost unlimited. In everyday life they are chaste, timid and puritanical, but when they drink there is a kind of licensed promiscuity, particularly among the women. These fiestas provide the main opportunities for courting, as well as discreet premarital and extramarital sex. Everyday norms are suspended while people are allowed to play alternate roles.

There are no special rules restricting behavior while the people are drinking, but sometimes sanctions may be imposed for very indiscreet sex, or excessive violence. Aggression is common, and people do not remember committing their drunken acts of violence. No one is blamed for these actions, nor is there a feeling of guilt.

How central is the tesguino complex? Kennedy tells us: "tesguino was part of, and prerequisite to all important activities. Conversations frequently concerned tesguinadas, and they also formed one of the dominant subjects of the dreams the Tarahumaras told me about" (p. 112). "The tesguinada is the religious group, the economic group, the entertainment group, and the group at which disputes are settled and marriages arranged" (Ibid.). And one cannot overlook the entertainment angle—the tesguinada is the prime time to joke, play, and participate in all forms of group activities. All social gatherings, whether for religious or other reasons, tend also to be parties, emphasizing gaiety and sociability. This sociability is facilitated, indeed lubricated by drinking tesguino. The tesguino complex is the most important and consistent Tarahumara social occasion.

Individuals seek intoxication frequently and seem to be happiest when they are drunk. The parties are occasions for tension release and tedium relief, providing alternate roles and novelty without responsibility. Kennedy suggests that the beer drinking complex is, in part, a psychological and social response to the isolation imposed by the mode of life in this rugged environment.

The institutionalized beer drinking reinforces obligations and social ties, enhancing the flexibility of the social system. These parties contribute to the formation of an important network, providing a stimulus for the development of a set of special social behaviors contrasting with those of daily life. Other extrinsic benefits result as well. Drinking patterns emphasize the host, group solidarity, reciprocal exchange of services and the relation of the group to the gods (to whom they offer beer). Tesguinadas bring people together to accomplish work goals. Further, tesguinades are ways of publicizing rank and power. Those men who have larger and more frequent tesguinadeas are publicizing their wealth. One can bring serious disputes to trial at tesguinadas.

There are, however, dysfunctional aspects to this drunken behavior. Each family uses all surplus corn for brewing beer, enough corn to feed a family of four for a month. Nearly 90% of all rule breaking, specifically illicit sex and assault, occurs within the context of beer parties. Sexual novelty is one of the greater rewards possible at a tesguinada, and sexual jealousy is usually the cause of fighting. While no one approves of illicit sex at these parties, it is acknowledged as commonplace, and people do not feel guilt as a result of such activities. But, remember, if one is too uncontrollable, one is not invited to any more beer parties.

There are also other, less frequent dysfunctions. Occasionally mothers with infants drunkenly roll on the child and smother it, or accidentally drop the child. People have frequent colds and pneumonia which Kennedy attributes to their habit of falling asleep on the hillside, unprotected, after a tesguinada. And rarely, someone drunkenly tumbles down a cliff.

Overall, otherwise forbidden behavior can accur in a relatively safe, neutral context, providing release for pent-up emotion. Much corn and energy is used to a seemingly non-productive end, but one must look again to the underlying importance of sociality in uniting the Tarahumaras in reciprocal networks of interaction. Beer drinking does not necessarily lead to positive functions (as we all know).

These functions are achieved by social channeling and structuring of these expressive behaviors. Important dysfunctions are averted by the temporal limitations, by the minimal social regulation of the behavior, and by the elimination of chronic troublemakers.

Data on the Santal come from Archer 1942-46. (1974) The Santal are an agricultural, cattle herding tribe of approximately 2 million people in East India. At the time of Archer's study, the Santal were the largest, most integrated tribe in East India. They were largely unaffected by either Hindu or Muslim practices. These people are known for their democratic equality. There are few differences in economic status, wealth matters little, and there are no social distinctions between various clans. A local council of headmen from various villages forms both the primary political unit and the court of appeals from village decisions.

To understand the central expressive behavior among the Santal, we first must understand their attitudes toward sexual behavior. From early youth to the onset of old age, sexual intercourse is "one of the chief ingredients in Santal happiness" (Archer, 1974, p. 222). Before marriage, it is considered the natural end of romantic love. The most important rule regarding sexual behavior is that a Santal must never have sex with a nonSantal; the same rule applies to close kin, members of one's own clan. Further, sex must always be private; if a couple is caught in the act, they are fined. Usually, the rules are followed. When serious rules of conduct are broken a bitlaha occurs, mobilizing the whole area, reinforcing the code of values. In the bitlaha the offenders are hunted like quarry, signifying the beast-like behavior of the culprits. The villagers expose the secret relationship, publicly announcing the deviants' intimacies. They sing mocking songs to shame and degrade the rulebreakers. The tribe's sense of defilement is expressed by public urination, and even defecation on the walls in the offender's village home. The suffering couple who have broken the incest or nonSantal sex rules suffer great shame as they experience the most serious sanction their society offers.

Attitudes about sex are expressed in a host of love songs, sung either privately in the forest, or openly in the village at weddings, at Sohrae festivals and other dances. Here, the division between the village and the forest is very important. The village and the forest are distinctly separate spheres of activity for the Santal. The forest is the place of secret recreation. In the forest men can talk about sex explicitly, away from women. Most importantly, the forest is the trysting place for lovers, where boys and girls meet in private, sing love songs, form attachments and have long term love affairs. Explicit sexual songs, and illicit sex are all banned in the village. Thus, to the Santal the forest remains vividly associated with early romance.

Children from the ages of 4 and 5 engage in sex play in this society. They very likely have their first sexual experiences long before puberty, and this sexual activity occurs in the forest. Once a boy and girl reach puberty and enter the romantic period, they engage in long term love affairs with fellow villagers, which last till marriage. These are serious affairs of the heart. Many last for as long as five years, but almost all will give each other up to marry the spouses picked for them by their parents.

These adolescent love affairs are regarded ambiguously by Santals. On the one hand, they are supposed to be the secret of the village youth and from an official point of view, they do not exist at all. On the other hand, every villager takes their existence for granted. What is most important is that affairs are conducted with discretion. Boys try to meet their girls at least once, if not twice a day. Meetings are usually prearranged and they do not last long. The safest, most obvious place to meet is in the forest, and a number of songs describe these secret encounters. From the day the romance begins, the young people know that family sentiment will oppose their ultimate union, so the love is only temporary. Few of the youths will flout their parents' wishes, although many suffer great emotional turmoil when they leave their young loves.

By the time a girl is 16, her parents are less inclined to let her meet her village boyfriend. Arranged marriage ends the romance and the young lovers are not to see each other again, except at the Sohrae festival. Occasionally, youths decide to flout the wishes of their parents and the village, and they choose to remain with their village lover. They may elope, or force a marriage, but in any case, everyone involved suffers a loss of dignity. The Santal think that even if it were desirable to prevent these love affairs, they could not. So public opinion leans toward two objectives: to maintain the love affairs on a secret basis, and to insist that such affairs end at marriage. Usually these objectives are met. But when young love proves too strong, the Santal reluctantly allow the young to have their way, although they neither admire nor encourage this. It is much preferred that parents arrange out-village marriages so one can start life in a new village, with a new family and be free of earlier entanglements. Couples are expected to maintain conjugal fidelity with the one important exception of the Sohrae festival. At the annual festival, married daughters return to their parents, brew rice beer, forget chores and for one week they may disregard the code of conjugal fidelity. The festival adds excitement to the marital state, offering sexual variety. The festival is most important for newlyweds, because during the early years of marriage, it is the loss of a girl's village lover which most upsets the young wife. At the Sohrae festival she is free to meet him again. Even if her husband is present, a girl is not deterred from seeking out her friend.

Indeed, the participants in the Sohrae festival are predominantly young newlyweds. Once a woman has a child, she begins to feel more a part of her husband's family, and when she has two or more children she will seldom change partners at the Sohrae. However, when people are much older, they often exchange partners as a joke. Married men tend to range more widely and even old men enjoy this week of sexual license.

While the Sohrae involves many public rituals of animal sacrifice to petition village spirts, bless cows and put the world in order, there is also much merrymaking. Songs, dances, and good humor flow. Some songs stress the importance of successful, long term marriages. Others, however, deal with the ways of lovers. They provide a running commentary on what is happening behind the scenes, as girls and boys encourage and chase each other, and husbands and wives avoid each other. In fact, in some of these songs marriage itself is mocked and brides are jokingly consoled. According to Archer there is "an air of laughing relaxation, modest fun and sportive daring" (Ibid., p. 205). During each evening lovers are reunited. When the festival ends, lovers part, returning to their spouses and relatively happy and stable marriages.

Thus, among the Santal, sex, the main expressive behavior, is restricted spatially to the forest, the private romantic sphere. Temporally, the freest sex is available to the young under 16 years, and once a year, to everyone theoretically, at the Sohrae festival. So sexual behavior is temporally structured over the life cycle as well as calendrically. The Sohrae festival functions as a carefully demarcated "licensed occasion" when ordinary rules are suspended. It is the younger boys and girls, and occasionally old people, who make the most of the relaxed norms. What are the benefits of this behavior? The tensions, frustrations, and disappointments of a broken love affair can be fortgotten for this week every year. One can return to a prior love and freely experience great pleasure in this meeting, with no penalty, no responsibility. It is temporally and spatially controlled, so the love affair cannot "go too far." At the same time, tensions and frustrations can be eased.

The costs of this behavior, as structured, appear to be few. Yearly meetings no doubt continue to remind people of their broken love affairs, sentimentalizing youth at the expense of age, and roman-ticizing the forest, which becomes a highly charged environment compared to the village. And if the young love becomes too strong, the couple can force their marriage on the village, even though all lose face. So the initial opportunities to meet can cause disruption to the society, but the majority of youths do not let love affairs disrupt the village, nor, apparently, their subsequent marriages. The Sohrae is an attempt to mix sexuality from a past highly charged relationship with a denial of long term romantic entanglement. People are allowed to indulge in play with no responsibility, to act out fantasies and pent up desires. "More than many people, infact, the Santals seem able to make the most of sex without destroying its finer aspects" (Archer, 1974, p. 225).

In every society, expressive behavior has both a functional and dysfunctional potential. Expressive behavior must be socially channeled and regulated if it is to have a positive functional value, and important dysfunctions are to be averted. A primary strategy in the social regulation of expressive behavior is to structure expressive license temporally, spatially, and/or according to social role. This structuring, then, is the focus of our larger study, a study in which the beer drinking of the Tarahumara and the sexual festivals of the Santal form two of sixty cases.

REFERENCES

Archer, W.G. *The hills of flutes: Life, love and poetry in tribal India.* Pittsburgh: University of Pittsburgh Press, 1974.

Bennett, Wendell C. and Robert M. Zingg. *Tarahumara: An Indian tribe of northern Mexico.* Rio Grande, 1935.

Kennedy, John G. *Tarahumara of the Sierra Madre, ecology and social organization.* AHM Publ., 1978.

chapter 2

PLAY, PERFORMANCE AND SOCIAL COMMENTARY:
THE ALIKALI DEVILS OF SIERRA LEONE

Jeanne Cannizzo
University of Western Ontario

The culture of childhood, where children inhabit a "self-regulating, autonomous world which does not necessarily reflect early developments of adult culture" (Hardman 1973:87), has been the subject of a small but growing number of anthropological investigations. However, it has been Robert Mackay who has most clearly linked the culture of childhood with concepts of children and models of socialization[1]. He rejects the adult assumption upon which most definitions of socialization rest—*i.e.* that the child is an incomplete being, unable to interpret his or her universe. He suggests instead that children *are* competent interpreters of the social world and that they possess a separate culture(s). Thus, "the study of adult-child interaction (formerly socialization) becomes substantively the study of cultural assimilation and theoretically the study of meaningful social interaction" (1974:184).

By comparing the masquerades of urban schoolboys in Bo, Sierra Leone, with those of rural Mende boys in the village of Torwama, this process of cultural assimilation can be examined. In the first instance it occurs within the culture of childhood through the peer group and in the second, it is product of encouragement by men and older youths taking place within the adult realm. The modes of interaction in these two arenas are as distinctive as the masquerades with which they are associated. The explanation of these differences lies in the changing set of identities and structures found in urban society in Sierra Leone.

On the major Muslim and Christian holidays, groups of boys in Bo, a town of 40,000 in central Sierra Leone, parade and perform on the streets with their *devils* or masquerades[2]. These creations are inspired in a general way by some of the local men's masquerades and based upon earlier antecedents which entered the country with Yoruba-speaking peoples in the 19th century. However, children's masquerades of the *Alikali* sort, as they are known, are of recent origin and appear in Freetown only after the Second World War.

The masquerade consists not only of a central costumed figure but also a carefully choreographed dance appropriate to each type of *devil* and a series of songs sung in Krio, which are often based on popular slogans from the radio, cinema and advertising. Each group performs before likely-looking spectators who will, it is hoped, *dash* the group a few pennies after the dance. Financial reward is an often stated reason for creating a *devil*; the boys use part of the money for elaborating and improving the next season's mask as it is thought that the *dash* is in proportion to the fineness of the performance. The rest is divided between payments to members for personal purchases and a common kitty which is used for outfitting football (soccer) teams whose membership is the same as the masking association.

These associations, usually having about eight or nine members all aged between seven and twelve, are residentially based[3]. All boys of the appropriate age who live on the street are asked to join regardless of ethnic background, religious preference, educational achievement or social status[4]. The boys so recruited, after payment of an initial subscription fee, assemble to "audition" for the offices which maintain performative and social order within the group. It is on the basis of ability and individual skill that the positions of headman, treasurer, controller, lead singer, dancer and chief musician are filled. These positions are not hierarchically ordered nor do certain offices receive larger proportions of monies collected.

All these talents are put to the test in the making and staging of the masquerades during festival periods. The four mask types, each with its distinctive visual aspects and choreography, form a kind of commentary on the nature of childhood and that of adulthood. The most popular, at least numerically, is the *Jolly* whose acrobatic tumbling is a fine demonstration of the physicality of the immature. The *Rainbow*, in his elaborate costume festooned with tinsel and expensive imported finery, is the epitome of youthful beauty. The *Talabi devil*, its back burgeoning with "medicine," plays its tricks on the adult world as a display of boyish power.

This trinity is in decided contrast to the *Kaka* or "shit" *devil* who deliberately violates aesthetic principles by appearing in dirty, torn costumes and dancing in inappropriate fashion. The *Kaka*, rather than embodying some aspect of youth, caricatures maturity. He represents the adult male and presents him in a state of advanced physical degeneracy—palsied, incontinent, inebriated and effeminate—for the process of maturation is one of progressive decay. It will be argued later that these *Alikali* masquerades celebrate "childhood" which is, in West Africa, a still emerging institution based on an equally new conception of "the child"[5].

These *Alikali Devils* of Bo town may be compared to the masquerades made by the boys of Torwama, a Muslim Mende village of about one hundred people some seven miles from Bo. Here children's masking is an integral, if not central, part of adult festivals. There are no boys' masking associations in the village and any boy who wishes to make a *devil* does so by himself or with the help of his father. Musicians are recruited on the spot from the boys and girls in the village, and everyone, including adults, sings in Mende. The *devil* does not parade from house to house but dances near the *barri* (a centrally located meeting place where old men hang their hammocks, women gossip and public announcements are made). Financial objectives do not prompt the performance and, indeed, monetary rewards from admirers are very rare, although words of encouragement and praise from both men and women reach the dancers from the circle of onlookers. The most popular masker was a small dancer of about six who wore a white cloth draped loosely over his head, with eyeholes cut into the fabric. Circlets of fresh green palm fronds were attached at the neck, wrists and waist, thus leaving large areas of the body exposed, although the child was wearing a pair of shorts. He identified himself as a *Nafali*, a Mende *devil* who wears a cloth hood studded with cowry shells in a cross pattern and shaped like a bishop's mitre. A long-sleeved, striped shirt and trousers accentuated with a raffia shoulder mantle, skirt and felt coverings make up the costume of the adult *Nafali*. The dance of the miniature *Nafali* also resembled that of the adult masquerader — both performances were characterized by very rapid hand trembling and foot shaking, punctuated by earth-touching sweeps, while the dancer was stationary.

This dancer appeared on December 2, the feast of Edi-ul-Ahda in the village and again on December 25th in conjunction with secular masquerades of the adult men's society, the Poro. He, along with the Torwama *Goboi* and *Falui* came into the Teachers' college compound, about half a mile from the village, to honor the principal with a performance[6]. Although the boy dancer was accompanied by an age mate on the *keilei* (a Mende log drum), most of the music for both his own performance and those of the society devils was furnished by the clapping and singing of village women with their *shake-shakes*, a young man playing a double sided bass drum which in a former life graced a North American high-school football field, and another young man on a snare drum. One music specialist played only for the *Goboi* on a low-voiced, muted horn whose tones exhorted the *Goboi* to more virtuoso displays. After the trio had performed for somewhat over two hours, the villagers returned *en masse* to Torwama.

The differences between the children's *devils* in Torwama and those created by the boys in Bo are very apparent. The physical setting of the town performances is very different, for the boys do not parade their *Alikalis* while adult maskers are on the streets, nor do they perform together. In many cases, town children were in awe of, if not actually frightened by, the men's society masquerades. In Torwama, of course, the children were not only at ease in the presence of the adult performers, but even engaged in duets with them, appearing at the same time and in the same place.

The elaborate code words and competition between *devils*, the fighting mythology, and the dual Yoruba and modern idioms are of negligible influence in the village. The Torwama songs are in Mende, known to both adults and children as they are traditional tunes and verses, not the thematic variations based on popular hit tunes and sung in Krio so favoured by the town boys. These differences stem from the actual nature of the two different styles of *devils*. The Bo *Alikalis* are ingenious improvisations inspired by the urban models of the Creole society *devils*, while the Torwama boys intend their masquerades to be, and successfully present them as, miniature versions of traditional Mende *devils* which contribute to.the continuity of the artistic traditions of which they are copies. The aesthetic considerations which shape these imitations of adult masquerades are childish attempts to implement the adult canons, rather than an original interpretation by the children themselves. Similarly, those aspects of cultural and social behaviour which children acquire within the context of participation in an adult festival are not generated within the peer group, but occur under the aegis of the society. The *Alikali* devils, on the other hand, are independent creations, art forms which are produced by and for children.

Both of these masking traditions, however, offer numerous examples of what David Lancy has described as "how play trains children for four major cultural subsystems (namely): (1) social relations (2) language (3) technology (4) ideology" (Schwartzman 1978:110). Both can be seen as lending some support to anthropological theories of play as fulfilling an enculturative function. In the case of the village the children are, in Mackay's words, assimilated culturally into the adult world while the boys of Bo are inducted into the culture of childhood by their peers[7]. But on another level, what thus may appear to the same sort of play is, in fact, very different sorts of "work."

The mask play in Torwama has what Sutton-Smith has called an "integrative function," *i.e.* it is part of "normative socializing" in which the boy is prepared through practice and imitation, to participate in Mende festivals which help define the divisions in rural society between male and female, chiefs and commoners, the initiated and the non-initiated.

The creation of the *Alikali devils*, on the other hand, provides a forum for socialization by innovation. "Play may socialize not simply by imparting behaviors that integrate the players into their cultural systems, but providing them with innovative alternatives that they may be able to use to change that cultural system" (Sutton-Smith: 1979:315). The world created by the boys in their masking associations is a meritocracy, a society characterized by an egalitarianism which runs counter to the hierarchies and boundaries which fracture adult life in Bo[8].

Of course, this innovative style is equally integrative, but it is normative socialization within the culture of childhood. Sutton-Smith has argued that

> the ratio of these two, integrative-innovative, changes with the kind of cultural system. In a more authoritarian system, the children's play is more strictly imitative; in a relatively open society like our own, the play is much more reversive and transformational as children feel free to attempt varying permutations of the possibilities before them (1979:315).

While the unstated equation of authoritarian: closed: traditional: non-authoritarian: open: modern is perhaps too strongly implied, it is within contemporary, urban West Africa that children *as* children are beginning to appear. It is here that the growth of the nuclear family and the emerging importance of education have made the child synonymous with the schoolboy[9]. However, education most often separates the child from his parents. It has been suggested that the scientific revolution in knowledge further segregated the child from knowledge, for the

> . . . differentation of knowledge . . . meant reality was no longer the same for all men. There were various canons of truth. Men could no longer make judgements in confidence and in terms of immediate perceptual information. The affairs and understandings of adults became increasingly invisible to the children. As a result children were, in fact, increasingly innocent (Sutton-Smith 1972:304).

In Sierra Leone where 75-80 per cent of the adult population is illiterate (in English), the situation is, in a sense, reversed. The affairs and understandings of children becoming increasingly invisible to adults, for the boys' modern education ensures that there are currently at least two canons of truth, one mature, and one immature in terms of age, if not in knowledge, of the modern world. The schoolboy is, however, increasingly dependent on his parents and family in a different way, for not only does his labour no longer make a significant contribution to the family income, but the family must provide his school fees and textbooks, as well as the annual tuition. As this dependency excludes the boys more and more from the world of men, they begin to create a children's world, where adults are excluded and where they themselves are interdependent.

Thus, while the *Nafali* masquerade is a celebration of creative and structural community, the *Alikali devils* mark artistic and social disjunction in a celebration of childhood itself.

NOTES

1. I am in agreement with Schwartzman's use of socialization to encompass enculturation (1978:106). Least anyone suspect that I am not aware that this panel is on work, not play, I must again refer to Schwartzman who has suggested that

> Perceptions of play are intimately related to one's culture. In the West, our understanding of play has been most significantly influenced by shared attitudes about what play is *not*. Play is not *work*; play is not *real*; play is not *serious*; play is not *productive*; and so forth. These attitudes, which are related to that complex of beliefs that has become known as the Protestant Ethic, have made it very difficult for Westerners to see that work can be playful while play can sometimes be experienced as work (particularly in the case of games); and, likewise, that players create worlds that are often more real, serious, and productive than so-called real life (1978:4).

2. Krio is a creole language found in Sierra Leone as the mother tongue of the Krios and as a *lingua franca* in many urban areas.

> *Devil* = Krio; a non-pejorative word for any masquerade
> *Alikali* = probably from the Arabic *al kadi* - "the judge"
> *Jolly* = Krio, probably taken from a young man's dancing company
> *Rainbow* = Krio, probably taken from a young man's masking society
> *Talabi* = a common Yoruba surname

3. See Olofson 1977 for a description of *Yak 'in Samari*, the "war of youths" waged in Hausa towns by boys 8-12 in residentially based groups.

4. See Salamone 1978 for an analysis of children's games as mechanisms for socialization and their role in establishing, maintaining or transcending ethnic identity.

5. See Lancy 1975 for a study of play forms in a rapidly changing Liberian town.

6. *Goboi* = an important secular mask of the Poro society whose costume consists of a full raffia cape adorned with miniature prayer boards and crowned with a squat, cylindrical headdress.

> *Falui* = another Mende mask which wears a baggy brown costume topped with a red cone and a feather tuft.

7. This is not to say that certain aspects of peer group socialization — including the inculcation of sexual stereotypes, politico-judicial skills and values such as courage and loyalty—are at variance with adult standards or that they are not acquired in other arenas under adult supervision.

8. Many adults in Bo operate both within an ascriptive system with a

rural origin and a more achievement-oriented society generated in town.

Whether achieved or ascribed, "traditional" or "modern," these status systems divide the adult world of Bo into many separate strata or spheres, be these segmented on the basis of birth into a chiefly family, or membership in an organization restricted to those of the same educational background and class. While it might be misleading to state that in their masking associations, the children resolve some of the conflicts which disturb the harmony of the parental generation, it can be suggested with some assurance that they dissolve some of the boundaries which confine adults to particular spheres. Whatever the conflicts within the *Alikali* groups, they are not generated by the same rivalries and prejudices which govern social relationships for men and women.

9. See Cannizzo 1978 for a fuller discussion of this process; the argument is similar to that first suggested by Phillip Aries in *Centuries of Childhood.*

REFERENCES

Cannizzo, J. "Alakali devils: Children's masquerading in a west African town." Ph.D. dissertation. University of Washington, 1978. "Alikali Devils of Sierra Leone." In: *African Arts* 1979, 12, 4:64-70, 92.

Hardman, C. Can there be an ethnology of children? *Journal of the Anthropological Society of Oxford.* 1973, 6, 2:85-99.

Lancy, D. The play behavior of Kpelle children during rapid cultural change. In D.F. Lancy (Ed.), *The Anthropological Study of Play: Problems and Prospects.* Cornwall, New York: Leisure Press, 1975.

Mackay, R.W. Conceptions of children and models of socialization. In Roy Turner (Ed.), *Ethnomethodology.* Penguin, 1974.

Olofson, H. Vertigo and social structure: Notes on Hausa children's play. In Phillips Stevens, Jr. (Ed.), *Studies in the Anthropology of Play.* Cornwall, New York: Leisure Press, 1977.

Salamone, F. Children's games as mechanisms for easing ethnic interaction in ethnically heterogeneous communities - a Nigerian case. *Ethnicity,* 1978, 5:203-212.

Schwartzman, H. *Transformations.* New York: Plenum Press, 1978.

Sutton-Smith, B. *The folk games of children,* Austin: University of Texas Press, 1972.

Epilogue: play as performance. In Brian Sutton-Smith (Ed.), *Play and Learning.* New York: Gardner Press, 1979.

chapter 3

CARNIVAL IN CANADA
THE POLITICS OF CELEBRATION

Frank E. Manning
University of Western Ontario

Celebration often exemplifies one of the central paradoxes of play. From one perspective, it is autotelic and purely expressive (Grimes, 1982, pps. 47-49), an ideal form of the ludic impulse in the classic sense described by Huizinga (1955). From another angle, however, celebration can be replete with studied political maneuvering and other instrumental stratagems. Their polarity notwithstanding, these two aspects of celebration are dialectically related in the "two-dimensional" process discerned by Cohen (1974, 1980). Power relations are represented, negotiated, and acted upon in the arena of celebration, while celebratory symbols derive much of their meaning and dramatic impact from underlying sociopolitical realities. Celebration, then, is both culture and politics. It is a "power play," ambiguous and moving.

I am concerned in this paper with the West Indian tradition of carnival, which has its source in Trinidad but which has diffused throughout most of the eastern Caribbean and, more recently, into several metropolitan areas in the United States, Canada, and Britain where large numbers of West Indians have settled. The politics of metropolitan carnivals are shaped by two distinctive factors: first the involvement of West Indians from many different Caribbean islands, whose cultural identities have traditionally been influenced by a thoroughgoing sense of isolation and alienation from each other; second, the social situation of West Indians as a racial-cultural immigrant minority. The Toronto Caribana, one of the most spectacular West Indian carnivals in North America and possibly Canada's outstanding ethnic celebration, richly illustrates the interpenetration of cultural festivity and political discourse.

Insularity on the Mainland

Caribana traces its beginning to 1967, when West Indians in Toronto were invited to participate in Canada's centennial observances. An *ad hoc* West Indian group brought to the city a contingent of Trinidadian masqueraders and musicians who were then in Montreal for Expo '67. A carnival-style parade was held downtown, and was reportedly the first major Caribbean cultural performance in Toronto.

Enthused by their success, the organizers constituted themselves the Caribbean Cultural Committee and determined to mount an annual summer festival. From the outset, however, they were deeply and acrimoniously divided along lines of island origin — a pattern that has been apparent in every metropolitan carnival with which I am familiar. To appreciate this archetypal conflict, one must be aware that the social category "West Indian" has had little positive meaning in the Caribbean. People view themselves, primarily and often exclusively, in terms of an island nationality and culture. Insular xenophobia is general and diffuse, but it is also structured hierarchically on the basis of island size. From the perspective of a given island, those from smaller islands are seen as "backward," and thus subject to ridicule, condescension, and contempt. Conversely, those from larger islands are seen as aggressive and domineering, a feeling which evokes a response of resentment, suspicion, and defiance. (The phenomenon is somewhat comparable to departmental isolation and disciplinary chauvinism in universities, but that can't be pursued here. Interestingly, it also parallels Canadian regionalism, the country's most powerful political and cultural force.)

The largest West Indian country, Jamaica, has traditionally been the most reluctant to deal at any level with any other island, and in turn is undoubtedly the most unliked by all the rest. Trinidad, the second largest country, is smugly viewed as a "small island" by the Jamaicans, but it dominates the eastern Caribbean. The remaining eastern Caribbean islands — there are eight principal ones—are relatively small compared to Trinidad, and will occasionally speak with one voice in distinguishing themselves from Trinidad or Jamaica. But this posture is invariably short-lived and ineffectual, as the smaller islands insist on ranking themselves according to size and thus preserving the overall hierarchy. The swift collapse of the West Indies Federation—the government created in 1958 to unite Britain's Caribbean colonies and lead them to independence — is only the best known of a litany of dismal failures at social and political integration. The Commonwealth Caribbean today is a melange of the world's smallest mini-states, each impotent on its own but unwilling to join forces with the others.

Insularity persists in Canada. Virtually all Caribbean institutions in the Toronto area—clubs, community associations, artistic groups, even student organizations — are oriented towards particular islands. Predictably, the most powerful group, numerically and politically, are the Jamaicans. But as Jamaica lacks a carnival tradition and has stigmatized that genre by associating it with the smaller islands, Jamaicans have had virtually nothing to do with Caribana. Their determination to "go it alone," as West Indians say, is dramatized on Caribana weekend when the Jamaican-Canadian Association runs an alternative celebration, Jamaicafest, in commemoration of Jamaica's national independence.

The non-involvement of the Jamaicans left the Caribbean Culture Committee, organizers of Caribana, to the Trinidadians and those from the smaller eastern Caribbean islands. The Trinidadians, many of them masquerade band leaders, insisted that the festival should preserve the format of the Trinidad Carnival, and that they should have the upper hand in running it. The claim was politically motivated, of course, but it also stemmed from a deeply felt allegiance to the notion that carnival is an exclusive Trinidadian birthright. As one masquerade band leader told me, "No one knows Carnival like a Trinidadian. We're born into it. It's in our blood."[1]

The Trinidadian position put the others in a dilemma. Most of their islands of origin have produced carnival celebrations in which local content and significance have been creatively incorporated into the basic carnival format (e.g., Abrahams, 1970; Abrahams and Bauman, 1978; Manning, 1978; de Albuquerque, note 1). One might reasonably conclude that this type of response — a carnival that articulated the Canadian experience — ought to be encouraged in Toronto. Acceptance of that premise, however, would have been tantamount to accepting Trinidadian leadership. The non-Trinidadians therefore insisted that the name "Caribana" was meant to indicate a distinctive type of festival in which carnival items—chiefly street masquerading, calypso shows, and steel band music—were only one component. The festival as a whole was to have pan-Caribbean scope and significance, and an overall emphasis on black racial identity. They sought to broaden Caribana as much as possible, introducing ferry cruises, fashion shows, picnics, art and craft exhibits, dramatic dance, and singing performances, merchandising displays, beauty contests, dance balls, and various other social and entertainment events that had little or no direct connection with the carnival genre.

After four years of embittered controversy, this tension produced an organizational split. The Trinidadians formed the Carnival Development Association, which ran what it called Carnival Extravaganza. This included the masquerade parade, a contest for king and queen of the masquerade bands, the display of prize-winning costumes from the Trinidad Carnival, a children's carnival, and a number of dances featuring calypso music played by steel or brass bands and highlighted by top name calypsonians from Trinidad. Dances, for example, were announced as "jump-ups," and the public encouraged to "jump," "jam," "wail," and "wine"—Trinidadian terms for dance movements, most of them erotic. Appropriating the Trinidadian calendar, the night before the masquerade was termed "jouvay," a patois term abbreviating *jour ouvert* (daybreak) and referring to the Trinidadian practice of revelling until the sun rises on the night before the first day of Carnival. Similarly, the concluding day of Carnival, was described as "las lap"—an occasion of reckless, unbridled abandon. As is said in Trinidad, "Las lap, we go make bassa bassa"—the final phrase being a Yoruba term for 'wanton destruction' (Hill, 1972, p. 99).

Meanwhile, the small-island remnant of the Caribbean Cultural Committee ran what it called the Caribana festival. The program had conscious symbolic intentions. It began with evening dance cruises, which were meant to represent the familiar eastern Caribbean experience of traveling on small boats. The symbolism here, however, was deliberately janus-like, as it included a distinctive Canadian image—the attractive, almost majestic view of Toronto's skyline that looms from a short distance off-shore. Another activity was a Miss Caribana contest in which great care was taken to select candidates from as many islands as possible, and, it was hoped, to rotate among the islands in choosing winners. There were also two major dances, one in honor of Miss Caribana and the other known as the Caribana Ball; both were held in prestige hotels. The popular highlight of the Caribana Festival was a series of picnics, exhibits, and shows spanning several days. This part of the program was held on Olympic Island, an island park in the Toronto Harbor chosen to represent a generalized Caribbean environment—an island with which every West Indian, regardless of origin, could identify. An informant spoke almost poetically about the island symbolism as a reminder of "home":

> I remember that, right from the very beginning, whenever I walked off that hot, steaming ferry, I felt that I was returning home—home meaning to someplace, anyplace in the Caribbean . . . . .—returning home with a lot of other people who felt the same way, returning home to a very beautiful part of my culture—such as the food, such as the music, such as the laughter, the humor that we grew up with. And it was a day to just forget everything else and pretend that you had never left wherever you had to leave, for whatever reason. . .

Race and Class

While the conflict between the Carnival Extravaganza and the Caribana Festival was drawn chiefly along lines of island origin, it assumed in time two other dimensions of significance: race and social class. Like inter-island distinctions, these identities have been articulated in the processual interplay—in the double sense—of symbolic expression and political strategy. Interestingly, it is in this secondary field of conflict that the celebration has been most appreciably affected by Canadian circumstances.

Trinidad is a racially plural society. The largest segments are blacks and East Indians, with smaller numbers of Chinese, Portuguese, Lebanese (called Syrians in Trinidad) and whites (northern Europeans). While carnival was introduced to Trinidad by the white plantocracy, it was taken over by Afro-Trinidadians after their emancipation from slavery in 1834, and it evolved as a black cele- bration for the next century. Many of its performance items, notably calypso and steel band, continue to be associated almost exclusively with blacks, and the event as a whole is still known jokingly as the "creole (black) bacchanal." Street masquerading, however, has drawn a variety of racial-ethnic groups, particularly at the organi- zational level where there are prominent Indian, Chinese, and Lebanese bandleaders. And the entertainment industry, like other businesses in Trinidad, is dominated by non-blacks. It is with some justification, then, that contemporary Trinidadian scholars of Carnival describe it as a national, rather than a racial, celebration (Pearse, 1956; Hill, 1972).

Vestiges of the Trinidadian pattern are seen in Toronto. The masquerade band leaders who made up the Carnival Development Association consisted of blacks and Indians, and the group was led by one of the latter. The Indian bands have attracted numbers of Indian masqueraders, and at least one of those bands has included Caribbean Chinese designers and white Canadian craft specialists. Masquerade afficianados encourage their white co-workers, friends, and neighbors to "play mas"—don a costume and join the street parade. Thus, in several of the bands there are whites, small in number but still noticeable enough to give the Toronto parade a dis- tinction that is lacking in most other metropolitan carnivals.

Carnival epitomizes Turner's (1969) sense of *communitas*, and there is no doubt that the recruitment of whites is in part inspired by this exuberant, egalitarian, and embracing ethos. But there are also practical reasons why whites are sought. For one, the bigger the band, the better the chances of winning prizes. For another, the presence of whites and other racial-ethnic groups resonates vibrantly with the the Canadian notion of multiculturalism. In 1971 Canada was officially declared a multicultural society. The many and diverse cultural groups were given the right, almost the duty, to preserve and display their heritage. This right, however, was expressed with reference to a higher ideal—the social responsibility to share one's culture and to learn about others as a step towards mutual enrichment and tolerance. Government policy, backed by substantial funding, is to promote this objective by "connecting" cul- tural groups (Ostry, 1978).

As the public highlight of the Carnival Extravaganza, the mas- querade parade was able to capitalize handsomely on its multicutural image. The parade begins near Queen's Park, seat of the Ontario Provincial Government. From there it proceeds along University Avenue, a wide, tree-lined boulevard that easily accomodates a crowd of 150,000 persons, many of them whites and tourists. The route is also flanked by several of Toronto's largest hospitals, affording patients an opportunity to watch the spectacle. The parade concludes at Harbourfront, a federal park on the shore of Lake Ontario that was first made available in 1976 — the year that the Carnival Development Association won a provincial grant of more than $20,000.

Trinidad's preeminent calypsonian, the Mighty Sparrow, described the scene in a 1972 calypso entitled Toronto Mas. The chorus went as follows:

> It's mas, Toronto gone wild
> It's mas, Trinidadian style
> Steel band play
> Lord, the sweet music
> All the white women
> Goin' be 'pon the street

The principal trope of calypso is the double-entendre, oral-aural as well as semantic. When sung, the last line of this chorus sounds deliberately like "honky on the street."

The multicultural popularity of the masquerade parade generated considerable publicity in the print and broadcast media. It also made it relatively easy to obtain commercial sponsorship, much of it from beer companies and from the travel industry. Finally, the parade has enjoyed an unbroken record of non-violence, which has kept its organizers in the good graces of the police and the public. One year, the leader of the Carnival Development Association was ceremoniously transported around the city in a police side-car.

On the other side, the Caribana Festival was differently situated and developed a different image. Most of the eastern Caribbean islands have been essentially monoracial since the collapse of the sugar plantation system in the early 19th century. Not surprisingly, all members of the Caribbean Cultural Committee were black. They saw racial identity as the basis of their own solidarity, and actively promoted it as a cultural counter-force to Trinidadian nationalism. Part of the strategy involved a choreographical tactic of integrating entertainment symbols from different islands in order to stress their underlying social unity. In the shows on Olympic Island, for example, there was typically a balance between calypso and other Caribbean rhythms such as spouge from Barbados and cadence from Dominica. There were also attempts to book top entertainers from as many Caribbean islands as possible. The committee's enthusiasm for black solidarity further prompted them to introduce black American styles and even to import black performers from the United States—a controversial move that incited West Indian entertainers in Toronto to call for tighter immigration laws! More recently there has been added a reggae component, partly because of the music's strong association with blackness, but also, and more pragmatically, because of its box office appeal to Jamaicans, the largest West Indian group in Toronto, and, ironically, to a growing constituency of whites drawn by the late Bob Marley, Peter Tosh, and other reggae superstars who have regularly played before sellout crowds in Toronto's largest concert halls.

The Caribana Festival's need to boost gate receipts has been chronic. Unlike the masquerade parade and outdoor costume competition, most Caribana events have been held in commercial premises and other private settings, and thus are dependent on ticket sales rather than government grants. Even on Olympic Island an entrance fee has been charged. Ticket prices have been steep, as West Indians, by their own admission are notoriously bad at managing money and scandalously prone to the leakage of profits. In 1981, for example, a couple who attended seven major events in Caribana faced ticket prices of nearly $175.

These circumstances gave the Caribana Festival an elitist aura, in contrast to the populist image of the Carnival Extravaganza. Class tension is strong in Caribbean societies, and, as Wilson (1973, pp. 105-111) has observed, some of it is played out in entertainment. There is, for example, a wide social gulf between public amusements and festivities, and private parties where admission is by fee or by special invitation. The bourgeois image of Caribana was reinforced by its boast of being not simply a "fete," but a more "serious" festival in which the arts were displayed and which had the long range "educational" objective of establishing a strong sense of black racial consciousness that would fuse West Indians into a united, powerful bloc in Canadian society. From this perspective, the Carnival Extravaganza was condescendingly dismissed as little more than a hedonistic outlet for the masses. In the critical words of a West Indian journalist "As far as I can see, it is simply a time to 'find a party, smoke a wattie, when you finish, drink a Guiness ' " (Solomon, 1979, p. 10). The latter phrase of this verse, which, ironically, was borrowed from a calypso, is a sarcastic allusion to the Trinidadian fondess for stout.

The organizational split between the Carnival Development Association and the Caribbean Cultural Committee was formally ended in 1980, when it became apparent that the rift had seriously eroded the efforts of both groups and that neither the West Indian population nor the city of Toronto were willing to support two competing festivals. The Trinidadians rejoined the Caribbean Cultural Committee, but acted within it as a caucus responsible for running the carnival program, even though the celebration as a whole became known again simply as Caribana. But despite the organizational rapprochement, the basic tension between the two modes of festivity is never far beneath the surface, and frequently rises well above it. In 1982, one of Toronto's top calypsonians, Lord Smokey, wrote a song in which he maligned "Mister Committee" for being dominated by "small island men," for promoting reggae instead of calypso, for importing expensive entertainers rather than relying on Toronto-based calypsonians, and for various other practices which he presented as indicative of the committee's inability to run the show. Thus, the fundamental symbolic and political conflict that I have examined here persists, even though some of the institutional structures in which it was once fought have undergone certain changes.

Made in Canada

Drawing these threads together, we see in this celebration an ongoing controversy along lines of island origin, race/color, and social class. These dimensions intersect and overlap, inextricably at times. But they are conceptually distinguishable, and each of itself is significant.

In the Caribbean, island identities are differentiated in terms of a variety of real or imputed factors. Behavioral norms are the most general consideration, but wealth, political power, education, and other attributes are often introduced to the social taxonymy of the islands. Among West Indians in Toronto, entertainment has become perhaps the most common focus of insular images and identities. This is particularly true for Trinidadians, who tend to see their love of calypso (the music and the "jump up" dancing style) at the core of their unique social personality. Interestingly, in Trinidad the calypso season lasts 6-8 weeks, from New Year's until Carnival. At other times, people listen to a variety of music, notably imported American trends. But in Toronto (and, I gather, in other metropolitan areas[2]), the calypso season is year round. Calypso is invariably the musical lingua franca at any social gathering dominated by Trinidadians. (Contrastingly, reggae has the same role in any gathering dominated by Jamaicans.)

In the Caribbean, race and class are important but shifting reference symbols in a dialectical process that Wilson (1973), borrowing a native metaphor for status climbing, calls "crab antics." Society is seen as a bunch of crabs in a barrel, each striving to climb up and out while the others scramble to pull it down again. High status derives from "respectability," a code of conduct based traditionally on stereotyped middle class values and white lifestyles. With nominal decolonization and the rise of a black elite, however, there has emerged a sense of black respectability which is as fully bourgeois as its white predecessor. As one Caribbean author put it, "Massa Day (elite domination) never ends in the Caribbean. It only grows blacker" (Coombs, 1974, p. xv).

In Toronto, the Caribana Festival assumed the aura of black respectability, consigning the Carnival Extravaganza to the bottom of the social barrel. The Caribbean Cultural Committee's cooption of that position is ironical, as it reverses the hierarchy based on island size. To compound the irony, the Caribbean Cultural Committee has sought symbolic rapport with the Jamaicans, the most aloof and chauvinistic of all "big island" peoples, in order to offset their opposition from the Trinidadians. It is the stuff of which a good calypso could be made, and it could only happen in a metropolitan setting.

These subtle developments, then, have given the Toronto celebration a "made in Canada" quality. The politics of festivity reveal a great deal about how West Indians in urban Canada are going about the contentious business of dealing with each other, as well as about how they are coming to terms with Canadian society and negotiating places for themselves within it.

NOTES

I have done field research on the Toronto Caribana each summer since 1980, and have also been involved in promoting West Indian entertainment in London, Ontario. For financial support of the Toronto study, I am grateful to two sources at the University of Western Ontario: the Dean of Social Science, and the Population Studies Centre.

1. This sentiment seems widely current among Trinidadians abroad. Cohen, for example, quotes a Trinidadian in London: "Carnival is in our blood. It is ours and cannot be taken away from us. . ." (1980, p. 73).

2. I am told by Linda Basch that Trinidadians in New York are similarly preoccupied with calypso throughout the year. Personal communication, December, 1981.

REFERENCE NOTE

de Albuquerque, K. The St. Thomas Carnival. Paper presented to the West Indian Association, East Lansing Michigan, 1979.

REFERENCES

Abrahams, R. Patterns of performance in the British West Indies. In N. Whitten and J. Szwed. (Eds.), *Afro-American Anthropology: Contemporary Perspectives.* New York: Free Press, 1970.

Abrahams, R. and Bauman, R. Ranges of festival behavior. In B. Babcock (Ed.), *The Reversible World: Symbolic Inversion in Art and Society.* Ithica and London: Cornell University Press, 1978.

Cohen, A. *Two-dimensional man: An essay on the anthropology of power and symbolism in complex society.* Berkeley and Los Angeles: University of California Press, 1974.

Cohen, A. Drama and politics in the development of a London carnival. *Man* (N.S.), 1980, *15*, 65-87.

Coombs, O. (Ed.) *Is massa day dead?* New York: Doubleday Anchor, 1974.

Grimes, R. *Beginnings in the ritual studies.* Washington: University Press of America, 1982.

Hill, E. *The Trinidad carnival: Mandate for a national theatre.* Austin: University of Texas Press, 1972.

Huizinga, J. *Homo ludens: A study of the play element in culture.* Boston: Beacon Press, 1955.

Manning, F. Carnival in Antigua: An indigenous festival in a tourist economy. *Anthropos,* 1978, *73*, 191-204.

Ostry, B. *The cultural connection.* Toronto: McClelland and Steward, 1978.

Pearse, A. Carnival in nineteenth century Trinidad. *Caribbean Quarterly,* 1956, *4,* 176-193.

Solomon, M. Is Caribana a true reflection of Caribbean culture? *Contrast* August 3, 1979, p. 10.

Turner, V. *The ritual process: Structure and anti-structure.* Chicago: Aldine, 1969.

Wilson, P. *Crab antics: The social anthropology of English-speaking peoples in the Caribbean.* New Haven and London: Yale University Press, 1973.

chapter 4

FESTIVALS AND ORGANIZATION OF MEANING: AN INTRODUCTION TO COMMUNITY FESTIVALS IN MINNESOTA

Robert H. Lavenda
Mark A. Lauer
JacLyn R. Norwood
Christopher E. Nelson
Antonya Evenson

During the summer of 1981, twenty-two undergraduate students from St. Cloud State University carried out research on two community festivals in central Minnesota.[1] We offer the results of this research to students of play, not just as pure description, but also as case studies of the application of a particular theoretical framework to materials from American culture. In this paper, it is argued that these festivals are cultural texts that are performed anew every year, providing participants with one way in which they may reflect upon experience, and hence make sense out of their lives. This theoretical position derives from the work of Turner (1974, 1977) and Geertz (1972), as well as from that of Ricoeur (1981), and holds that it is the experiential, metasocial nature of such events that makes them significant.

Significant, but not, perhaps dominant. There are other texts, other performances, other experiences in central Minnesota towns; summer festivals are not the only ones. They do, however, serve in these towns as the only common experience of the entire population. Differences in religious denomination, political affiliation, class, ethnic group, friendship, and interest group serve to separate people in these towns; summer festivals, if they do not "bring them together," at least provide a meeting place and a set of common experiences which may be summoned up as reference points for interaction and reflection during the rest of the year. These common experiences, however, differ from community to community in Minnesota in ways which are both interesting and important, telling the participants (and us) different stories about themselves and their social situations.

The two Minnesota communities studied in 1981 were Foley and Glenwood, chosen because they provide striking contrasts both in their composition and in their festivals, and hence, provide the comparison necessary for a deeper understanding of festivals as texts. Foley is located in central Minnesota, some fifteen miles east of the city of St. Cloud. It is a community of some 1400 people, the county seat for a rural agricultural county, and serves a trade area of approximately 400 square miles. Until very recently, Foley was a farm service town—banks, bars, churches, physicians, veterinarians, farm and dairy supply stores, clothing stores, grain elevators, farm implement and automobile dealers, and the like. During the 1970s, however, some light industry came to Foley, as did a Land o'Lakes turkey hatchery. The city of St. Cloud has been expanding its regional influence, and by 1981, nearly one-fourth of a sample of full-time workers in Foley were employed in St. Cloud (Erickson: Personal Communication). An advertising campaign designed to attract rural and small town shoppers to St. Cloud was begun in 1979, and by late 1981, a business-person in Foley admitted that it had been all too successful—more and more trade was being drawn away from Foley to St. Cloud (Otto: Personal Communication). The ethnic makeup of the community is predominantly German and Polish; most people are Catholics. Foley has the reputation in the surrounding areas of being a very conservative, very inwardly-directed community. Its festival, Foley Fun Days, began in 1962, and with the exception of one four-year period, it has been organized by a single person.[2] It was conceived as, and has remained, a festival for Foley and its immediate area.

Glenwood is quite different. It is located 75 miles west of Foley, on the edge of the Great Plains. Although also the seat of a rural, agricultural county, it is scenically situated on the eastern shore of one of the largest lakes in Minnesota. Part of its survival, as well as part of its character, is due to the summer residents and tourists who have lake houses or who camp there every summer. A local grocer estimates that his business increases by 30 percent every summer, and our research team felt that the town was quite a bit more accustomed to strangers than was Foley. Glenwood is nearly twice the size of Foley (2600 people), and its economy is rather more diversified, depending on tourism, the surrounding farm area, the railroad (Glenwood is a division point on the Soo Line), and on a small amount of light manufacturing. Additionally, the business district of Glenwood is owned by relative newcomers. Although at first glance it seems to be made up of businesses that have been in the same family for generations, few businesses have not been sold to newcomers at least once over the past twenty-five years. An "oldtimer" in Glenwood has lived in town for fifteen years or more. Since the population has not grown dramatically over the past quarter-century, it is clear that there has been a significant flow of population out of the town to balance the newcomers. This was confirmed by informants in the town, who talked of having to re-set the type in the telephone book every year, and of watching most of every high school graduating class leave town.

The Glenwood Waterama was established in 1956, and has become the largest water-festival in the state outside of the Minneapolis Aquatennial. Visitors come from all over Minnesota, as well as from Iowa and the Dakotas. The festival depends on outsiders for its very survival, and its organization, in contrast to Foley's, makes this clear. As noted above, in Foley, one woman is in charge of the entire festival, and her word is the final (and sometimes the first) word on all issues relating to the festival. When she needs help in doing the work for Fun Days, she asks for it; as she noted, "I don't ask anybody to help unless it's really necessary. So most of the time when I ask for help, they're there." There are, therefore, people who are in charge of organizing the different events, but they clear things through the woman in overall charge. She, in turn, reports to the Business Bureau, which serves as the sponsor of the event, but it is generally agreed that the organizer has a free hand. She and her husband, both self-made people, own and operate a floral and gift shop, and have no official position in the community. One of the authors has characterized this form of organization as "a mom-and-pop operation," and indeed, it resembles very closely a family form of organization.

Glenwood contrasts sharply with this: Waterama is a legal corporation, and is organized on two levels. At the top is a controlling hierarchy, made up of three men, the Admiral (in over-all charge), the Commodore and the Vice-Commodore. The Admiral, who has become one of the symbols of Waterama, oversees all the work on the festival and travels to various festivals around the state, promoting Waterama. He is responsible for grooming his successor, the Commodore, who serves on committees and often travels with the Admiral to other festivals. The third man in the hierarchy is the Vice-Commodore, the "entry-level" position. He is chosen by the preceding Vice-Commodore, usually on the grounds of friendship and business acumen.

The second level of organization is where the day-to-day work of organizing the events and finances of the festival occurs. Each event, the publicity apparatus, and the financing system have a separate committee, usually made up of three couples. Each committee is responsible for ensuring the success of its particular task. Here, again, a minimum three-year involvement in the festival is assumed, and recruitment to the committees often invovles friendship. Often, but not always, the committees serve to incorporate new business and professional people into the community. If such people have not volunteered to work on Waterama within 2 years or so of their arrival, they are approached by a representative of Waterama and asked if they would like to volunteer to work on a committee. Refusal, we were told, results in negative sanctions, including (it is said) avoidance and withdrawal of support. Whether the cautionary tales told are apocryphal or not, it is certainly the case that the business and professional people of the town are heavily involved in, or have been involved in, Waterama. It will be recalled that Glenwood has undergone a great deal of population movement, so that, in effect, a rapid, effective means of socializing people whose roots are elsewhere is required by the social system. This is a function fulfilled by the organization of Waterama. Additionally, the constant infusion of new people into the organization leads to a greater degree of freedom to become innovative and creative than that found in the Foley case. This is not to imply that freedom and creativity are absent in Foley Fun Days; they are not, but they are contingent. In the Waterama, these factors are structural: because new people are always involved in the festival, new ideas and practices are inevitable and, indeed, expected.

Further, we were struck by the way in which the organization of the two festivals seems to replicate the organization of sex-roles in the two towns and the orientation of the two towns toward outsiders. Counts of spectators and participants at Foley Fun Days indicated that very few events at the festival attracted men and women in equal proportion. Those events traditionally associated with the home and women's concerns—street sale, craft show, queen pageant and story hour—attracted two to three times as many women as men, while those events traditionally associated with men—firemen's water fight, softball, trap shooting—attracted far more men. Thus, the organizers' ideas that there should be something for everyone seem to lead to a selection of events that will appeal to men or to women. The lone event which attracted men and women in equal proportions was the parade, an event which was attended by a very substantial number of outsiders. In Glenwood, by contrast, there were far more events, (indeed, most of them) that attracted men and women in approximately equal proportions.

This contrast is replicated in the organizational system of the two festivals as well. In Foley, either men or women organized different events. In Glenwood, couples worked together to organize the festival. Although men got the official credit on the Waterama letterhead, it was universally recognized that both men and women worked together in the committees. We argue that these divisions according to sex are not just reflections of the status quo in the two communities, but also serve to shape people's perceptions of appropriate interests and behaviors for men and women.

So, too, with the communities' orientations toward outsiders, Foley Fun Days is organized in such a way as to minimize participation by outsiders. This was not, in our estimation, a conscious attempt to be unfriendly, but rather a way of focussing on Foley and its immediate hinterland. While Fun Days begins officially on Saturday, the events of that day and a great portion of the next are not the most significant. A mini-marathon and a softball tournament are the major events of the weekend, and both involve significant numbers of outsiders. The "core" of Fun Days begins on Sunday night with the

Queen Pageant, and continues on Monday, Tuesday, and Wednesday with a street sale, carnival, beer trailer, firemen's water fight, and children's events. By scheduling these during the week, people not from the immediate vicinity who might have been interested in attending would find it very difficult to get there. In this way, the core is protected, as it were, and intensifies the community of Foleyites while excluding outsiders.

Waterama is completely the opposite. As noted above, Waterama depends for its very survival on outsiders, and the festival is scheduled in such a way as to maximize their attendance. The festival always begins late on Friday afternoon with a mini-marathon which attracts runners (and often their families) from a considerable distance, continues with a water-ski thrill show and lighted pontoon parade on Saturday, and concludes with a huge parade, queen coronation with state-level celebrity and drawing for cash prizes on Sunday. There are enough things of interest to keep a family in Glenwood for the entire weekend, but each day is scheduled so carefully that even those who can stay but a day will feel they have spent their time and money well. The care of the organizers to attract people may be seen in their research into summer rainfall in Glenwood early in the history of the festival. Careful investigation showed that the last full weekend in July is the least likely to have rain, and the festival has been on that weekend ever since. For Glenwood residents, then, the festival is always shared with outsiders, and is always a time for displaying the community. Such an outward orientation is inevitable in a community that is itself in constant flux.

What is clear from the organization of the two festivals is that the very different ethos of the two communities is expressed clearly through the way in which the festival is conceived and brought about. Foley, an inwardly-directed, conservative town, still very much tied to its own hinterland, has a festival organization which reflects this, but which also gives these characteristics a concrete form. The same is true of Glenwood. The organization of Waterama (a highly effective one) is corporate and hierarchical, corresponding to an image of orderliness and stability. It provides continuity in a community where, for the small businessmen and professionals, continuity is sometimes hard to achieve, and also provides a way of rapidly integrating new members of the community into active participation. Thus, although the experience of organizing the festivals is different, the net result is the same—the expression of certain general characteristics of the community in specific form.

Significant experiential differences also emerge in considered social control in the two festivals. For purposes of this paper, social control will be taken to be those methods that are employed by a group of people to ensure compliance to confidence in the values and expected behavior patterns of the society. For analytic purposes, we distinguished two types of social control — formal and informal.

Formal control was taken to encompass police procedures and formal criminal law, local ordinance, and festival rules. This form of control, in the festival context, could be considered the "rules of the game" of the festival. For example, in Foley, drinking was allowed in public places, while in Glenwood it was prohibited. These can be considered different rules of play. On the one hand, in Foley the people are allowed to engage in behavior that for most of the year is considered to be against the norm, while on the other hand, Waterama enforces behavior that is expected during the year, i.e. public sobriety. This particular issue will be considered in greater detail later.

Informal control is rather more ambiguous. This division also encompasses a broader spectrum of social and cultural attitudes and conventions than does formal social control. Informal control was taken to encompass such elements as peer pressure and gossip, parental control over children, control of older siblings over younger, festival organization and timing of events. Although the latter two elements may appear unlikely parts of informal social control, when events are organized and scheduled so that people are led in an orderly fashion from event to event, crowd control is certainly being practiced. The crowd is not aware that it is being controlled, and therefore, the control may be called informal.

The police force of Foley is made up of two officers and a chief. Also located in the town is the county sheriff's department, composed of eight deputies and the sheriff. Ordinarily, the three police officers are considered adequate protection for the town. However, during the festival, the police chief felt that he needed help from the sheriff's department, especially for the crowds expected for the parade on the festival's final night. Although the chief was concerned that his small force would not be sufficient, the history of the festival has shown that three policemen has been sufficient. There have never been reports of major disturbances, nor of disorderly conduct or radical departures from the ordinary events recorded on the police blotter on any other weekend. The attitude of a sample of townspeople was that the police presence at the festival was just enough.

By contrast, Glenwood has a police force of six regular officers and a chief. During the festival, the chief hires extra officers from other communities. In 1981, he hired fourteen such officers, feeling that twenty police were sufficient. He noted, however, that he drops hints of having hired forty officers to certain "big mouths" in town, and lets them spread the word, exaggerating the number if they pleased. By keeping his officers visible at as many events as possible, he reinforced the gossip, making it appear that he had an army at his disposal, and rather neatly combined formal and informal methods of social control.

The Pope County Sheriff's Department assists the Glenwood Police Department to a greater degree than do their counterparts in Foley. They help handle traffic control, needed because of the massive influx of people from out of town. They also patrol the campgrounds in the county, which though out of police jurisdiction, house festival-goers. The police in both communities enforce laws that are normally enforced during the year (driving while intoxicated, vandalism, theft, etc.), but in the case of Glenwood, the police also enforced an ordinance of considerable importance to the festival.

This is the ordinance that prohibits the consumption of alcoholic beverages in city parks and on city streets. Violation of the ordinance is punishable by a $100 fine. The ordinance grew out of the trouble that arose from excessive drinking at the city-owned campground, the Chalet Park. Each year, because the festival draws people from around the state and from out of state, the local camping areas fill up rapidly. In the past, this caused a spillover into the city campground which became more and more crowded every year. By 1979, more than 3,000 people were crowded into an area designed to hold a maximum of 200. Most of these campers were young and came from out of town, carrying their alcoholic beverages with them. Many were former residents of Glenwood who had moved away or were attending colleges and universities in other towns. Waterama, then, became a good reason to hold reunions as well as the obligatory parties which accompany reunions. These parties sometimes induced indecent exposure, public drunkenness, and vandalism. One police officer related that in 1979, ten picnic tables were used for firewood, and about fourteen garbage trucks and three days were required to clear away the paper, beer and soda pop cans, bottles, and other litter from the park at the end of the festival. After these reports of vandalism and excessive behavior, as well as fear of drunk drivers, pressure was put on the city council to close the park during the festival, and to bar drinking in other areas of town, as well.

It must be noted that there were few complaints from the citizens of Glenwood concerning public drinking, or about the crowds, noise, and events at the Chalet Park, nor were there any incidents of insulting, impertinent or dangerous behavior. The people who camped in the park generally never left the area and created very few problems for the people of the town. But it was felt by the city council that *no* vandalism and *no* public drinking could be tolerated. The police chief was very much in favor of the ordinance, and felt that he had a good deal of support. Indeed, 73 percent of the women interviewed after the festival were in favor of the ordinance, and although only forty percent of the men thought that it was a good idea, this still represents a majority in favor of the ordinance. We argue that this change in the festival, part of the process of "bourgeoisization" of the festival, is a significant one, reflecting changes in how the powers in the town view themselves, their audience, and the Waterama.

In Foley, social control in the area of festival events is almost entirely informal. For example, at the queen pageant, there is no need for the police since the event is held indoors and admission is charged. Ostensibly, the admission fee is used to pay for the expenses of the pageant, but may also serve the latent function of control. Regardless of how little it costs to get into the pageant, the charge may discourage those who would want to disrupt the proceedings; why pay for the opportunity to disrupt when there is ample opportunity later in the festival to disrupt for free? The police were absent from the pageant because in the estimation of the organizers, such a presence was deemed unnecessary.

The audience for the pageant, held in the high school gymnasium, was composed primarily of adults in the 30 to 45 year-old group, with a fringe group of young people primarily of teen age. The older people sat in folding chairs on the floor of the gym, while the youngsters sat in the bleachers, the quieter ones sitting up front and the more boisterous ones in the back. Here, informal control varies inversely with distance: those youngsters sitting near the adults had to tone down their comments in order to avoid retribution or expulsion.

In Glenwood, the arrangement of the crowd was much the same as it was in Foley, but the event was outdoors, the crowd was much larger, and the police were in evidence. There was a tendency towards family groups in the crowd; also significant for social control was the presence of a very well-known Minnesota celebrity who acted as master-of-ceremonies for the coronation. Many in the crowd, we believe, attended in order to see him, and we would argue that the crowd's desire to indicate to this person its civic pride and respect for the event was a factor in the peacefulness of the event.

We would argue that the relative absence of police in Foley and their quite obvious presence in Glenwood was due, in part, to the differential power of peer pressure and gossip in the two towns. In Foley, because of the closeness and inner-directedness of the community, these informal control mechanisms work effectively; indeed the Police Chief in Foley felt that he did not have to exercise much police control because the people in the community viewed fighting among themselves as "fighting in the family." By contrast, in the Glendale Waterama, because it is outwardly-directed and attracts many people not from the community, there is less pressure for an individual not known in the community to behave in a dignified manner.

This sort of "familial" informal control is strikingly manifested in the attitude toward public drinking in Foley. During Fun Days, drinking is permitted on the streets, and the Lions Club-sponsored beer wagon takes a central place in the festival. Very large quantities of 3.2 beer are consumed by adults and underage adolescents as well.

Although an effort is made to control the drinking of the latter group, responses to a questionnaire after the festival indicated that very few people were disturbed by underage drinking. Those who noticed any tended to pass it off with, "Boys will be boys," or "It's okay because it's during the festival," or "It's only 3.2 beer; what's so bad about that?" We are inclined to see these responses as indicative of an acceptance of certain kinds of behavior as being as much a part of the festival as the parade or carnival. Ordinarily, public drinking and public underage drinking are unnacceptable, but during the festival, these strictures are loosened or ignored. The festival is a game, and in order to be part of the game, it is necessary to ignore the excesses of some co-celebrants.

In sum, from the perspective of social control, festivals are times which have potential for the reversal of norms. The rules of behavior may change. But at the same time, rules must be followed. If we look at the festival as a form of game, social control is the method of keeping the game on an acceptable level of play. Without this control, the game soon falls apart and ends because the players no longer know how to play and begin to make up their own rules. This sort of behavior is not acceptable in the context of a game, nor is it acceptable to the people who hold a festival. The text of a festival emerges out of and is part of the total social and cultural world of the community that creates it.

In the case of Foley, we can see that these game rules sometimes include the suspension of everyday public rules. Drinking in the street, not officially sanctioned during the rest of the year, is viewed as part of the game during the festival. The text here seems to read, "We agree that we will not do this after the festival is over, but for now, we're only playing." It is important to note that in the case of Foley Fun Days, the activities are geared to the people of the community. The festival is small, inwardly-directed, and designed to coincide with the first alfalfa harvest of the year as a thank-you to local townspeople and farmers for patronizing the businesses in town during the year. So this festival is, in effect, saying, "come downtown and have a good time. You've been working hard and now it is time to play." With this as the text, it is possible to see the permissive attitude toward drinking in public as either a reward, or, indeed, as part of the game.

On the other hand, when we look at Glenwood we see quite a different story. Drinking was allowed at one time but is no longer. This is an entirely new game. This is an entirely different festival, one geared toward a wider, and indeed different, audience. The activities are made to be enjoyed by anyone, not just the local citizens. The festival here, as has been seen, is designed to bring in tourists to use the lake and to aid the businesses in town as well as the area campgrounds. The rule prohibiting drinking can be seen as a slap in the face to the rural permissiveness found in a community like Foley. Waterama is not a festival of reward to the local farmer. Rather, it represents the triumph of urban middle-class values of control over a tradition of excessive drinking heretofore characteristic of rural Minnesota, and may be seen as a demonstration of the rise of centralized urban power in a generally rural location. This "bourgeoisization" of the festival is also sharply revealed in the contrast between the queen pageants in the two communities. A common characteristic of many of the festivals in central Minnesota is the selection of a young woman to act as a public representative of the local community. The purpose of our research on queen pageants was to see whether the different focus of each festival and their varying organizational structures resulted in differences in the women ultimately selected. Would a particular type of woman be interested in participating and why? What influence would the organizers have on those who entered? Did the guidelines single out certain characteristics? How would the way in which the women were judged affect the outcome?

The formal guidelines in both communities are quite similar: the women must be single and between the ages of 17 and 21, and must also be from a specified area. In Foley, this is the trade area, while in Glenwood, it is the county, a much wider area, encompassing three towns, Glenwood, Starbuck, and Villard. Glenwood adds high school graduation as a further stipulation, thus setting up an accomplishment as well as age for participation. The results of these two differences are significant. Of the ten candidates in Foley, two had just completed their junior year in high school, while the other eight had just graduated. In Glenwood, all the candidates had graduated from high school, and one had completed her freshman year at the nearby university. In Foley, all the candidates were known more or less by the audience at the pageant, while in Glenwood, none of the candidates was known by all of the audience. This difference at once set up different affective fields within the events-in-drawing in Foley, as the audience is drawn into the event through acquaintance with the participants or their families, not as in Glenwood, where all that is known is what is seen.

In Foley, it was the overall organizer who, eight years after the foundation of the festival, suggested that a queen pageant be added. In her recollection, the suggestion was made because queen pageants were part of the festivals in neighboring communities, such pageants adding "a little bit of glitter" to the festival, and because the pageant would provide the community with a representative to send to other festivals and parades, particularly if the high school band was unable to attend. The young women themselves were not left out in her reasons for the pageant, although they were not primary. The organizer hoped that the pageant would provide the participants with a "positive experience" and a chance to meet new people. As a businesswoman in the community, she also acted as a sponsor of a candidate in the pageant. Her reason for doing this was to acquire a "good representative for the community." This theme of "good representative" was repeated often by sponsors, parents, candidates, and particularly by the women directly overseeing the pageant.

Although the primary organizer of the festival took a keen interest in the pageant, details were handled by other women in the community. With the exception of the four-year period when the Jaycees ran the festival, the membership of the queen pageant committee had not changed until 1981. All three women were members of the Business Bureau, the sponsoring organization of the festival. Two of the members were active in family businesses, while the husband of the third owned a business in the town. All these organizers have lived in the area for most of their lives and appeared to be members of the middle class in the community.

Toward the end of the planning period for the 1980 pageant, two younger women became involved. In 1981, one of them acted as primary spokesperson for the pageant and planned to be the primary organizer for the next year. Unlike the original organizers, she did not belong to the business community. Although raised in Foley, she had only recently returned to the town. Furthermore, neither she nor her husband were involved in community functions as were the previous owners. She decided to become involved with the pageant because she had been a contestant in one of the first years of the event, and having enjoyed participating, felt it to be a valuable experience for the young women. A main concern of hers was to make the pageant more "professional" by involving older participants and choreographing the pageant, as well as by encouraging participation by the winners in further state competitions. Her concern for change was shared by the other young woman involved. This desire for change put her somewhat at odds with the festival organizer, and was indicative of a potential "bourgeoisization" of the festival.

By contrast, the organizers of the Waterama queen coronation, as with the members of other communities as a whole, are married couples and are involved with the event for three years. In 1981, membership on the coronation committee was very much based on friendship and a sense of obligation. The three couples involved were all relatively recent arrivals, and in contrast to Foley, rather than being interested in the coronation, talked of fulfilling a committment to the festival itself. Numerous times it was stressed that their involvement was a way of being seen in the community, a way of becoming integrated into a town. Being involved in the festival was seen as an obligation and as a way of improving business or community relations. The occupations of the committee-members were attorney, social work case aide, commercial photographer, hospital administrator and secretary.

Given this orientation toward festival service rather than the coronation itself, the members' reasons for choosing the queen committee are revealing. Principally, all three couples saw the responsibilities of that committee as the easiest to fulfill and the least time consuming. Overall, the committment by the members of the group to the coronation was not as strong as in Foley, and all talked about being glad when their service was completed. None expressed any interest in being on the committee a second time.

Sponsorship for the two queen competitions is similar in the two communities. In both communities, businesses sponsor the candidates and are assessed a fee to help defray the cost of the pageant. There is no financial obligation on the part of the contestants. In both cases, the sponsors usually give their candidates some small token of appreciation. There are two significant differences between the communities, however. The first concerns the actual candidate selection process. In Foley, the sponsors always select their candidates, while in Glenwood there are three additional selection methods: application by a potential candidate to the queen coronation committee; contact of a potential candidate by the organizers; and contact of a potential sponsor by a potential candidate. None of these is impossible in Foley, but they have never been done. There, it is always the sponsors who select the candidates, and their tastes only shape the pageant.

The second significant difference involves the qualities in a candidate sought by the sponsor. In Foley, much concern was expressed over the personal attributes of the candidates: it was not enough to select a good representative from the community; she had to be a "nice girl." In Glenwood, the sponsors tended not to know their candidates as well as did the Foley sponsors, and when asked why they chose to sponsor a candidate, many tended to reply that it was a way to be involved in the festival without having to put a lot of time and energy into it. Furthermore, it was mentioned by sponsors in Glenwood that it was important for the candidate to be able to conduct herself well in public, a response which focused less on the personal characteristics of the candidate and more on public appearance skills.

With regard to judges and judging, although there are revelatory differences in selection and procedure in the two towns, very similar results occur. In both communities, the judges are from outside the community and are chosen by the pageant's organizers. In Foley, the judges' occupations were bank officer, child-care worker, clothing buyer, construction worker, and secretary. Of the five, only the bank officer had any judging experience. In Glenwood, the occupations were lawyer, construction worker, physical therapist, and secretary. In Glenwood the judges were two married couples who stated that they had accepted the position in order to have a free weekend and spend time with their friends. In both towns, the judges are very serious about the job and tried hard to select the appropriate candidates.

It is clear from the way in which the judges were selected and their occupations that they were, in a certain sense, reflections of the organizers and shared similar values with them. In an important way, this set of shared values and "outsiderness" of the judges super-cedes all else in the pageant, and explains why particular women are selected.

The nature of the judging process is a significant difference between the two pageants. In Foley, 80 per cent of the judging is done at the pageant itself, while in Glenwood, judging goes on during the entire festival, and the actual public event is a coronation, not a pageant—the winner is already selected before the candidates set foot on the stage. In Foley, the system is modeled after contests on the state level. There is an evening gown competition, a talent com-petition, and on-stage questioning, as well as a ten-minute private interview with the judges. The judges are not aware of how the others have scored the candidates until the final tally is made. In contrast, the judges in Glenwood view and talk with the candidates on a more extended basis. The personal interview is longer, and the judges are able to discuss their reactions to the candidates. The final decision is made by consensus. In 1981, there was some conflict among the judges concerning the winner, and a great deal of time was spent going over observations made of the candidates.

Although the sponsorship and the judging were quite different at the two pageants, and although the pageants differed significantly in terms of audience interaction and in terms of structural position in the festival, the candidates were quite similar, and the winners were almost interchangeable. All the young women involved claimed that post-secondary education was important to them, and all had been heavily involved in school, church, and community activities. The winners in both communities had neither more nor fewer activities than the other contestants. In Foley, the winner listed the following activi-ties: basketball, track, tennis, speech, chorus, yearbook, National Honor Society and 4-H. In Glenwood, the winner had been involved in cheerleading, band, choir, basketball, track, volleyball, National Honor Society and 4-H.

Inasmuch as these lists are similar to all participants, what is it, then, that sets the winner apart? Particularly in the case of the winners (rather than the runners-up), the willingness to compete openly seems to be the answer. Both winners talked freely about the competition between themselves and among their peers and felt that it was good. The queen in Foley talked of the surface "niceness" of all those involved, but that on a deeper level, it was "blood and guts." Obviously, from the activities in which all the participants had engaged, none were strangers to competition. These two, however, were very frank in expressing their desire to win, and felt that they would be a good representative of their respective community. Throughout the judging process, it was clear that they were conscious of their relationship to the judges and would modify their behavior accordingly. In Glenwood, where the judges were free to discuss the candidates among themselves, the judges talked approvingly of the competetive nature of the candidate ultimately selected queen. It was their opinion that her ability and willingness to act in the way she saw necessary would work to her advantage in effectively representing the festival. It should be noted that neither queen was the the popular choice of her peers, perhaps precisely because of their willingness to shed the illusion of cooperation and friendship and to compete straightforwardly.

In our overall analysis of the results of the two queen pageants, it seems clear that the pageant text operates on two distinct, and in some ways, mutually exclusive levels. Within the level of the individual festival, it is seen that a particular segment of the community— from organizers to candidates—is participating in the event. It would not be inappropriate to characterize this segment as "upwardly mobile" in relation to the rest of the community and bourgeois in orientation. Class membership is particularly significant in the pageant's organization and selection process, and even the contestants seemed confident that they could walk through their school halls and point out those of their peers who would or would not be asked to participate. On this level, then, the text seems to be about the ability of a small town to produce young women who are bright, attractive and active. The young women involved are a businessman's dream of young American womanhood, and are quite literally, the girls next door. On this level, the power of queen pageants in small towns cannot be overestimated: they are debutante presentations and coming-out parties, they are meditations on the passage of time for those who have watched girls grow into the young women now before them, they are about pride and striving. They are also about class, and our American dream of transcending it. For a moment the doctor's daughter, the lawyer's daughter and the banker's daughter are on the same stage as the teacher's daughter, the farmer's daughter and the carpenter's daughter. They all have achieved great things, they all look lovely and they all have great hopes. Many, perhaps most, of these hopes will come to naught: some will never finish the college that is so important to them now; few indeed will gain wealth, or power, or influence. But at the moment of the queen pageant, none of this matters in a small town in Minnesota.

But the process does not stop there, with the young women singing or dancing or twirling batons on stage. A judgement is made, and one of them becomes queen. This very different level of judgement does not belong to the town. It belongs to the judges, who are

outsiders. The judges, in selecting a queen and one or more prin-
cesses, are applying somewhat different criteria than are the busi-
ness-people who select the candidates. Given the way judges are
selected and the occupations they pursue, they certainly have many
similarities to those in the communities directing the festival and are,
by and large, from the same class. Because they are from the
outside, however, they are not aware of the dynamics involved in the
position of the women or their families within the communities.
Knowing nothing of this, they judge only on what they see. But what
they see is mediated by a particular image of the right kind of woman,
and more specifically we found, the right kind of woman for the community in which they found themselves. Thus, the judges are continually reflecting upon and interpreting everything around them. They
seem to have an ideal in mind, but recognize that their ideal may not
fit the town in which they are judging. Here, too, however, is reflection,
because it is their interpretation of what the town wants that is, in fact,
that which guides. The complex interplay is between these two
images, as well as the judges' interpretations of the candidates'
behavior toward each other and toward them and, additionally, the
audience's response to the candidates. The significance of this
context-free application of ideal and interpretation is highlighted
when it is noted that in both festivals, neither winner was the
audience's popular choice, nor was either much liked by our informants throughout the community, but both fit the ideal.

This, we argue, is where the significance of queen pageants lies.
They are a continuous series of interpretations and reinterpretations
by all those concerned: for the contestants, aware of each other and
of their impact upon the judges; for the audience, interpreting and
responding to the behavior of the contestants; and for the judges,
trying to make their interpretations of the contestants and the community coincide with their interpretation of the community's criteria
for a representative. Although class is an unstated base upon which
the pageant is constructed, queen pageants are not straightforward
reflections of class. Rather, they are an interpretation and shaping of
a particular image of the ideal young American woman for general
consumption—emerging from, but not completely determined by, the
vision of a particular class.

Festivals, in general, like the queen pageants within them, are
interpretations and shapings. It is not just ideals that they interpret
and shape, however, it is experience. Festivals in central Minnesota
are ways of reflecting upon experience through the interaction of
organizers, participants, and audience. Each of these groups is
forced to draw upon their fund of past experience in order to carry out
effectively their respective roles. At the same time, of course, participation in any form in the festival itself *creates* experience, and this is a
twofold process. On the one hand, the experience of the festival is

conditioned by the reflection upon prior experience necessary to participate effectively. On the other hand, it is through participation in the festival that common, although not perhaps identical, experience in a small town is created. The centrifugal forces in a small town today are manifold—religion, politics, class, patterns of kinship, friendship, mutual interest, work and climate all serve to separate people into variously sized cross-cutting, and sometimes opposing, groups. Attendance at the summer festival becomes one of the only experiences (perhaps the only) shared by all of these people. Despite their potentially conflicting interpretations of the festival, they at least have a common ground for future interaction, even if that interaction never transcends the level of small-talk between barber and banker or desultory conversation over mid-morning coffee in the cafe. For some, however, particularly in Glenwood, it becomes the common basis for cooperative action through year-round participation in planning Waterama.

The actual interpretations of the festival are manifold, ranging from those who attend but are offended or disappointed, to those who look forward with keen anticipation to the festival. It is probably safe to say that most of the small community groups identified above have differing interpretations of the festival, and even within the organizing committees of Waterama, we found different groups attached different meanings to the festival. This double sense to the festival—common shared experience on one level and different interpretations of it—give the festival its power, inasmuch as it can at the same time be all things to all people and one thing to all people. The festivals we have discussed simultaneously convince the participants that they are one community and allow each group to interpret that community in its own way.

There is a second significant duality to the festival which emerges from the earlier analysis. The festivals we have examined are double texts. On the one hand, they are planned—events are selected and scheduled, bands are contacted, a carnival is hired, a queen pageant is organized, the beer wagon is set up, the police notified—and all of this, a plan for social action, is written down. It becomes a text which is designed to be performed, and it is a text with distinct authors. It is not the gods, or the ancestors, or "custom" dictating the action, it is a group of people from the town with very distinct ideas about that which they wish to accomplish. But as Ricoeur (1981:201) notes, "the text's career escapes the finite horizon lived by its author." The festival text, as it is performed, inevitably breaks the bounds of the original intentions of its authors, becoming a shifting field of kaleidoscopic images, interpretations, and actions. Once the enacted festival is over, however, it becomes a new text itself, having now been "inscribed" in the collective experience of the group. Herein lies the festival's power to affect and to effect as well.

NOTES

1. Research on central Minnesota festivals, supervised by the senior author, was made possible by a Student-Faculty Research Grant from the Bush Foundation. The students involved were Amy Adams, Joel Barthelamy, Macaela Cashman, Andria Christenson, Garth DeNio, Gina Dircks, Rene Doerfler, Antonya Evenson, Kevin Gwost, Motoko Iki, Marybeth Christenson-Jones, Mark Lauer, Gayle Loehrer, Anna Leisen, Christopher Nelson, JacLyn Norwood, Maurice Patrick, Laurie Pattison, Pamela Rudolph, Thomas Schmitt, Patrick Stokes and Susan Waller. The junior authors, as well as Gwost and Patrick, were group leaders. The senior author wishes to thank Emily Schultz and Don Handleman for their useful comments.
2. In 1982, the festival was first cancelled by the Business Bureau, and then resurrected by a new group representing somewhat different interests. The old organizer was not invited to the organizational meeting of the new festival.

REFERENCES

Geertz, Clifford. Deep play: Notes on the Balinese cockfight. *Daedalus*, 1972, *101*, 1-37.

Ricoeur, Paul. *Hermeneutics and the human sciences* (J.B. Thompson, Tr. and Ed.) Cambridge. Cambridge University Press, 1981.

Turner, Victor. Liminal to liminoid, in play, flow and ritual: An essay in comparative symbology. *Rice University Studies,* 1974, *60,* 53-92.

Turner, Victor. Variations on a theme of liminality. In S. Moore and B. Myerhoff (Eds.), *Secular Ritual.* Assen: Van Gorcum, 1977.

chapter 5

BOYS INTO MEN—STATE INTO NATION: *RITES DE PASSAGE* IN STUDENT LIFE AND COLLEGE ATHLETICS, 1890-1905[1]

Roberta J. Park
TAASP Convention, London

In his Introduction to *The Past Before Us: Contempory Historical Writing in the United States,* edited on behalf of the American Historical Association, Michael Kammen (1981) noted that during the 1970s historians began to read ethnographies, ethnohistories and works in cultural and symbolic anthropology in an attempt to better ". . .understand the interplay between values and customs on the one hand and their social environment on the other" (p. 41-42). Gordon S. Wood (1979) has gone so far as to state: ". . . of all the social sciences, anthropology seems to have the greatest kinship with history because it treats the people it studies on their own terms and begins with the assumption that such people do things differently. . ." (p. 29).

A large number of epistemological and methodological problems may arise when scholars attempt to undertake research utilising theories from another discipline. MacAloon (1981), for example, referred to ". . .the notorious tendencies of the cultural category, psychobiological, and symbolic approaches to run away with those who employ them" (p. xiii-xiv). Nevertheless, it is consistent with current thinking to suggest that many of our attempts to increase our understanding of the past might benefit from a consideration of some of the more recent insights of the social sciences, especially anthropology. It is this belief which has given rise to the subject with which this paper deals.

Numerous and varied studies have sought to explain the origins and development of intercollegiate athletics—especially football—at the turn of the century. Explanations which have been advanced to account for the meteoric rise of institutionalized athleticism for men in American colleges and universities after 1876 include: Modern sports reflect dominant American values, especially those associated with the industrialization, urbanization, bureaucracy and competition; administrators purposefully capitalized upon students' interests in games to subdue unruly youthful exuberance and develop a sense of pride in and loyalty to *alma mater,* largely for pecuniary reasons; modern forms of sport consist of and reflect male ceremonial combat rooted in psychological and sociobiological events. Taken in aggregate, these views have contributed a great deal to our understanding of the power and persistence of athletics in American college life. Yet, we are still far from understanding this ubiquitous phenomenon, either at its origins or as it now exists. In particular, relatively few historical studies have paid much attention to intercollegiate athletics as symbolic cultural phenomena, and even fewer have attempted an understanding from the standpoint of the students who originated and nurtured them.

Focus of the Investigation

An examination of the cultural contexts and the accoutrements of college athletics offers an intriguing possiblity for deepening our understanding of the period between 1890 and 1905. Within a short time after a post-Civil War American college or university had organized athletic teams, its students had also created a variety of rallies, songs, yells, mascots, emblems, trophies, and all sorts of support groups which were closely associated with the actual contests. The presence of an "arch rival" in the form of a neighboring and comparable college or university served as a stimulus to intensify efforts. Indeed, the athletic contests themselves rapidly became embedded in the whole series of "frames" which must be considered as important, if not in some ways more important, than the games themselves (cf: Bateson, 1955; Goffman, 1974).

The present paper is a pilot study. It focuses upon student customs and the rise of athletics at one institution—the University of California—between 1890 and 1905, as these were viewed by the students within the general context of college life. Some attention is also given to the wider context of life beyond the college community. The effort was stimulated by Geertz' (1973) assertion that ritual functions as a vehicle to remind people of the basic ideology which underlies a society's organization, and by Turner's (1974a; 1974b) discussions of *liminal* and *liminoid* and spontaneous and institutionalized communitas. The study also owes a great deal to various historical accounts of the "Gilded Age" and the "Progressive Era," particularly Oscar and Mary Handlin's (1970) examination of the socializing functions of higher education in the United States; Burton Bledstein's (1976) analysis of the role of universities in the formation of a post-Civil War "culture of professionalism"; Robert Wiebe's (1967) account of the breakdown of traditional agrarian communities between 1970 and 1920 and a search for organizing principles around which a new social order could be established; and Laurence Veysey's (1965) study of the emergence of a uniquely American form of higher education between 1865 and 1910 and the college degree as a ". . .syndicated emblem of social and economic arrival" (p. 440).

Methods of Investigation

There are two reasons for the focus upon a single institution. The first is the obvious practicality of the accessibility of documents and memorabilia; the second, and methodologically more important, reason is summed up by Veysey's (1965) observation that careful comparison lies close to the heart of historical explanation. If, therefore, the approach suggested here has merit, other scholars may wish to study other colleges and universities.

If one is to try to understand the perspectives of students, it is obvious that the products of student life must be carefully examined. In conducting this investigation, yearbooks, handbooks, minute books, souvenirs, daily and monthly publications of all types, game programs, song books, photographs and artifacts of every description were inspected. Publications of alumni associations and the publications and correspondence of various university administrators and faculty were also consulted, as were selected publications of the larger community in which the University of California was—and is—situated.[2]

The dates which frame this study are significant. The University of California was founded in 1868. In 1873 it moved to the then remote hills of the small town of Berkeley. Prior to 1891, when Stanford University opened, no university of comparable stature existed in the State which could be considered a potential "arch rival" for the new institution by the Golden Gate. The 1891 *Blue and Gold* (the student yearbook) emphatically made this point when referring to athletics. Those college traditions which did exist were relatively few in number and largely in a formative stage. By 1905, however, a considerable number of traditions, frequently in the form of annual rites, had been established; the University of California had met Stanford University for over a dozen years as intercollegiate athletic contests; rooters clubs, a rally committee and an alumni association had been formed; a symbolic trophy, emblematic of athletic prowess, had been "captured" in an atmosphere of intrigue and contest; the "Big C" award in the five major sports—football, baseball, track, boating (crew) and tennis—had each been given its unique shape; and the emphasis was clearly upon "varsity" rather than "class" athletic contests. Significantly, the 1905 *Blue and Gold* opened with a lengthy essay dealing with the evolution and maturation of student traditions at Berkeley, concluding that *college* spirit had come to replace *class* spirit, and attributing the change largely to the development of intercollegiate athletic teams (p. 17-32).

General Historical Context

Americans who lived in the decades between the end of the Civil War and the outbreak of World War I were witness to a society experiencing the dislocations of rapid change and the conflict of old and new ideologies. Numerous works have analyzed the impact of the modern scientific attitude upon traditional beliefs in religion, health and hygiene, business practices, government, and many other human concerns. Industrialization, urbanization, immigration, and changing demographic patterns precipitated a host of impersonal, hierarchical regulative agencies, the centralization of authority, and the breakdown of traditional agrarian community structures. Conceptions of work and leisure were altered (Rodgers, 1974). A new middle class emerged in which men came to define themselves largely in terms of their professional training and careers. Between 1870 and 1900 over a dozen professional associations were formed (Haskell, 1977), and new attitudes regarding success, authority, merit and worth emerged. Aspiring young men increasingly became aware of the need to prepare themselves for entry into various specialized careers. The rapid growth of universities after the Civil War, and a new conception of the university's mission provided the major mechanisms for achieving this new orientation. Rudolph (1962) notes the growing importance of ". . .the environment of friendships, social development, fraternity houses, good sportsmanship, athletic teams" (p. 289) in the decades following the Civil War, and especially during the 1890s and early 1900s (pp. 373-393). Veysey (1965) describes how "the custodianship of popular values comprised the primary responsibility of the American university" (p. 440) after 1890, and contends that college athletics—especially football—". . .increasingly channeled into one major outlet what had previously been a far wider variety of possibilities for student high-spiritedness" (pp. 276-277).

Success in a professional career was to ensure—or at least make more likely—success in all spheres of life. Advancement and status depended upon the possession of specialized technical knowledge and the assimilation of the proper forms of social behavior. It also depended upon the individual's understanding of how he was to fit into a newly emerging social order. At college a young man would learn from both the formal curriculum (which would provide him with technical training for a profession) and from the student extracurriculum (which would enculturate him into the values of the broader society which he was about to enter). Everything increasingly required specialized skills and information, a tendency which Bledstein (1976) finds was reflected in a growing demarcation between public and private space, the careful regulation of that space, and the assignment of various symbols and ceremonies to the activities which took place within that space. It was in the last decades of the nineteenth century that many previously rather informally organized pastimes also became regulated, formalized, even bureaucratic, sports, each with its own sub-culture, codes, symbols and ceremonies.

Between 1870 and 1915 the dominant American view also

". . .tended to divide the life of a person not yet an adult into fixed spans correlated with the stages of education" (Handlin and Handlin, 1970, p. 48). In a society oriented toward the hope of upward social mobility, youth needed to be offered inducements to postpone the gratifications that adulthood was supposed to confer. "In the pleasant interlude of independence that the college bestowed on young men before they were expected to settle down into the routine of affairs," Oscar and Mary Handlin (1970) have written, "they were 'sympathetically encouraged to instruct themselves and educate one another' after their own fashions" (p. 51). While the four years in college could certainly provide such an interlude, they were also very important years in which students were instructed about the structures and values which were increasingly coming to dominate the sectors of American society which they aspired to enter. The campus was at once its own self-contained community in which young men could criticize and critique the values of the larger society and a microcosm which reflected and reinforced the values of that society, with the far stronger emphasis being placed upon the latter. In the late 1800s and early 1900s, as Veysey (1965) has clearly stated, "the road to social success usually involved strenuous participation in the 'right,' that is, the prestigious campus organizations and activities" (p. 275). This tendency has persisted, with some slight modifications, into the decade of the 1980s.

Events at the University of California, 1890-1905

At the University of California, in the 1870s and 1880s the focus of a student's interest and activity had revolved largely around his class of entry. This was substantially the case for athletics as well as for other aspects of the student initiated and controlled extra-curriculum. By the mid-1890s increasing emphasis had begun to be placed upon activities which united the individual student as part of the total campus community, and by 1905 this trend was virtually complete. While elements of class activities certainly did continue to exist, the emphasis turned demonstrably to creating "campus" rather than "class" spirit. Each student had to be incorporated into the university family and also prepared to leave the institution at the end of four years and take his place in a society in which the dominant values were changing from the traditional American ideals of individual initiative and local community to the realities of urban society, centralized authority and corporate responsibility. (The collision of these changing values often found expression in the rhetoric regarding "values" in intercollegiate athletics. Some commentators in the 1880s and the 1890s found athletic contests to be "educative" and wholesome because they taught decisiveness and a sense of corporate behavior. Others considered athletic contests to have become "brutalizing" and demoralizing, largely because increasing reliance upon external authority [the referee] and the proliferation of codified rules were shifting the site of ultimate responsibility for behavior away from the individual player [Park, Reference Note 1]). In the four years at college the student was returned to infancy and then raised to manhood according to the value system needed to get on in this newly emerging society.

A male student entered Berkeley in the decade and a half between 1890 and 1905 a baby and left four years later a man prepared to meet the tests of society and, ostensibly, ready to contribute to his profession and his country. During the four years he passed through a series of carefully defined stages, each framed by its symbols, rituals and ceremonies. The initial activities served to separate him from his former family and community and incorporate him, at the lowest level, into the new family of the university community—and, by extension, into the community of all those who had undergone the same experiences and had reentered the larger society upon graduation. It is significant that the majority of the activities were exclusively male. Except for dances, the Senior Pilgrimage and similar activities, when female students were involved it was almost always as spectators. (It must be recognized that women students also had a variety of organizations and activities of their own; however, these were generally seen to be peripheral, at best.) It is also significant that intercollegiate *debates* were often spoken of in student publications in much the same manner as were intercollegiate athletic contests. Ong (1981), for example, finds certain similarities between the oral tradition in academia and aspects of modern agonistic sports.

For the Freshman the entire year was a liminoid-like experience in which numerous prescribed events took place. The new arrival and his classmates were constantly reminded of the stages through which they would be expected to pass. The iconography and the essays in the student yearbook, for example, made this abundantly clear. Freshmen were usually depicted as babies; Seniors as men about to enter the world. The designations for each class's annual dance (the Frosh Glee, Sophomore Hop, Junior Prom, Senior Ball) and the sartorial splendor of a unique headpiece for each class reinforced such distinctions. Interestingly, the hats of the two upper classes were of the same shape. The grey Junior "plug" was very individualistically decorated according to its owner's tastes, while the black Senior "plug" was largely devoid of decoration, reinforcing the message that the Senior was about to be reincorporated into a world in which conformity was important, and individuality must be confined within rather carefully prescribed bounds.

The task of initiating the new arrival fell to the Sophomore class, which itself had only recently emerged from its own year of trial, and the tensions between adjacent classes persisted throughout the four undergraduate years, possibly because the two perceived each other as the closest rivals for the scarce resources they would have to contest for after reentry into the broader society. The clashes between the Freshman and Sophomore classes culminated in a biannual "rush"—a wild, physical melee. These might be fought out in the dead of night, which added suspense and intensity to the event. (The element of surprise on the part of the Sophomores was deemed to be an important part of the rush.) The Spring rush preceded Charter Day, the University of California's public celebration of its own birthday, with its own academic traditions and dress reaching back into the Middle Ages. Custom required that the Freshmen place their class numerals on the hillside above the site where Charter Day was held, and that the Sophomores attempt to prevent their success. If the Freshmen were successful, the emblem was permitted to stay for the remainder of the year. The annual Bourdon rush at the end of the school year marked the last time that these two classes would be permitted to rush each other. The Bourdon was shorn of much of its original disorderly activity by the administration when a student was badly injured in 1897. It may also be that the growth of the other student events, like athletic rallies, had begun to take over some of the functions that the earlier wild rushes had performed.

The passage from the first two to the last two years of campus life was not marked by formal public ceremonies, but a number of student traditions acknowledged the transformation of boy into man. The activities of the Junior and Senior classes were routinely described in student publications as being far more "dignified" than the melees of their younger brothers. Junior Day, marked by speeches, music, essays and a three-act farce, was modeled on Senior Commencement activities. During Commencement Week the Senior class underwent its final rituals in preparation for return to the broader society. Ties with the University, to be maintained after graduation through participation in alumni events such as class reunions and the "Big Game," were reinforced during this last week. (Events like the "Big Game" and class reunions may constitute a form of *normative communitas,* and the topic merits further study.) The Senior Class Pilgrimage, with all the men dressed in a similar manner—and all the Senior co-eds attired in white dresses—saw the entire class proceeding as a group, revisiting important campus landmarks and listening to speeches which were at once nostalgic and prophetic. Just prior to the Senior Pilgrimage *all* the classes met at Senior Oak for impromptu graduation exercises. The president of the graduating class transferred his black Senior "plug" to the Junior class president, the Sophomore president received the Junior "plug" and the Freshman donned the Sophomore cap. In an interesting reversal of roles, on this day the two upper classes indulged in the horseplay while the two lower classes were uncharacteristically subdued. (For an interesting and informative discussion of the possibility of studying "role reversals" as a means to achieving a better understanding of certain aspects of the past, see Babcock, 1978.) The Senior ball, Senior banquet, library reception and an alumni reception culminated Senior Week, the last event serving to welcome the departing class into the larger university family community of those who had already graduated.

Athletics at Berkeley, 1890-1905

In baseball, both class teams and a University Baseball Nine had been organized in the 1870s. Football was a rather desultory affair consisting of contests between the various classes until a University of California Football Team was created in 1882. Its first game, with the Phoenix Club of San Francisco on December 2nd, ended in an 8 to 6 defeat for the University team. For a decade Berkeley had to be content with football contests against various local clubs composed of young businessmen, many of whom increasingly were graduates of the University. Sizeable crowds often turned out to witness these games, but as Weaver (1893), Ferrier (1930) and other have observed, the students were anxious to test their skills and prowess against teams from comparable institutions of higher learning. For several years students of the University of California, and not a few faculty members, had referred approvingly to the extracurricular affairs of established Eastern colleges, especially Harvard and Yale. (Indeed, Berkeley had chosen Yale blue as one of her colors, the other being gold for the Golden Gate and the color of the flowers on the surrounding hills. Her second president had been Daniel Coit Gilman, a graduate of Yale.) The 1891 *Blue and Gold,* the student annual, lamented: "We have often wished that a college existed near us, with whose students we might engage in friendly contests. . .We have no other in these parts worthy of the name" (p. 140). (The students at the State normal college at San Jose were not considered to be sufficiently meritorious for the men of the University to contest with.) This situation changed dramatically with the founding of Stanford University in 1891 and the rapid establishment of athletic teams at this four-year institution. The first U.C.-Stanford football game was played in San Francisco on March 19, 1892. The February 1893 *Overland Monthly,* commenting upon the rapid rise of football on the Pacific coast, declared that it was the founding of a rival institution and the importation of football coaches from the East which had brought football to a place of prominence in Northern California (Weaver, 1893).

A major contributor to the changing interest in and emphasis upon *intercollegiate* as opposed to *class* athletic contests was Berkeley's highly successful 1895 "Eastern Track Tour." Since 1891 an Intercollegiate Field Day (track athletics) had been held with Stanford Univeristy, but the achievements of the 12-man 1895 track team, the first University of California athletic team to compete outside the State, symbolized for many students, faculty and towns-people Berkeley's incorporation as a full partner into the fraternity of the nation's most prestigious colleges and universities. Classes were suspended as both "gown" and "town" turned out to welcome the returning team. Shortly thereafter, the Associated Students sent a delegation East to secure a qualified "varsity" football coach. A 1902 track team, which did not fare as well as had the 1895 squad, was sent East with the following sentiment: "The sending of a good track team East does much to establish a favorable reputation for the University of California among Eastern institutions. . .[showing that] men of the same character are being molded in this Western University as in the older institutions of the East" (*The University of California Magazine,* 1902, p. 41).

Systematic yelling began at the 1895 Cal-Stanford football game. An event of considerable importance in the development of both campus-wide and community-wide interest in Berkeley-Stanford athletic rivalry occurred on April 15, 1899. A Stanford yell leader had brought a broadaxe to the final—and deciding—baseball game of the season with the idea of using the weapon to punctuate a yell which declared "Give 'em the axe," and an effigy dressed in blue and gold was beheaded in full view of the Berkeley spectators. After the game, victorious California students and alumni managed to wrest the axe from its owners and a wild chase, widely reported in the local press, ensued. A panel of professors from each institution finally ruled that possession belonged to the captors as the axe was "a prize by reason of conquest." The trophy, which became the most enduring tangible symbol of rivalry between the two universities, was placed in the guardianship of a prominent athlete chosen annually by his predecessor. It was brought out only for the "Axe Rally," at which time the story of its capture was routinely retold and alumni and undergraduates sought to outdo each other in exhorting the football team to victory (Ferrier, 1930; *California Monthly,* 1981). While there had been numerous rallies for several years, it was in August 1901 that the Associated Students appointed a seven-man California Rally Committee to serve as the guardians of the University's emblems and traditions.

Between 1892 and 1903 it had been necessary to hold the annual Cal-Stanford football game in San Francisco. California Field, a stadium of considerable capacity, was built on the campus in 1904 at a cost of around forty thousand dollars. In 1905 the Freshman and Sophomore classes agreed to jointly construct a concrete "C" on the hillside above the Greek Theater, the site of the University's annual Charter Day ceremonies, the "Big Game Rally," and other campus-wide events. This act, in effect, ended the tumultous "rushes" in which these two classes had previously engaged as the Freshmen class sought to place its year of entry numerals on the hillside. A metal plate was affixed to the new "C" with the inscription: "In memory of the Rush — Buried by the Classes of 1907 and 1908." The *Blue and Gold* subsequently declared that the two would go down in history as the two classes which ". . . sacrificed class spirit for the love of Alma Mater" (*Blue and Gold,* 1905). (The older tradition was, in part, revived when the Freshman class took up the practice of attempting to paint the golden "C" green.)

The iconography of athletics and the symbolic frameworks within which these contests had come to be embedded were so well-established by 1905 that the administration's decision the following year to abandon American football in favor of English rugby (University of California, 1905) had no perceptible effect upon the accoutrements or the contexts of intercollegiate athletics. In a functional analysis of rugby at the University of California between 1906 and 1916 (Berkeley returned to the American game in 1915), Allen Tindall (1969) found that the imposed game performed the same functions as had football in the years preceding the change to rugby.

The dominating annual celebration was the "Big Game" which was embedded in a host of yells, songs, emblems, trophies, rallies and similar events which, by tradition, were passed from one student generation to the next. The model provided by the "Big Game" also served as the scenario, but on a less grand scale, for other athletic contests, thereby reinforcing throughout the year the types of symbolic messages which were incorporated into the annual football extravaganza. Before the unifying power of the athletic ceremonies, such "class" activities as did continue were relatively insignificant. The game itself, whose outcome as identified by *score* might very well be uncertain, was set within a highly regularized framework of predictable and prescribed activites which were communicated, in largely symbolic ways, within and across the entire campus "community" (students, alumni, faculty—even townpeople might vicariously participate). Moreover, because other colleges and universities had similar accoutrements (the specifics being unique to each institution), the University of California extended family could share in a "college culture" which extended across the entire nation.

REFERENCE NOTE

1. Park, R.J. Action as moral necessity: Reflections on healthful exercise and 'wholesome' sport, 1815-1915. Seward Staley Address. Annual Convention of the North American Society for Sport History, Austin, 1979.

NOTES

1. Acknowledgement is gratefully extended to Mr. Patrick Miller, doctoral student, Department of History at the University of Cali-

fornia, whose perceptive insights have been very valuable to the author in the investigation of this topic.

2. These materials are located in the Bancroft Library; the archives and library of the Associated Students, University of California, Eshleman Hall; the historical collection of the Department of Physical Education, Hearst Gymnasium, University of California, Berkeley.

REFERENCES

Babcock, B. A. (Ed.), *The reversible world: Symbolic inversion in art and society.* Ithaca: Cornell University Press, 1978.

Bateson, G. Theory of play and phantasy. *Psychiatric Research Reports,* 1955, *2,* 39-51.

Bledstein, B.J. *The culture of professinalism: The middle class and the development of higher education in America.* New York: Norton and Co., Inc., 1976.

California Monthly, December 1981, 15-18, 30.

Ferrier, W. W. *Origin and development of the University of California.* Berkeley: The Sather Gate Book Shop, 1930.

Geertz, C. *The interpretation of cultures.* New York: Basic Books, 1973.

Goffman, E. *Frame analysis.* New York: Harper & Row, Pub., 1974.

Handlin, O. and Handlin, M. F. *The American college and American culture: Socialization as a function of higher education.* New York: McGraw-Hill Book Co., 1970.

Haskell, T. L. *The emergence of professional social science: The American Social Science Association and the nineteenth-century crisis of authority.* Urbana: University of Illinois Press, 1977.

Kammen, M. (Ed.) *The past before us: Contemporary historical writing in the United States.* Ithaca: Cornell University, 1980.

MacAloon, J. J. *This great symbol: Pierre de Coubertin and the origins of the modern Olympic games.* Chicago: The University of Chicago Press, 1981.

Ong, W. J. *Fighting for life: Contest, sexuality, and consciousness.* Ithaca: Cornell University Press, 1981.

Rodgers, D. T. *The work ethic in industrial America, 1850-1920.* Chicago: The University of Chicago Press, 1974.

Rudolph, F. *The American college and university: A history.* New York: Alfred A. Knopf, 1962.

Tindall, A. *A functional comparison of football and rugby at the University of California, 1900-1916.* M. A. Thesis, University of California, 1969.

Turner, V. Liminal to liminoid, in play, flow and ritual: An essay in comparative symbology. In E. Norbeck (Ed.), *Rice University Studies: The anthropological study of human play,* 1974, *60* (3), 53-92. (a).

Turner, V. Passages, margins, and poverty: Religious symbols of communitas. In V. Turner, *Dramas, fields and metaphors: Symbolic action in human society.* Ithaca: Cornell University Press, 1974. (b).

University of California. *Report on the football situation, by the Committee on Athletics of the Academic Council.* December 23, 1905.

The University of California Magazine, 1902, *8* (1), 41.

Veysey, L. *The emergence of the American university.* Chicago: The University of Chicago Press, 1965.

Weaver, P. Jr. Intercollegiate football on the Pacific coast. The *Overland Monthly,* 1893, *21,* 113-131.

Wiebe, R.H. *The search for order; 1877-1920.* New York: Hill & Wang, 1967.

Wood, G.S. Intellectual history and the social sciences. In J. Higham and P.K. Conklin (Eds.), *New directions in American intellectual history.* Baltimore: The John Hopkins University Press, 1979.

chapter 6

THE FOOL AND THE HIPPIES:
RITUAL/PLAY AND SOCIAL INCONSISTENCIES
AMONG THE MZEINA BEDOUIN OF THE SINAI

Smadar Lavie
University of California Berkeley

What I am about to describe happened only once, though other versions occurred about twice a week during my twenty-seven months of field research in the Southern Sinai.

It is around eight o'clock on a summer evening in Dahab. This main oasis along the Aqaba Gulf is inhabited by 500 of the approximately 5000 Mzeina who dwell in the Southern Sinai desert. At that hour dinner odors are still in the air, mingling with the smell of salt brought from the sea by the whispering breeze, softly blowing among the palm trees scattered in clusters on the coastline. In the distance a mother's undulating melancholy voice singing a lullaby tenderly echoes the cry of the *muezzin* bursting forth, calling the community of believers for the evening prayer. Answering the call, the twenty-four men who have been sitting in a circle on the ground in a fenced-off area, their men's club, rise and enter the nearby mosque in order to pray in unison. After ten minutes, the first ones come back to the club (*maq 'ad rejjal*). Some stay a few minutes longer for private prayer and meditation. The moon throws light on the tranquil faces of people who have just fulfilled another duty of their religious routine. One of the men serves small glasses of sweet, dark tea, which has been heated on glowing embers in the center of the sitting circle. A quiet conversation slowly begins to flow, each man taking his turn, without interrupting the other, even in cases of disagreement. They speak of what has been said in the latest news broadcast and the way it may effect the Sinai, the high inflation rates, the quickly changing prices of various goods. The conversation continues, flowing into issues of wage-work.

Most of these men, ages from 22 to 60, earn their income from selling services and goods to the many tourists who visit the Southern Sinai peninsula. Dahab is among the "pilgrimage sites" for foreign and Israeli hippy backpackers, who come for a vacation of a week or two, desiring to have an "authentic" experience of living "as Bedouin" amidst the palm trees on the beach. These hippies, nevertheless, lie naked on the beach suntanning, and engage day and night in explicit, public sex. The Bedouin — fully and traditionally dressed — sell them "Bedouin-style" hospitality. They rent them huts in the fake Bedouin village they have built only a mile from their home village; they organize camel tours; and sell them Bedouin caftans and food, as well as narcotics and alcoholic drinks. Hospitality is a core value among the Mzeina. Selling hospitality to other Bedouin never happens, since it would be considered a degradation of oneself. The Bedouin refer to the tourists as "beatniks," and in a collective group name (*nisba*) as Batanka. They are sure that the word emenates from the colloquial Arab verb *naka* which means to fuck.

"Oh, God," says one of them men sitting in the club, "today there was such a fat, healthy-looking, nice girl on the beach! Have you seen her — the one who is with that skinny, dark guy, under the palms of Freij. . .? Too bad she sunbathed. Her white skin turned red like a roasted lobster." "Ya —, she came to me asking for tobacco," continues another. "I told her I smoke only dope [since the Sinai-grown green tobacco smells the same] and asked her if she would like to buy some. Finally I sold her a cigarette for four bucks." All laugh. "She bought three." Some laugh again. "I think she dyes her hair. Her pubic hair was a different color," responds the man sitting next to him. "Oh, Abu-Zayed! — [a folk heroic figure], oh, evil of disaster (*ya shar al-balawa*)—" says somebody else, puzzled, to himself, while the rest laugh. Then silence prevails again for a moment. "I swear on my life, I can't figure out what she sees in that guy, he's so dark and skinny" [which is considered ugly by the Mzeina]. All laugh. "This summer, the nakeds have increased like rubbish on the sand." The atmosphere is serious again. "What do you want?" asks a man in a louder voice. "It's their vacation. This is the way they enjoy themselves. Tell me, isn't it fun that you take your girlfriend, or even come by yourself, everybody is naked, and you — just pick the one you like? And according to their money rates, such a vacation is pretty cheap." Soon there is a reply in a louder voice, "Pray to the Prophet! You two have become beatniks! Aren't you fed up with staring at the genitals of godless, naked girls? Should we discuss it every evening here, in our men's club, near the mosque?" Another man responds, "We all have become like beatniks. Today I was praying the noon prayer, and two guys — whose penises were hanging, and whose only clothes were their cameras — took pictures of me." He angrily waves his hands and shouts, "What do they think? Are we there as their free movie show (*cinema balash*)? I am already fed up with them, stretched out on the beach, being like a free movie show for us!"

Another man, sitting nearby, replies, shouting and using sharp hand gestures to supplement his statement, "In other places there isn't such a mess. People live like they used to in the past. The hell with money! Which life do we live?" A shouting voice is heard from the other part of the circle, "Have you ever seen an Arab praying in the midst of nakeds?" The man sitting next to him continues, "Great Lord, the Bedouin dwell in the desert, in Egypt, in Saudi Arabia, everywhere, without touching this pollution. Why is our luck such that our source of income is this [working with hippies]?" Quietly, and so lowering the volume and tempo of the discussion, which by now is turning into a dispute, another man continues, "What do you want? Do you have problems? Try to raise goats in this desert — Within a week you will spend all your money buying them food. In our desert there is a lot of grass, but not the kind we need." [This is meant as a pun, because the word *hashish* means both herding grass and also dope, but there are only few grins in response]. Then one flares up, "We are like beatniks, living on money, spending money," he scolds the rest. "What property do we own? Our homeland is all rugged, bare mountains and cutting corals, which are good for nothing except for crazy tourists, diving, climbing, endangering their lives for their pleasure. The Bedouin have fields and flocks. Every once in a while they go to the market and exchange some goats for goods. These dollars have killed us!" His neighbor elaborates on how Bedouin are supposed to behave, and says sharply and loudly, "The Bedouin are people of honor! They justify God and his disciple [Muhammad]! The Bedouin despise money!" A bitterly bemused voice responds to the challenge, "We all saw you yesterday, haggling with those dirties over exchange rates [of Israeli and foreign money] down to the pennies, and then counting your dollars nervously and delightedly. Oh Great Lord, we are not like the rest of the Bedouin!" Another man burst in, interrupting the speaker, asking furiously, "Who needs money? The Bedouin need freedom! Let them travel around in the desert, reciting caravan songs (*hejeni*) and courting the veiled shepherdess."

A very old man immediately shouts with authority, "The Bedouin don't pay attention money; one helps the other: a father his sons, the sons support their old father, everyone and his uncles and cousins. They are organized better than Eged Corporation!" [Eged is a large, monopolist, Israeli public transportation cooperative. The sentence is meant to be a joke, and I have heard people laughing on other occasions when comparing the Mzeina agnatic organization to the powerful Eged]. Now, when the atmosphere is stormy, when all dispute in search for their identity as Bedouin, nobody laughs. Another old voice exclaims strongly, "For the Bedouin it's *Ad-damm dhamm, ma fi khramm* (the blood is protected, there are no holes)." This statement, meaning that there are no gaps in a social network organized on the basis of blood relationship, is taken from the Mzeina's judicial jargon, but it is also uttered in routine discourse, at moments of crisis, when a conversation cannot proceed.

Suddenly, a neglected figure, very short, skinny, and sharp-boned, sloppily dressed, rises up, weaving its hands, shouting wordlessly, "Ho!" This is Shgetef, who is also known by his nickname, "the Fool" (al-Ahabal). The disputants, recognizing that he has something to say, and that he has not participated in the discussion till now, quiet down. Then, in a very solemn voice, the fool says, "—but the Bedouin pee while sitting —." [In the Southern Sinai dialect of Arabic, sitting means squatting. Squatting is the proper way in which a Muslim should urinate in order not to become polluted by drops of urine.] All burst out with laughter. They know through the fool's utterance what makes them different from the nearby hippies. In that paradoxical context, peeing while squatting means existing in the world as Bedouin.

The fool goes on, describing the "bizarre" life of the hippies in their false Bedouin village. He stages his story as a theatrical "show," using exaggerated hand motions and grotesque facial mimicry. "Yesterday a couple came to me. They wanted to rent a hut. I think they were from a kibbutz, but the guy looked Swedish. She drove the car and he unloaded it." The fool pauses, letting his audience laugh. [When local migration occurs, Bedouin men load and drive their pickup trucks, and women do most of the unloading.] The fool continues, "The guy shut up while she haggled with me on the price, and then she tried to cheat when paying." All laugh again [since Bedouin men are the ones to haggle with foreign merchants, and sometimes, intentionally, they pay them less. Bedouin women haggle only with local Mzeina merchants, and when paying they carefully count the exact amount of money.] The fool waits till the laughter fades and continues, "Finally they undressed and went to the beach." He moves gracefully the upper part of his body, putting his hands on his chest, imitating the bouncing breasts of a woman. Another peal of laughter emerges from the audience. "And that Swede — he had the largest foreskin I've ever seen in my life! He was so hairy!" All laugh. [According to the Muslim law, Bedouin men are circumcised. The word tuhur, circumcision, is derived from the verb tatahar, which connotes purification. Both men and women remove their pubic hair, which is also associated with pollution.] The fool pulls his face with disgust and continues, "In the afternoon she pulled the guy away from the beach and took him to the hut. They did there all sorts of things which people never do." He then kisses, caresses, and embraces an unseen figure. "And at the end she was on top!" The audience roars with laughter for about two minutes. [According to the Mzeina interpretation of Muslim matrimonial laws, only married couples can have sexual relations, and these take place only during the night. Mzeina couples express their emotions reciting metaphorical poetry in one-gender company. During intercourse they hardly touch each other.]

The fool continues with his buffoonery for ten minutes more. Then, when the last laughter has faded out, he shrugs his shoulders, showing that he does not care very much for the characters in his story and says, "And that's the way it is (wahadha hia kidhi)!" a common statement at the end of solo speeches. After some minutes of agitated silence, conversation begins again to flow. Now the topic is prices and stocks of caftans.

At the start the fool seriously intruded a jocular punchline into the dispute, making with it a sharp distinction separating Mzeina-as-Bedouin from hippy-tourists-as-outsiders. When telling the story about the tourist couple, who behaved exactly the opposite from Bedouin, he expanded on the distinction. The fool is actually a wealthy, talented businessman. He, however, is always dressed in rags. He makes his living from renting huts to the hippies and exchanging American dollars and German marks. He nevertheless, contributes generously to the maintenance of the village mosque and has participated twice in the expensive pilgrimage to Mecca. He demonstratively prays the noon and afternoon prayers during work-time, when in the midst of naked hippies stretched out suntanning on the beach. In his parodic performance at the men's club, the fool epitomizes the existential paradox of the pious Mzeina, who make a relatively good living from selling sins to naked outsiders. There are naked foreigners in the midst of pious Muslims because none of the Israeli authorities, who governed the Sinai after the 1967 war, bothered about the impact of exposing some "decadent" Western lifestyles before one of the "exotic" components of the attractive Sinai landscape, i.e., its inhabitants. The Mzeina, for their part, could not force the hippies to at least wear bathing suits, since, according to Egyptian law, which was continued by the Israeli military government, they were not allowed to impose their legal institutions on outsiders.

The fool brings his theatrical talent and symbolic capacity to bear upon the inconsistent, insecure living situation in which the Mzeina are placed. From 1972, with the opening of the asphalt road connecting the Israeli city of Eilat with Sharm A-Sheikh, till April 1982, with the return of the whole Southern Sinai peninsula to Egyptian hands, the Mzeina made their living mainly out of tourism while under Israeli military control. During the '50s and most of the '60s Mzeina men worked as unskilled migrant laborers in the Sinai, in the Egyptian oil towns and in the manganese mines on the coast of the Suez Gulf; they also smuggled hashish and opium through the Southern Sinai from Jordan and Saudi Arabia to Egypt, and even went to the Nile valley seeking jobs in cities. From the 1967 war till 1972 they lived mainly on goods and money they had stockpiled during the previous Egyptian period. As they stated in their discussion, they cannot rely on pastoral nomadism or large-scale fishing for their subsistence. It is now hard to predict what will be their major wage-work occupation from this April on, when the Sinai pawn is again changing hands for the seventh time during the last thirty-four years, between Israel and Egypt.

The fool is an allegorical figure — belonging to the peripheries of social deviation — in the course of acting out a theatrical "show" about itself. The fool's comic "show" communicates a message about his course of action and also an implicit metamessage about the general structure and action of Mzeina life. He is likely to appear in a situation when the unity of the social context cannot be maintained, when a shift from the flow of everyday routine to the spatially and temporarlly closed frame of ritual/play is about to occur. The fool shouts his "Ho!" only after somebody has uttered, "The blood is protected, there are no holes," a statement brought from the reservoir of agnatic ideology only in times of logical and contextual crisis. In the ritual/play frame social knowledge from the various fragmentary domains of routine is stylistically reflected and communicated. The frame, although bounded within limits of time and space, has dynamic, transformational properties. The fool transforms all the ad hoc disputants in the men's club into partakers in a cycle of ritual/play which he creates, beginning with his shout of "Ho!" and ending with his statement, "And that's the way it is."

The fool first appears in a situation of social inconsistency, in which routine typifications of the reality of "being a Bedouin" become contradictory and paradoxical to Mzeina men. Such social opacity occurs when Mzeina men, in the midst of ordinary routine, reflect about themselves in a reductionist fashion. During certain moments in that routine they ask themselves what the essence is of their existence as Bedouin. The fool, by his very intrusion into the inconsistent social situation, restructures the meaning of the social context. The Mzeina know that they are Bedouin like the other Bedouin after the fool states, "The Bedouin pee while sitting." In this manner he bridges paradox at a humoristic, higher level of abstraction. When performing his antics at the men's club, the fool treats it as a theater stage. He does not interact with his audience in the Goffmanian sense. By being a solo actor on the stage he can choose to end the dispute. The fool is the situational embodiment of the Mzeina, and thus he cannot be reduced to a simple term such as a prototype, stereotype or social role. In contrast to the latter, the reality of the fool is total, and there is no room in it for any negotiations. When the wealthy fool mockingly imitates the hippies, no one interrupts him to ask about exchange rates or his camel. He is his own rationale, or as some Mzeina stated to me, "The fool is a Fool." When his evocator chooses to be a fool, and not a devotee or a merchant, others cannot ignore him, but are forced to participate in this farcical world. In this manner the fool can rearrange reality for the rest of the men sitting in the club in keeping with his own image.

During the course of the fool's performance, the social selves of the others become irrelevant, but the fool demonstrates some identity which they have sensed in themselves prior to his ludicrious intrusion into their everyday conversation. His audience have admitted ambiguously that they are Bedouin, beatniks and fools. The fool, on the contrary, clearly, coherently and unambiguously communicates a message about the foolish beatniks, which entaiïs a metamessage dissociating the Mzeina Bedouin from the beatniks. In his performance the fool dramatizes the antistructure of Dahab Bedouin life. When demonstrating this antistructure, he becomes a source of humor because of the bisociation imminent in his appearance: a rich man in rags, a devotee discussing proper urination, and the like. The fool thus reifies and affirms the Mzeina Bedouin identity.

Two days after the dispute in the men's club, I was sitting on the beach, leaning against a palm trunk during twilight time, when the sharp red granite cliffs seem to glide into the red Red Sea, mirrored in its water. At this time of the day, men wash themselves at the seashore in preparation for the early evening prayer (*maghrib*). Then they sit beneath the palms on the beach, eight or ten feet distant from each other, silently waiting for the *muezzin* cry. Smells of cooked fish and ground spices gradually drift into the air. I remarked to no one in particular, "Shgetef made me laugh a lot the evening of the day before yesterday." There was a very long pause which I timed with my watch. Then one man responded slowly, choosing his words carefully, "Shgetef — his mind is sharp as a knife. This summer he earned more than all of us from the tourists. But at times — his mind goes with the twilight breeze (*tarawa*). His tongue does not know what it says." There were two minutes of silence. A faraway man said nonchalantly, with a cynical intonation, "The fool is a Fool." My neighbor responded immediately, with dramatic irony, "Is *he* a fool?! *All of us* have become fools!" I waited a bit, and asked, "*Are* you all fools?! What do you mean?" My neighbor replied at once, "The tourists have made us fools. They photograph us, they make movies of us. There is not any mountain left they have not climbed, any wadi they have not hiked, any coral reef they have not scubadived to. They want to eat our bread, drink our tea, and then they complain of constipation." He paused, then laughed sarcastically. He grimaced, his furrowed face probably reflecting his generation's humiliation, and continued slowly and bitterly, "Our children do not know this desert, their homeland, as well as some of the tourists. They want to hang around Eilat [An Israeli city on the Gulf of 'Aqaba], eat white bread soaked in pasturized milk. They want to drive only Mercedes taxis—" And the man who sat in the distance added, completing the sentence, "—and seek sexual adventures (*yaghawu 'ind*) with our daughters."

There were five minutes of quiet. I assume we all thought of the ways romantic pasts relate to global futures at that sunset/moonrise, moody time of the day. Then somebody slowly and monotonously recited a traditional poem (*gasid*) on the fool. The rest joined, repeating the rhymed syllables. The recitation of the poem underscored the importance of the fool as a cultural asset of the Mzeina. He is a defense mechanism to be used against external chaos. By his ritual/play he helps the members of the tribe shield themselves from the impingement of external, inconsistent forces beyond their control.

NOTES

This article is based on 27 months of field work conducted between February 1976 and August 1979, in the southern Sinai peninsula. I also spent August 1981 in the Sinai in order to update the research. I wish to thank William A. Shack and Grace Buzaljko of the University of California at Berkeley for their valuable comments.

REFERENCES

Cohen, A. Symbolic action and the structure of the self. In I. Lewis (Ed.), *Symbol and sentiment: Cross-cultural studies in symbolism.* London: Academic Press, 1978, pp. 117-128.

Douglas M. The social control of cognition: Some factors in joke perception, *Man*, 1968, *3*, pp. 361-376.

Goffman, E. *The presentation of the self in everyday life.* Tel Aviv; Reshafim. (Hebrew translation, 1980). 1959.

Grathoff, R. *The structure of social inconsistencies: A contribution to a unified theory of play, game and sccial action.* The Hague: Martinus Nijhoff, 1970.

Handleman, D. Play and ritual: Complementary frames of meta-communication. In A. J. Chapman and H. Foot (Eds.), *It's a funny thing, humour.* Oxford; Pergamon Press, 1977, pp. 185-192.

Handleman, D. & Kapferer, B. Symbolic types, meditation and the transformation of ritual context; Sinhalese demons and Tewa clowns. *Semiotica,* 1980, 30 (1/2): 41-71.

Klapp, Orin E. The fool as a social type. *American Journal of Sociology*, 1949, 55: 157-162.

Marx, E. Changing employment patterns among Bedouin of South Sinai. In A. Palerm & R. Owen (Eds.), *An Anthropological View of Labour.* Mexico City: NAH, 1975.

Turner, V. *The ritual press.* Chicago: Aldine, 1969.

Turner, V. *Liminal to liminoid in play, flow and ritual: An essay in comparative symbology.* Rice University Studies, 1974, 60 *(3)*, 53-92.

CONCLUSION

We note that modern festival occasions are complex events which might include games (softball), exhibitions, commerce, parades, beauty contests, dance, song, music, bands, picnics, cruises, art and craft exhibits, fashion shows, water fights and nocturnal "rushes." Clearly, many kinds of persons and many kinds of motives are at work in these complex events. In the simpler ones of the Tarahumara or Santal, we recognize that the major purposes include the licensing of behavior not usually exhibited. The Tamahumara are free to get drunk, be violent and indulge in illicit sex. The Santal are permitted their once a year sexual binge with their erstwhile youthful lover or others. The Hippies are permitted to walk about naked and indulge openly in sex, despite the distaste of the nearby Bedouin. The Bedouin, for their part, allow their "fool" to imitate this same distasteful behavior in order to mock what they abhor. In Sierra Leone the festivals permit costumed display of immaturity, of "shit," of degeneracy, of trickery and the behavior of "devils."

The Toronto Carabana includes erotic dances, revelling until sun-up the day before the parade, and on the last day reckless and unbridled abandon at least in the West Indian original versions. In Minnesota it might not be quite so wild, except that in Greenwood the drinking and vandalism required town ordinances to the contrary; in Foley drinking, which was not usually permitted in the streets, was allowed on the day of the festival. At Berkeley in the 1890s the violence of the Spring rushes between the classmen of different years, the injuries, the horseplay, the wild chasing, the wrestling for the axe all moved the authorities to move towards more careful institutionalization.

From these cases it is not hard to argue that if there is indeed play on these occasions, then one of its features seems to be *the permitting of a license not available at other times*. Whether the behavior is sexual, aggressive or vertiginous (alcohol and drugs), in all cases it is something that is not usually permitted. There is certainly support here for the view of a number of writers (Babcock, 1978) that the festival world is a reversible world. That is, a sphere in which one finds behaviors antithetical to those regarded as normative in the society concerned. In the festival one may do things that are not usually done. At the mildest, this is simply that the participant is at leisure, not at work. Better still, one can participate vicariously and perhaps vividly in the unusual antics of the performers. Again one can participate by eating unusual foods, or by becoming a performer in game contests and dances. And finally, there is always the possibility of participating in excesses of sex or violence or gluttony or altered states of consciousness.

But this is a description of festivals. Is the obtaining of license for antithetical behaviors also play? Or is it merely what one does when one is encouraged by the society to participate in these other forms of behavior on these special occasions? We do not need to call it play. Perhaps festivals center on license, and perhaps play does also. At this point, all we need to keep in mind is that it might be useful to think of play in the same way, as always some kind of antithetical behavior, some kind of licensing of what is usually forbidden. A verdict on this can be postponed until later.

A second obvious characteristic of all these events is that they are *sanctioned by their communities*. They are openly occasions for emphasizing social bonds, from the socially starved Tarahumara to the folk of Foley, wanting to preserve their own identity, there is also an open recognition of the importance of these events for the local sense of community. Even the Bedouin, who abhor the passing Hippie Parade and are the most ambivalent about this festival on their beach, are unable to give it up as it represents their livelihood. Their own brief and festive moment with their fool is, of course, what draws them emotionally together again and transcends their conflict on that occasion. Festivals create community. Does play also create community? It would seem that it does insofar as games and sports create and maintain their groups of players and even their groups of supporters. What of more informal play? Does it create community? Again, a case can be made for social bonding as a major outcome of play, and the case has even been made that that is one of the major outcomes of animal play (Baldwin, 1982) but we will return to this point later when more evidence is in hand from our Child's Play section.

There are a couple of points often made about play that can perhaps be disposed of if what is being discussed here is indeed play. Thus, it is usually said in this century that play is always something that is optional, something we choose to do. It is a voluntary behavior. Looking at the more traditional festival behavior, however, we see that that is less true. One was expected to participate in those occasions (Tarahumara, Santal, Sierra Leone) because that was what everyone else was doing. One could argue that in modern festivals also, one often goes along because everyone else is doing so, and only later becomes drawn into what is either festive or playful. One perhaps goes to the festival because it offers the promise of impulse rewards, rather than as a manifestation of freedom. One can even join games because others need an extra player or because one is supposed to be virile. It is true that the central definition for leisure in the modern world must surely be the absence of the obligations of work. But it would seem that play need not always take place in a leisure context, even though it usually does.

In short, play need not be defined in terms of the obligator-optional bipolarity. As Turner has argued, it tended in traditional societies to be discussed instead in terms of events that are sacred or profane, and play was usually classed amongst those things regarded as sacred (1982).

It is a modern habit also to think of play as functional, socializing or enculturative. The nineteenth century notion of its triviality or evil character has given way to the view that it is a preparation for life, it is a form of mental adjustment, of cognitive consolidation, of information acquisition, of cognitive divergence, or a fundamental form through which we construct social reality; to sum up briefly some major modern kinds of play theory. Yet as Alford demonstrates most directly and the other authors indirectly, these festival occasions can lead to death, to accidents, to quarreling, to violence and to the ostracization of offending members. Amongst the Tarahumara, drunken members of the celebration fall down steep cliffs, develop pneumonia lying out drunkenly in the cold, step on and smother babies, use up all their hard-won corn in making the beer, have violent quarrels over the illicit sex in which they indulge. As Manning shows, the Toronto Carabana has exacerbated existing political hostilities between the West Indian Island groups as much as it has celebrated their distinctively different heritages. In Minnesota, the police in Glenwood have had to enforce a ban on alcholic consumption during their festival because of the excessive drinking, public exposure and vandalism which ensued at the local camping grounds. Park provides a history of the University of California's recurrent need to exercise control of student athletic institutions which are constantly veering out of control. And Lavie recounts the story of the embattled Mzeina Bedouin who both make their living off of and play host to a hippie, and extremely liminoid, festival exhibiting nakedness and fornication to which they have extreme moral aversion and from which they can be salved at least in part only by their own "playing the fool." In reading these cases, we realize that excess is always potentially intrinsic to the character of festival. If festival is play, if such license is play, we see that play cannot be defined alone by its functional contribution to the individual or the society. Play is a more dangerous frame than that.

The point of view of some of the writers of these articles, taken from Geertz, is that the members of the society can read the events like *texts* (1973). They are a metacommunication about the society of which they are a part. The idea is that the members of the festival walk away from it with a sentimental or moral message, a communication of something more fundamental about themselves or their society at an intuitive level. And yet from all the above mentioned license and dysfunctional behavior, one would have to declare that if these festivals be texts, then they are inversive texts in part, more akin to pornography than to the Bible.

In sum, if we use the festivals presented here as a help in defining play, then we must say that play cannot be defined as being solely obligatory or solely optional because either condition can apply. It cannot be defined as solely functional or dysfunctional. Either condition can apply, and presumably all of these conditions might apply.

But there is reason to believe that if play is like a festival, then it might well be a genre that allows license to impulses not usually given, that it expresses socially antithetical behaviors and that it both creates and contributes to a sense of communitas amongst the players. All these points (license, antithesis and community) have been framed by Victor Turner in his accounts of festivals and play (1982, 1983).

part *two*

ADULT RECREATION AND GAMES

INTRODUCTION

In this section we deal with the recreation of bicycle riding, the bowling game of Bocce, gambling on the race track and in the casino. As with festivals, these are all thought of as kinds of leisure. In the modern situation, leisure is the usual context for festivals, recreation, games and play. In the modern world, leisure is the most fundamental of these terms, and it is defined largely in terms of escape from the bondage of the work life. It is some kind of preservation of the energies of the organism in the face of those pressures of space, time and action which declare the character and deprivations of industrial society. The contrast with tribal societies is quite profound. Unless such tribes are in a state of deprivation (as is often the case in their contacts with colonial powers), or slavery, they have no equivalent of the modern monolith of external government and the organization of all the phases of life, including that clearly structured and articulately differentiated sphere called work (Diamond, 1974; Cherfas & Lewin, 1980). This profound and overwhelming temporal regulation of life by the routines of work and their accompanying technologies and architectures is the context without which modern leisure is inconceivable. It is not surprising that within this cultural context: "The central dimension of all definitions of leisure is freedom. Leisure is chosen, not required, discretionary not obligatory . . . The second universal dimension is derived from the first. Since work must be done and leisure cannot be 'necessary' then leisure is not work" (Kelly, 1981, p. 183). Those who are specialists in the study of play find little trouble with this definition because at the very least it dignifies their scholarly pursuit. And yet when the most common forms of leisure of the masses of mankind are examined, they somehow do not seem to match up with this concept. In study after study we find that people spend most of their leisure time doing such relatively inactive things as daydreaming, visiting, talking, eating and being entertained. As Roberts has shown, the major forms of British leisure are watching television, smoking, gambling, drinking and either preparing for or have sex (1978). There is nothing particularly dignifying or particularly illustrative of freedom's finest hour in most of this. Modern leisure is rather the complement of modern work. Its key characteristic is that you don't have to work. It is freedom from the captivity of work time, not freedom for a very active pursuit of life's opportunities, though it can be that. *Leisure is primarily a state of being idle,* of being labile, of being undriven and unrequired, of being responsive to passing novelties. Its pleasure lies in its escape from those determined passages of time and events that industrial society requires.

The pleasure that is foremost, then, is the release of restraint. After that come the most varied pleasures of the mind or body thus liberated. Most typically these are the relatively mild pleasures of easy going sociability, conversation and eating and drinking. But occasionally, as our study of festivals has shown, they can be the more dramatic pleasures of watching spectacular events, of indulging in licentious behavior through sex, or gluttony or violence or altered states of consciousness. None of these mild or excessive pleasures in itself is play, though it seems most probably that it is easier for playfulness to break through into performance in these settings, a point to which we will return later. Between idling and festival, however, there is a place for those more moderate forms of excitement called active recreation, including in this section bicycling and games and gambling.

chapter 7

THE DIVERGENT EVOLUTION OF COMPETITIVE CYCLING IN THE UNITED STATES AND EUROPE: A MATERIALIST PERSPECTIVE

David N. Maynard
University of Pittsburgh

This paper addresses several general issues in the social analysis of games in complex societies through the framework of one empirical case study. The case study examines the divergent evolution of competitive cycling in the United States and Western Europe from 1890 to the present. More specifically, the investigation entails several distinct problem areas. First, why was competitive bicycle racing equally popular as a mass participation spectator sport from 1890-1915 in both Europe and America? Second, why did cycling cease to be popular (or even exist as an observable systemic pattern) in both competitive and recreational forms within a very short time span after 1915 in the United States but not in Europe? Third, what economic variables are responsible for the persistence of cycling in Western Europe at present? Finally, what material causal factors and psychological processes at the population level account for the reappearance of competitive cycling and other structurally equivalent expressive activities in the contemporary United States?

Current anthropological approaches may treat games symbolically or functionally as forms of ritual (Norbeck, 1974; Turner, 1974; Blanchard, 1980; Dunleavy and Miracle, 1981), as models of social structure or of antecedent psychological conflicts in childrearing practices (Sutton-Smith and Roberts, 1982; Arens, 1976) or as is often the case, in terms of functional analysis. Methodologically, there is a strong dichotomy between qualitative, subjective interpretations that lack intersubjectivity and reliablility (as in symbolic analysis or the game as ritual metaphor) or highly empirical, operationally explicit mathematical studies of games as cognitive domains (as in behavioral space analysis).

Materialist analyses are somewhat less common in the anthropological literature on games. At a paradigmatic level, I cannot assume that a game can be properly understood solely through an examination of the psychological motivations or cognitive maps of participants in that game. Nor is it necessary to assume that games represent a metaphor or model of other systemic features. Rather, I attempt to establish causal relationships between games (or sport) and associated material factors and psychological processes at the population level through both historical and ethnographic research. Most notably, such a perspective is useful in examining the origins and transformations of specific sports, the political and ideological function of sport in society and the relationship of sport to social stratification and economy — all of which are central concerns of contemporary sport sociology (Loy et al, 1978; Edwards, 1973).

A Brief History and Ethnology of Competitive Cycling

For a short period of time, bicycling was a major recreational and competitive sport in the United States. Although there was a minor surge of interest in the late 1860s, it required technological improvement in the bicycle itself — namely the appearance of the safety bicycle with pneumatic tires, components using ball bearings and chain drive — to initiate a trend that would turn bicycling into an expressive craze of the 1890s.

This mass participation activity was confined mainly to urban areas of the northeastern United States. It was a short lived phenomenon since by 1904 the bicycle was mourned as "dead" by the League of American Wheelmen (LAW). Although prices of new machines fell to reasonable levels by 1900, cycling was primarily a middle and upper class participation sport. Participation rates are difficult to reconstruct, but it is estimated that there were hundreds of cycling clubs by the middle of the 1890s. On one Sunday in August 1898, an estimated 100,000 bicyclists left New York City to tour through the countryside while an additional 50,000 stayed in the city itself.

Some picture of the significance of the cycling boom of the late 1890s can be derived from bicycle industry statistics. It is estimated that the bicycle was a 500 million dollar business in 1896 with 400,000 new machines being sold. By 1898, there were approximately 1.25 million cycles in use in the United States. Other collateral industries benefitted as well: iron, steel, rubber, repair shops, hotels, inns and the clothing manufacturers (Smith, 1972; Aronson, 1952).

Bicycle manufacturers (of which there were over 400 in 1895) encouraged the growth of cycling by financing the first publications and cycling clubs and by supporting litigation to make cycling legal on public roads. Later, manufactuers and organizations such as the LAW lobbied successfully for road improvement. Many features of the bicycle industry may be seen as precursors of the automobile industry: mechanized mass production, product testing, speed and distance trails as advertising, a dealer network selling standardized products with factory warranties and planned obsolescence with the appearance of yearly models with stylistic changes. After a trade-price war, the bicycle industry (by then controlled through the American Bicycle Company Trust of J.D. Rockefeller and Albert

Pope) collapsed in 1903 from overcapitalization and overproduction (Smith, 1972).

It is in this milieu that competitive cycling flourished for little more than a decade. Cycle racing fell into two basic categories: amateur road racing and professional track racing. Most major cities in the United States (Chicago, Denver, Buffalo, New York, etc.) held point-to-point road events as an annual affair. Starting fields consisted mainly of weekend cyclists and were often quite large — up to 500 riders. Professionals avoided these events since roads were poor, mass crashes were a frequent occurrence and prizes were minimal or non-existent. In spite of its general popularity, road racing was handicapped as a spectator sport since it was difficult to view the entire event and road sides were dirty and uncomfortable.

Professional cycle racing was conducted on a circuit of several dozen dirt or board tracks in cities throughout the eastern United States. Top cyclists like A.A. Zimmerman or Charles "Mile a Minute" Murphy were nationally recognized and acclaimed. Up to 10,000 paying spectators watched Six-Day races in New York and elsewhere. Illegal betting on contests was common. By 1896, there were 2,000 professional riders, the best of whom could make up to $20,000 per season. Corporate sponsors consisted primarily of bicycle manufacturers. The overall popularity of cycling as a spectator sport is difficult to estimate, but several historical sources rank it as roughly equal in media coverage and live attendance with baseball, prize fighting and horse racing, the other major American spectator sports of the late 19th and early 20th centuries. By 1915, bicycle racing had lost most of this popularity and by 1929 had ceased to exist as an observable systemic pattern in the United States until its revival in the early 1970s (Smith, 1972; McCullaugh, 1976; Betts, 1969, 1974).

Competitive cycling in Europe developed quite differently. First, both amateurs and professionals competed in road and track events. Second, road events became the principle focus of the professional end of the sport. Third, there were multiple corporate sponsors apart from bicycle manufactuers. In particular, major daily newspapers tended to initiate and help finance important one-day races held annually as well as the national tours or stage races, the Tour de France being the most prominent of these (Henderson, 1970; Saunders, 1971). The relevance of the contrasts between European and American forms of competitive cycling will be discussed in the next section of the paper.

Professional bicycle racing is one of the most popular spectator sports in Western Europe today, ranked only behind soccer (Arlott, 1976). It has been estimated that 30 million spectators view the three week long Tour de France held in July. More than 100,000 paying fans attended the 1975 World Championships in Mettet, Belgium.

Over a season that stretches from early February to the end of October, competitive cycling receives extensive media coverage in daily newspapers and live television broadcasts as well as through specialized sports publications. By contrast, competitive cycling in North America remains an obscure, "underground" sport, despite some growth in the number of active participants and expansion in corporate sponsorship and media coverage in the latter part of the 1970s.

A Structural and Historical Analysis

The divergent evolution of competitive cycling in Western Europe and the United States may be conceptualized as a problem of "cultural fatigue" — the playing out and disappearance of systemic patterns (or style patterns) from both internal and external change factors (Kroeber, 1948). What are some of the historically and institutionally rooted variables that account for the demise of competitive cycling as a systemic pattern in America and its persistence as a systemic pattern in Europe?

The rapid technological replacement of the bicycle by the automobile after 1905 in the United States was a significant factor in the demise of the bicycle manufacturing industry and of cycling as an adult recreational activity (Betts, 1974; Smith, 1972). In one sense, technological and organizational trends in the expressive craze of cycling in the 1890s generated the preconditions that favored the rapid diffusion of the automobile. We have already noted that production and marketing features of the bicycle industry were later reproduced in the automobile industry. Many of the personnel, retail outlets and capitalist firms in the early automobile industry of the United States had originally participated in the bicycle business (Smith, 1972). Various technological improvements in the bicycle (pneumatic tires, ball bearings, braking systems) contributed to the technical feasibility of the automobile. Finally, litigation initiated by cyclists which resulted in road improvement served to benefit motorists by making early automobile use easier and more convenient.

In Europe several material factors including different socio-spatial organization of urban areas and lower per capita income combined to slow the adoption of the privately-owned automobile as a mode of transportation and maintain bicycle use in both expressive and utilitarian contexts. I would argue that this allowed a longer period of time for institutional replication of the game of cycling to occur in Western Europe. Institutional replication refers to a set of mechanisms that recruit personnel and spectators as well as avenues of information transmission which perpetuate a specific culture pattern as a socially recognized field of activity.

A related consideration is that the underlying economic basis of competitive cycling was much narrower and therefore more vulnerable to disruption in the United States than in Europe. Since racing was supported and organized largely by bicycle makers in America, it seems reasonable that when the bicycle industry collapsed suddenly about 1905, competitive cycling should also have collapsed. In Europe, major economic supports for racing came at an early date from newspapers and other extra-sportive sponsors as well as bicycle makers, all largely for purposes of advertising.

Several objections present themselves to the argument I have outlined up to now. First, if cycling was so popular as a spectator sport in the 1890s, why didn't it survive after the appearance of the auto-mobile? Horse racing as a spectator sport endured both the intro-duction of the railroad and the automobile. Second, why didn't other businesses fill in the vacuum when the bicycle industry ceased to sponsor competitive cycling?

One reply to these objections lies in the amount of time neces-sary for institutional replication of a mass participation spectator sport to take place. Another answer is related to the much greater number of competing sports in the United States. As Neale (1969: 219) puts it "competition exists not between teams of leagues but between sports." Regardless of the psychological motivation for participation of individuals in sports as expressive activities, it is also true that sports compete in economic terms for spectators, media coverage and so on. In the United States, at least half a dozen more institutionally stable sports could fill in any void in the supply of sports consumption when cycling ceased to exist as a large scale pheno-menon. In Europe, there are very few competing mass participation spectator sports at present. This was also true in the early part of the century.

In summary, major factors in the demise of competitive cycling as a systemic pattern in the United States after 1903 include collapse of sponsoring industries, initiation of a new expressive craze (the automobile), too short a period of existence for institutional repli-cation to occur, and a large number of competing mass participation spectator sports to which fans could shift their attention after the demise of cycling. From a materialist perspective, the collapse of bicycle industry sponsorship in America is a process involving cor-porate mergers in periods of economic downturn (Bergesen 1981; Wright, 1978) and a rapid shift in patterns of capital investment to new and different sectors of commodity production. In Europe, continued use of the bicycle in both utilitarian and recreational modes by con-sumers made it profitable for capitalist firms to support competitive cycling for advertising purposes. The explanation of underlying structural causes of the differing numbers of competing sports in Europe versus America, however, is beyond the scope of the present analysis.

The preceding analysis suggests several paths of inquiry into the factors affecting the persistence of competitive cycling as a systemic pattern in Europe up to the present time. Cycling is a business in the same way as other professional sports are. Promoters, corporate sponsors, newspapers that sponsor major stage races, and towns that host races, all wish to sustain interest in cycling to show a continued profit. The profit motive leads to attempts to make cycling as entertaining as possible. Some of these attempts include inducements to competitors to put on as good a show as they can for the spectators. Other attempts include minimizing any negative publicity about bicycle racing. For example, doping (use of illegal stimulants or other drugs) has long been a major problem in European cycling (Woodland, 1980). Many observers of the sport claim that each new doping scandal has decreased cycling's popularity by giving fans the impression of unfair competition. Hence, most newspapers try to gloss over occasions when top cyclists are found guilty of using illegal substances. (For general perspectives on the interlock of media and sports teams see Loy *et al*, 1978: 314-16.)

Competitive and recreational cycling have undergone a resurgence of interest in the United States since 1970. At the same time, other sports — nordic skiing, backpacking and especially running — have also grown in popularity. The above mentioned leisure time activities — whether games in the technical sense (cf Roberts *et al*, 1959) or otherwise — are structurally equivalent expressive activities. That is, they share common features and are often amicably viewed as being mutually compatible personal fitness activities. Important similarities include:

- all are anaerobic threshold sports;
- all involve similar physiological changes, notably the production of a hormone known as nonrephredrine — a consequence of aerobic exercise for periods of longer than 30 minutes;
- all are organized through formal and informal quasi-groups but may be practiced individually as well;
- nearly all involve a potential for equipment fetishism — the conscious attempt to purchase and display high priced, elite consumption items.

Empirically, the situation is more complicated on a psychological level since a certain amount of "expressive intolerance" (cf Roberts, 1981) exists between participants in these different sports; for example, cyclists and runners may have have little regard or respect for other aerobic sports that they do not happen to participate in.

How can the growth in popularity of such sports be explained? To begin with, there are some readily apparent economic dimensions. Physical fitness is a $30 billion a year service and manufacturing industry. (Reed, 1981) and the institutional linkages between the media that encourage attitudes extolling the virtues of fitness and youth and this industry could be examined empirically.

Another perspective that may contribute to an understanding of this phenomenon is Robert LeVine's model of "evolutionary population psychology" (1973: 132-134). LeVine's model consists of four interdependent components.

• Adaption of early child care customs to ecological pressures (page 132.)

• Deliberate socializations of children by adults so that they conform to societal norms (page 132).

• Secondary adaptions of individual personality to normative environments through selective social behavior (page 133) including behavior in socially defined roles.

• Adaptations of aggregate personality characteristics of populations to normative environments through the selective pressures of social sanctions (page 133).

Assuming that any regularities in behavior and underlying psychological states (propensity to become involved in specific expressive activities, for instance) are normally distributed within a population, then selective pressures will affect that distribution through various

Relevant selective pressures that have affected changes in interest and participation in personal fitness expressive activities over time include:

• concerns over health problems resulting from contemporary lifestyle, specifically degenerative cardiovascular diseases;

• concerns about meeting normative expectations of youth, beauty and fitness;

• the intensity of exposure to others already engaged in these activities, whether through interpersonal contact or media diffusion.

If this line of explanation is correct, one should expect any change or minor cyclicity of selective pressures to be correlated with changes in participation rates in aerobic expressive activities. I am currently conducting empirical research to see if this is the case.

If cycling, running, nordic skiing and so on are structurally equivalent activities, how does one account for differential participation across them? The number of runners who competed in the New York City marathon in October 1981 exceeded the total number of competitive cyclists in the United States by ten times. In this case, there are probably aspects of content that contribute to differential popularity-relative costs, perceived safety, perceived aerobic benefits per unit of time invested and the nature of the competition itself. Running races permit an individual to perform at his or her own pace, while cycling, due to the aerodynamics of group riding in races, forces a competitor to ride at the same speed as everyone else — or drop out of the race. The difference may help explain the pleasant camaraderie of a marathon as opposed to the fierce competitiveness of a bicycle race.

I do not mean to suggest that the current expansion of participation in running or cycling should be attributed solely to individual motivations regarding health and beauty, nor, for that matter, to the sociological truism that the adoption of innovation is related to how prevalent that innovation happens to be in one's immediate environment. Once again, it is necessary to consider structural factors of an economic nature. For instance, between 1977 and 1982, membership in the United States Cycling Federation (the governing body of amateur cycling in the United States) has nearly doubled to 15,000 license holders. An increase in media coverage, particularly television, may be partly responsible. On the other hand, more extensive corporate sponsorship of events and teams for both national-class and beginning competitors is also important. Simply put, as more resources become available, the sport of cycling attracts more competitors and spectators, thereby creating larger events which are more likely to receive media coverage and so on in a positive feedback process. Here, we have come full circle in the analysis: firms like the Southland Corporation (parent company of the 7-11 convenience food store chain), Lowenbrau, Coors, etc. are willing to invest nearly a million dollars in cycling because the sport happens to fit in with the desired image of their products in advertising. A similar situation exists in the socio-economic organization of running in the contemporary United States. Ironically, companies that now support cycling do so in part because the sport is so little known in this country, thereby making it both a novel promotional venue and a relatively inexpensive one since there were no major financial interests involved in American cycling prior to 1977.

In summary, I have used the history of competitive cycling to suggest ways that anthropologists might analyze games in complex societies in contrast to the more conventional theoretical frameworks represented in the TAASP proceedings of previous years. I do not deny that games have a cognitive dimension (or even a ritual one!) which is worthwhile to study; however, it might also be worthwhile for anthropologists to devote more attention to material determinants of games.

I noted at the beginning of the essay that materialist analyses of games are somewhat rare in the anthropological literature. One wonders why this should be so. I suspect that part of the answer lies in the apparent triviality of studying games. Materialists are often strident in their insistence that *they* study theoretically and politically relevant problems while their cognitively oriented colleagues are theoretically wrong-headed and politically obscurantist (see for example, Harris, 1980). Indeed, studies of contemporary American society (eg. Kottak, 1981) that focus primarily on Star Trek, McDonalds, football, single's bars (or even, God forbid, bicycle racing) may well be lacking in substantive significance when compared to the study of issues like poverty, racism, the exacerbated class conflict characteristic of late capitalism, restricted access to the American legal system for the poor (Nader, 1980) and so on. But what critics like Harris overlook is that the academic study of triviality (however it is to be defined) is in itself the product and consequence of definite material processes. During the 1960s, the growth of the academic establishment made it possible for all sorts of new specialties in the social sciences to appear. Now that the contraction of that system has begun, it is inevitable in the ecological sense that individuals who have made (or are making) an investment in an academic career will seek out, or more intensively exploit, a given niche (like the topical study of games) and attempt to rationalize it as a legitimate arena of scholarly inquiry. It, therefore, seems reasonable to expect that for as long as humans play, there will be anthropologists interested in studying play.

NOTES

1. I would like to thank Professors John M. Roberts and Laurel Bossen as well as Ron Sacco, Cliff Stevenson and Michael Coy for comments and suggestions on a previous draft of the paper.

REFERENCES

Arens, W. Professional football: An American symbol and ritual. In W. Arens and S.P. Montague (Eds.), *The American dimension: Cultural myths and social realities.* Port Washington: New York: Alfred, 1976.

Arlott, J. *World Encyclopedia of sports and games.* London, 1976.

Aronson, S.H. The sociology of the bicycle. *Social Forces,* 1952, 30, 305-312.

Bergesen, Albert. Long economic cycles and the size of industrial enterprise. In R. Rubinson (Ed.), *Dynamics of world development.* Beverly Hills: California: Sage Press, 1981.

Betts, J.R. *America's sporting heritage: 1850-1950.* Reading: Mass: Addison-Wesley, 1974.

Blanchard, Kendall. Introduction to the ritual dimension of play:

Structure and Perspective. In Helen B. Schwartzman (Ed.), *Play and Culture*. West Point: New York: Leisure Press, 1980.

Dunleavy, A. O. and Miracle, A. W., Jr. Sport: An experimental setting for the development of a theory of ritual. In Alyce Taylor Cheska (Ed), *Play as Context*. West Point: New York: Leisure Press, 1981.

Edwards, H. *The sociology of sport.* Homewood: Illinois: Dorsey Press, 1973.

Harris, Marvin. Historical and ideological significance of the separation of social and cultural anthropology. In E.R. Ross (Ed.), *Beyond the myths of culture.* New York: Academic, 1980.

Henderson, Noel G. *Continental cycle racing.* London, 1970.

Kottak, Conrad P. (Ed). *Researching American culture.* Ann Arbor: University of Michigan Press, 1981.

Kroeber, Alfred. *Anthropology.* New York: Harcourt, Brace, 1948.

LeVine, Robert A. *Culture, behavior and personality.* Chicago: Aldine, 1973.

Loy, John W. Jr., McPherson, Barry D. and Kenyon, Gerald (Eds.) *Sport and social systems.* Reading: Mass: Addison-Wesley, 1978.

McCullaugh, James C. (Ed). *American bicycle racing.* Emmaus: Pennsylvania: Rodale Press, 1976.

Nader, Laura (ed.). *No access to law: Alternative to the American judicial system.* New York: Adadimic Press, 1980.

Neale, Walter C. The peculiar economics of professional sports. In John W. Loy and Gerald S. Kenyon (Eds.), *Sport, culture and society.* New York: Macmillan, 1969.

Norbeck, Edward. The anthropological study of human play. Rice University Studies, 1974, 60, 1-8.

Reed, J.D. *et al.* America shapes up. *Time* magazine, November 2, 1981, 94-106.

Roberts, John M. Natural games: A cultural perspective. Colloquium presented in the Department of Anthropology, University of Pittsburgh, November 25, 1981.

Roberts, John M., Arth, M.J., and Bush, R.R. Games in culture. *American Anthropologist,* 1959, 61, 577-605.

Saunders, David. *Cycling in the sixties.* London, 1971.

Smith, Robert A. *The social history of the bicycle.* New York: American Heritage Press, 1972.

Sutton-Smith, Brian and Roberts, John M. Play, games and sports. In Harry C. Triandis and Alistar Heron (Eds.), *Handbook of cross-cultural psychology.* New York: Allyn and Bacon, 1982.

Turner, Victor. Liminal to liminoid in play, flow and ritual: An Essay in Comparative Symbology. Rice University Studies, 1974, 60, 53-92.

Woodland, Les. *Dope: The use of drugs in sport.* David and Charles: Newton Abbot: United Kingdom, 1980.

Wright, Erick Olin. *Class, crisis and the state.* London: New Left, 1978.

chapter 8

PLAY OR PATHOLOGY:
A NEW LOOK AT THE GAMBLER
AND HIS WORLD

Martin McGurrin
Vicki Abt
James Smith

> *True, we personally negotiate aspects of all the arrangements under which we live, but often once these are negotiated, we continue on mechanically as though the matter had always been settled.*
>
> (Goffman, *Frame Analysis*)

Behavioral preferences and decisions, especially those somehow dealing with vaguely illicit conduct such as gambling, are usually explained almost exclusively by individual psychopathological traits and attitudes. The more undesirable the activity, the greater the emphasis on individual pathology. Unfortunately, this reductionist approach, while in keeping with our cultural emphasis on individualism (people free to create their unique experiences) ignores the conventional nature of much social behavior, particularly those behaviors considered deviant.

While it is certainly true that individuals may have their own psychological goals and that they are capable of personal perception and interpretation, the sources of individual "worlds of reality" are situational. The resulting structure of experience relies heavily on socially constructed meaning systems, on norms which define game-plans as well as determine what constitutes "winning." These meaning systems generate role identities and may both reflect and contribute to the actual physical layout of the enacted social situation. Role theory suggests that much of the continuing motivation for various behaviors can be explained by reference to the social situation and the roles themselves. Indeed, humans define reality, but those who are in the situation ordinarily do not create this definition personally, although society can be said to have done so. As an illustration, the traveler wishing to visit relatives across the state, drives on a pre-existing network of highways (in various states of repair), taking into account local traffic ordinances and the driving behavior of other travelers. He is not free to drive on a neighbor's lawn to save time. Also, whatever the original motivation for undertaking the trip, it may be changed along the way. The traveler may begin to enjoy driving for its own sake, or look at the scenery, or take pride in his ability to outmaneuver other drivers for road space. Experience is constantly being transformed; situations create new enticements, meanings, and motivations. The same principles hold true for gambling behavior. The gambler cannot gamble without a socially constructed game, with or without other players, and a whole accoutrement of game-defining rules, organization, and artifacts. The answer to why people gamble at race tracks and casinos, how often they gamble, and how much they gamble may largely be found in relating perception of opportunities, risks, and goals to social experiences within the physical and normative system of the gambling situation itself.

It is not surprising that a 1974 survey of gambling behaviors found that the amount and kind of gambling, as well as beliefs surrounding the behaviors, were associated with gaming laws and the numbers of existing racing and casino facilities in the various locales (Kallick, Suits, Dielman and Hybels, 1977). The essentially conventional nature of gambling is demonstrated by the reported fact that over half the population said they placed bets with one or more of the popular forms of commercial gambling. Moreover, over half these persons bet less than fifty dollars a year. The low level of heavy betting clearly undermines the traditional view of gambling as a psycho-pathological, self-destructive compulsion leading inevitably to the economic and social ruin of the individual. As we have suggested in previous papers, gambling is most often a popular, conventional form of play and gaming, the outcome of a series of consumer leisure decisions mediated by the surrounding worlds of work and family, that engenders its own justifications supporting apparently safe levels of risk that serve to maintain the socially constructed games of chance over time (Abt, Smith, and McGurrin, 1981).

Having said this, it is still legitimate to ask what, if anything, distinguishes the regular gamblers from those who rarely if ever attend commercial gambling locales? The related questions of which predisposing social characteristics and beliefs, experiences of gambling in a socially constructed game, and resulting perceptions of future gambling chances and values influence gambling behavior is a more difficult one to analyze. Even if we find that gamblers distinguish themselves from nongamblers in their riskiness, in their fatalism, or in their perception of their ability to win (Ladoucoeur and Maryrand, 1981), we still have the problem of determining causal links because it is not clear whether these attitudinal differences cause initial entrance into gambling arenas or whether they are themselves a result of a process of differential association (Sutherland, 1960) with the cognitive norms of experienced gamblers. Cognitive dissonance principles suggest that one's perceptions constantly interact with and are altered by actual behavioral choices (Festinger, 1957; Totman, 1979). "The capacity to bring off an activity as one wants to — ordinarily defined as the possession of skills — is itself motivating" (Goffman, 1974, p. 59). "As one wants to" need not entail only winning money; it may well include making social contacts, partaking in ceremonials, playing with icons and symbols, enhancing presentation of self, or simply learning the rules well since a player need not *win* a well-played game. Additionally, unless personal identity is transformed by the gambling role, gambling may be an accidental or totally situational option, one of many vying for a person's leisure choices. In this case we would expect little difference between player and nonplayer.

The Present Study of Gamblers

In terms of the sociology and normalizing of human behavior through social structures and cultural integration, race track and casino gambling are two of the most socially constructed and conventional forms of gambling. Our previous papers deal with descriptions of the race track and casino experience in terms of available roles, rules, action and physical layouts of the locale. These descriptions were a result of several years of participant observation, of in-depth interviewing of casino and track personnel, and of a generally impressionistic research plan. We concluded that gambling behavior could be explained using a situational approach which views the gambling locales as containing transformation rules that linked outside worlds to the enclosed world of the track and casino. These locales seem to embody their own mechanisms for maintaining interest and a constant, steady level of betting behavior.

Nevertheless we did not address the empirical question of personal attributes that might distinguish the gambler from those persons choosing not to gamble and influence the gambler's choice of games or bets within the track and casino. Relevant data was collected through a 155 item survey administered to gamblers and nongamblers in the Philadelphia area. Conventional sampling techniques cannot be employed successfully in a study of social behaviors such as gambling because the universe of true gamblers is not defined in terms of number or location of cases. We do not know how many gamblers there are, nor do we know their individual residential addresses. Consequently, it is not possible to design and execute a standard probability sample. Instead a field survey quota sampling technique was used in which a set number of cases was subjectively agreed upon by the investigtors as a minimum number to generate preliminary findings. Meanwhile, administration of the survey would be ongoing and the case numbers increased as accumulated. Since sampling was done at the gambling locale (race track or casino) it was understood that the population being surveyed was intensely comprised of gamblers; however, the number of actual respondants was limited because their voluntary participation in the survey was required. The equivalent number of nongamblers employed in this study was obtained through a stratified random sample of the general population of southeastern Pennsylvania. Survey interviews were both by telephone and in face-to-face conditions. It has taken six months to accumulate 120 casino gamblers and 150 race track gamblers because of the problems inherent in convincing gamblers to trust the investigators and to cooperate in the study. However, we are still engaged in attempts to increase our number of cases.

The survey questionnaire contains open ended and precoded questions and deals with the following potential factors relevant to gambling attitudes and behavior suggested by the sociological literature on leisure choices.

- Status characteristics of respondents (including socio-economic status variables, educational background, marital characteristics, sex, age, etc.)
- An index of social integration and stability (length of neighborhood residence, relatives within the community, number of good friends, length of current employment situation, organizational memberships, etc.)
- A leisure behavior and preference inventory (comparison over time)
- Perception of significant others' beliefs concerning gambling
- Reasons for attendance at track and casino (over time)
- Social networks at track and casino.
- Familarity with track and casino rules and games
- Perceptions about ability to be successful at track and casino
- General riskiness and beliefs about planning for the future
- Life satisaction index
- Patterns of betting (over time)

Present Findings

We are in the process of developing a comprehensive synoptic model for explaining gambling motivation and behaviors. Our present analysis, however, has progressed only to the point where we can report on the status characteristics of race track and casino gamblers as they compare with nongamblers. We can also offer some information on the belief systems, attitudes, and perceptions of our sample. Analysis in terms of the full model, with reference to the remaining potential factors listed above, remains to be completed.

A basic issue examined was the validity of the stereotype of the gambler as a pathological deviant who carries out a lonely, alienated, and unconstrained existence on the fringes of normal society. In this respect, let us summarize the findings of a typical study of the gambler which equates gambling with social pathology. The gambler is described as experiencing unsatisfactory marital situations including divorce, constant arguments with spouse over money, and generally turbulent family situations. Work is another major area of life dissatisfaction for the stereotypical gambler and he typically experiences low job satisfaction, and frequent job changes related to geographical mobility. Our findings dramatically and consistently contradict this profile of the gambler as a maladjusted social misfit. Gamblers are no more likely to live alone, outside of a family or friendship bond, than are nongamblers[1]. In fact, among our sample, the gambler tends to be married and living with his spouse more often than does the nongambler: While only 43.7% of the nongamblers were married, 50% of casino gamblers, 57% of race track and casino gamblers, and 80% of race track only gamblers were married. Furthermore, while 18.7% of nongamblers lived alone, only 10.7% of casino gamblers and none of the track and casino or track only gamblers lived alone. Typically, then, the gambler was married and lived with spouse, or if unmarried lived with a companion or with family (See Table 1).

.Our gamblers also compared very closely with the general population along several other dimensions of traditional family life and wholesome social integration. First, they were just as likely to have become parents as nongamblers, with 68% of gamblers having at least one child compared to 68.5% of nongamblers. Second, 71.4% of casino gamblers and 80.2% track players have lived within ten miles of their present residence for four years or more, while only 50% of nongamblers displayed the same degree of residential stability. Furthermore, 51.7% of casino gamblers and 57.1% of race track and casino gamblers had three or more relatives other than wife/husband or children who live within fifty miles, while only 25% of nongamblers reported a similar family proximity. When asked "How many of your friends do you feel you can confide in about personal matters?" only 10.7% of casino gamblers and 7.1% of race track gamblers said they had none. At the other end of the scale, 39.3% of casino gamblers and 42.8% of race track gamblers claimed they had three or more such confidants while only 31.2% of nongamblers claimed as many confidants.

It is clear from these findings, then, that the popular stereotype of the alienated gambler without family or friends must be seriously questioned. Our data suggest that far from being a lonely outcast, the gambler is typically as much invested and integrated into stable family life, friendship, and neighborhood as the nongambler.

Similarly, our findings challenge the traditional, unflattering image of the gambler as a failure at work who finds little, if any, satisfaction in conventional employment and who drifts from job to job as his involvement in the gambling life demands. Only 2.2% of our gamblers were presently unemployed compared to 12.6% of the nongamblers surveyed. Moreover, 53.6% of casino gamblers and 71.4 % of race track and casino gamblers had been employed in their present jobs for six years or more. Only 43.7% of nongamblers reported the same degree of employment stability and tenure. Furthermore, 89.7% of the gamblers reported either satisfaction or great satisfaction with their occupation compared with 81.3% of the nongamblers claiming similar degrees of work satisfaction.

The gross misrepresentation of the gambler through traditional stereotypes and social science literature is underscored by our findings that gamblers are typically more religious and religiously active than nongamblers, as much involved in community and other social organization activity as nongamblers, and profess as much responsibility for and commitment to the general welfare as nongamblers. All in all, one might say that the most common gambler is just another "good citizen" who happens to enjoy race tracks and casino games among his chosen forms of recreation.

If gamblers and nongamblers do not differ on the basis of social status and role characteristics which influence social integration and stability, do they differ in terms of their belief and attitude systems, particularly in the area of self-determination and fatalism? The literature reports that gamblers tend to be much more inclined to hold a fatalistic orientation to life than nongamblers and that gamblers believe external and cosmic forces have a greater effect on the future than self-determination and personal planning. In response to the proposition that "when your number is up, your number is up," gamblers tended to agree or strongly agree much more often than nongamblers (gamblers 72.2% vs. nongamblers 56.3%), but there were gamblers who rejected this fatalism very strongly (See Table 2). When asked if they agree that some people are born lucky, gamblers much more strongly endorsed this belief than do nongamblers (gamblers, 74.4% vs. nongamblers, 37.5%). When asked whether we each can generally control what happens to us, gamblers tend to be less likely to endorse this notion than nongamblers (gamblers 69.6% vs. nongamblers 93.8%), but there was a surprising proportion of gamblers who professed a belief that individuals can exercise personal control over life events. Overall, when asked if there is much reason to make plans for the future, gamblers were virtually identical with nongamblers in their support of this proposition (gamblers, 62.6% vs. nongamblers, 62.5%). We should not be surprised by this congruence as studies of actual watering patterns continuously attest to a rational market approach among bettors. Race track gamblers show a distinct shift to caution when betting as a group. Furthermore, there is little overlay, indicating that gamblers tend to bet the most probable winners, thus maximizing their chances of success (Bolton, 1981 and Hausch, 1981). In addition, Ladoucoeur found that, on a sequence of coin tosses, gamblers did indeed overestimate their chances of success in guessing the sequence of tosses. In other words, they thought they had more control over the outcome of the trial than statistical probability dictated (Ladoucoeur, Maryrand, 1981). These findings attest to the question of control over destiny as well as to the additional question of relative optimism.

Finally, in response to the proposition "I generally take too many risks," gamblers certainly view themselves as more likely to be risk takers than nongamblers and race track gamblers agree more than casino gamblers (race track, 41.2% versus casino, 24% versus nongamblers, 15%). And again, when responding to the question "I enjoy a sense of physical danger," gamblers tend to answer yes more often than do nongamblers (gamblers, 40%, nongamblers, 17%). These findings tend to agree with other studies characterizing the gambler as a person who is attracted by the experience of taking risks. However, it should be pointed out that while risk-taking is more prevalent among gamblers than among nongamblers, the majority of gamblers themselves do not prefer exaggerated risk-taking; within the gambling world, they usually choose the wagers with the greatest success probability.

Thus, it seems clear that at this time, our findings tend to challenge fundamentally, if not refute, the traditional stereotype of the gambler as a socially isolated, psychopathological deviant, with no internal controls, and a compulsive drive to destroy himself socially as well as others who depend on him. Instead we have found that the gambler is characterized well within socially acceptable limits and that he may even tend to be *more* stable and conventional in some areas than the nongambler. There seems to be an aspect of ritualism in the stability of both the gambler's social life and his gambling behavior. The fact that the gambler continues to return to the track or casino without any consistent economic reward suggests that the gambler is motivated much more by success in conformity to established situational norms than by actual financial success in rationally calculating and manipulating reality. The ritualistic person converts the instrumental means, the playing of gambling games, into ends in themselves. For most recreational gamblers, the real payoff is the satisfaction of participating in the socially constructed reality of gaming which provides them with meaning and direction rather than demanding innovation. The gambler simultaneously entertains himself through the patterned experience of excitement, suspense, and release as he experiences ego enhancement through the temporary resolution of frustrations and tensions in the fantasy world of gaming. He creates an acceptable pattern of temporary escape from the restrictions and limitations of real life. The play, then, is the thing!

TABLE 1
Comparative Sociodemographic Profiles of Gamblers and Nongamblers

	Casino (N=105)	Gamblers Race Track (N=90)	Race Track & Casino (N=75)	Nongamblers (N=325)
Mean Age	36 yrs.	50 yrs.	40 yrs.	35.6 yrs.
Sex Ratio: M/F	52/48	85/15	65/35	49/51
Marital Status				
% Single	21.4	17.0	22.0	31.3
% Sep., Divorced, or				
Widowed	28.6	13.0	29.7	25.0
% Married	50.0	80.0	57.0	43.7
Parental Status				
% No Child	35.7	28.7	29.6	31.5
% Children	64.3	71.3	70.4	68.5
Residential Stability				
% High	71.4	80.2	78.7	50.0
% Moderate	17.9	10.3	14.3	18.7
% Low	10.7	9.5	8.0	31.3
Close Friend as Confidant				
% None	10.7	7.1	10.5	6.3
% 1-2	50.0	50.1	49.3	62.5
% 3-4	39.3	42.8	40.2	31.2
Job Stability				
% Unemployed	3.5	2.1	1.1	12.6
At present job				
% 1 year or less	10.7	27.2	21.4	22.7
% 1-5 years	32.2	10.3	7.2	21.0
% 6 or more	53.6	62.5	71.4	43.7

TABLE 2
Comparison of Belief Systems of
Gamblers and Nongamblers

Belief Item	Percent Agree		X^2	Sig. Level
	Gamblers	Nongamblers		
When your number is up, your number is up.	72.2	56.3	16.2	.001
Some people are just born lucky.	74.4	37.5	81.3	.001
We each generally control what happens to us.	69.6	93.8	61.42	.001
There isn't much reason to make too many advanced plans.	62.6	62.5	0.0	n.s.
I generally take too many risks.	33.3	15.0	55.19	.001
I enjoy a sense of physical danger.	40.0	17.0	39.38	.001

NOTES

1. Respondents indicating that they had wagered at a race track and/or at a casino and had done so within the last three months were included as gamblers in our sample. Further distinctions as to amount gambled, frequency of gambling, and number of different gambling preferences are not variables in the present discussion.

REFERENCES

Abt, V., and Smith, J. "Playing the game in mainstream America," paper presented to the Association for the Anthropological Study of Play, Fort Worth, April 1981.

Abt, V., Smith, J. and McGurrin, M. "Ritual, risk and reward: A role analysis of race track and casino encounters," paper presented to the Fifth National Conference on Gambling and Risk Taking, Lake Tahoe, October 1981.

Bolton, R., and Chapman, R. "An empirical analysis of an optimal wagering system," paper presented to the Fifth National Conference on Gambling and Risk Taking, Lake Tahoe, October 1981.

Dielman, T. E. Gambling: A social problem? *Journal of Social Issues,* Vol. 35, (3), 1979.

Festinger, Leon *A theory of cognitive dissonance.* Evanston, Ill.: Row, Peterson & Co. 1957.

Goffman, Erving. *Frame analysis.* Harvard University Press, 1974.

Hausch, D., Ziemba, W., and Rubinstein, M. "Efficiency of the market for race track betting," paper presented to the Fifth National Conference on Gambling and Risk Taking, Lake Tahoe, October 1981.

Kallick, M., Suits, D., Dielman, T., and Hybels, J. *A survey of American gambling attitudes and behavior,* Appendix 2 to *Gambling in America,* Washington, C.C., U.S. Government Printing Office. 052-003-00254-0, 1977.

Ladoucoeur,R.,and Maryrand, M. "Evaluation of the illusion of control," paper presented at the Fifth National Conference on Gambling and Risk Taking, Lake Tahoe, October 1981.

Sutherland, E. H., and Cressey, D. R. *Principles of criminology,* 6th ed. Philadelphia, Lippincott, 1960.

Totman, R. *Social causes of illness.* New York: Pantheon, 1979.

chapter 9

"MORTI, MORTI, MORTI":
THE DEATH OF A BOCCE BALL CLUB

Bruce Pierini
California State University at Sacramento

Bocce was brought to America by Italian immigrants of the late 19th and early 20th centuries. A 1903 photograph of Genoese settlers in the Napa Valley of California shows adults and children holding bocce balls at a Christmas celebration. Elsewhere in northern California the popularity of bocce among Italians is amply demonstrated in the 1920s and 1930s through oral and written accounts in San Francisco (*San Francisco Chronicle*, August 31, 1935: H-15), Oakland (*The Express,* February 27, 1981), Martinez (personal interviews), Sacramento (personal interviews) and San Diego (Ciruzzi, 1980:64). It is quite likely that bocce was played in California in the 19th century since many of the earliest immigrants were from Piedmont, long a center of bocce in Italy (Gumina, 1978: 3-4; Radin, 1935: 39). By the time of the great migrations of the latter part of the 19th century bocce had been popular for at least 50 years and quite probably for much longer yet. A court case involving bocce near Asti in 1826 attests to the popularity of the sport then (Eydoux, 1980). Piedmontese immigrants would likely have brought this inexpensive pastime with them to America.

Bocce is now played all over America by thousands of people; the largest percentage of players in California by far is made up of Italian-American males in their 60's, 70's and 80's. I wanted to know the importance of bocce in these elderly mens' lives. Besides enjoyment of a simple recreational activity, what other satisfactions did the men derive from the bocce associations that could account for bocce's continued popularity? What is the social setting of a bocce association like? What is the predominant view of the world expressed from within the bocce group? What is the relationship between the social relations of the group and its cosmology? What is the future of bocce in California?

Methodology

Data collection using participant-observation occurred over an eight-month period and included interviews with and observations of players in four cities in northern California and Lucca, Rome, and Fiuggi, Italy. Most of the roughly 100 hours of fieldwork took place at one bocce association in a park and clubhouse in northern California. Approximately 35% of interviews took place in Italian, the remainder in English.

Data

Bocce is a simple game. Customarily four to six players divide themselves by blind chip selection into two or three teams. The game is similar to lawn bowling, the object in bocce being to throw a bocce ball as close to the "pallino" or jack as possible. After all balls are tossed, points are totaled and kept on a board until the winning score of twelve is achieved by one of the teams.

Daily bocce club activity begins at 1:00 P.M. and ends at 5 P.M. The average number of men who arrive at the small, city-built and maintained clubhouse is 12 to 15. Members usually arrive singly and are often greeted with good-natured teasing, customarily in Italian. The following is a typical vignette. A member arrives and asks why a certain member is absent:

"Che ha successo?" ("What happened to him?")

"E andato a puttana a Roma." ("He went whoring around in Rome.")

With the exception of one club in northern California, only men play bocce publicly in the clubs visited. In the study club the average age is 74. Most of the core group are blue collar and semi-skilled retirees. They are mostly immigrant, first-generation, northern Italians with the largest percentage from the area of Lucca in Tuscany. There are two non-Italians who regularly participate. While eight of the regulars live in the neighborhood of the park, another seven live an average of four miles from it. On a typical day, most of the men will play two or three games of Pidro (a traditional Italian card game) or pinochle. Members continue to arrive throughout the afternoon with most settling into a card game. Some simply watch and/or converse. Occasionally a member will play "Solo" (Solitaire). In good weather, usually in the earlier afternoon, a member or two will solicit others to have a game of bocce. If four members decide to play, they walk about 15 yards outside to the bocce courts. Others may follow them out, observe the games, exchange gossip or news and usually go inside the clubhouse to play cards and continue conversations.

When asked why they come to the park, the men, with few exceptions, give brief, simple answers such as "to pass the time," "to kill some time," or "there's nothing to do." Only a few talked about the obvious sociability of the club. When asked why the men come, the president rhetorically asked "Where would they go, what would they do?" Another member, quite unsolicited, came to me and said: "In the summer it's cool under the trees. In winter it's warm and dry inside. This is how our lives get hope."

One of the most salient features in interviewing the players is they all talked about the impending death of the club: ". . . the club's dying"; "all the good players are dead"; "they die, you know. Ol' age"; "the men are dying." The impending death of the present and future is contrasted with the vitality of the past. In one of the most memorable moments in the field, an elderly man asked me to turn my head and look out the clubhouse windows at the benches flanking the covered bocce courts. He said they used to be "full of people playing and watching bocce ball." He was referring to the time when he began coming to the bocce courts in 1967. This contrasted sharply with the dozen or so present regulars. Another reminisced that on Saturdays and Sundays the courts used to be full of "giocatori" (players) and "spetatori" (spectators), and that all four courts used to be filled in contrast with the one now occasionally used. In recounting the deaths of the old players and the loss of the halcyon days of bocce, he intoned: "Morti, morti, morti" (Dead, dead, dead). In 1980 the membership of the club fell from 62 to 36. The men attribute this decline as primarily due to deaths of members. They do not mention those who simply dropped out due to apathy or for other reasons. Two informants only mentioned that some players didn't enjoy coming to the park any longer and so quit the club. The men are not morose about the club's demise, however. What one hears is a sense of resignation. During the study, a long-standing member of the club died. The president was polling individuals present at the clubhouse as to whether they could act as pallbearers. One by one the excuses were given. One of the members, concerned, asked aloud: "What will happen if they don't find anyone?" The anonymously delivered answer caused convulsive ripples of laughter in the group: "They'd make him walk!"

Analysis

In analyzing the relationship between the predominant view of the world and the social environment of the club, I used notions presented by Mary Douglas in two books *Natural Symbols* (1973) and *Cultural Bias* (1978). I found it useful to look at the social environment of the club in terms of Douglas' notions of "grid" and "group." By "grid" Douglas refers to: "The cross-hatch of rules to which individuals are subject in the course of their interaction" (Douglas, 1978: 8). In a social unit with strong grid, individuals do not interact freely, there are hierarchy and status differences expressed in clothing, food and other physical signs. Douglas defines "group" in terms of the "claims it makes over its constituent members, the boundary it draws around them, the rights it confers on them to use its name and other protections, and the levies and constraints it applies" (Douglas, 1978: 7-8). The degree of "grid" and "group" is assessed and charted on continua expressed as X and Y axes respectively. Accordingly, there are four distinctive types of social environments possible: (A) "Individualist" with weak grid and weak group; (B) "Insulated" with strong grid and weak group; (C) "Strong Group" with strong grid and group, and (D) "Small Group" with weak grid and strong group (Figure 1).

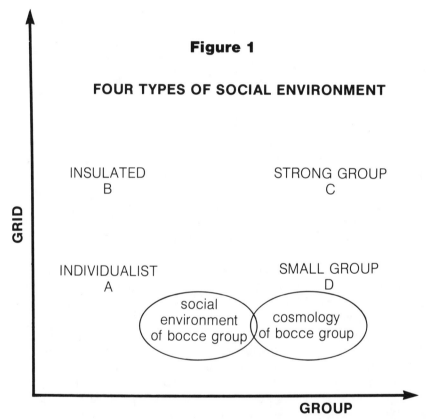

Figure 1

FOUR TYPES OF SOCIAL ENVIRONMENT

In all, Douglas (1978) lists ten generalizations for the kind of tightly sealed social context found in groups with weak classification supporting a vulnerable, small group cosmology like the one found in interviews in the bocce club. In discovering an implicit cosmology and in surveying the social environment, I must emphasize that I will be using data acquired in two different social contexts. The first is the interaction among the men. The second is a series of dyadic interviews I conducted with them. The distinction between the two is crucial. For it seems that the social environment of the group, judged from observed interaction, differs from the cosmology implicit and explicit in interviews. In those interviews notions of a small, well-bounded association that can provide safety from the potentially inimical outside world are present. The group's social environment, however, seems not to be in the lower right (D) of weak classification and strong group boundaries (as is the cosmology) but on the border of (D) and (A), toward individualist competition. While there seems to be some boundedness and emotional commitment to the group, it is not the strong identification with a tightly sealed social unit one expects in small groups on the lower right side. This is where one would find cults and sequestered groups which put great pressure on their members to participate in and conform to group life. These men are in no way so highly controlled by group life. This is a voluntary association without any significant constraints on its constituent members. Members can come to the park if they wish — no one can coerce others to attend bocce or card games. Thus, this group's social environment seems to fall toward the individualist in (A) but at the border with (D).

But if one looks at the cosmology of the group, one finds notions of a caring, meaningful inside contrasted with a somewhat dangerous or indifferent outside. I found the men implicitly and explicitly making such contrasts. Ideas that the park is safe, the trees shady and nurturing, the clubhouse warm, dry and protective and the members freely and eagerly transacting are current. The men, conversely, found danger in the "low-riders" around the perimeter of the park, indifference or minimal concern with their needs by the city government, and generally an uncaring attitude about their concerns on the part of society outside the club ("Where would they go, what would they do?"). This is the kind of cosmology one expects in small groups far to the right of the map — too far to the right to describe the bocce association. I did note elements of "rugged individualism" in interviews exemplified by statements such as "I come to kill some time." One does not find the highly competitive, individualist cosmology in interviews that Douglas predicts for groups whose social environment is like that of the bocce group. Why the disparity between the two realities, social and cosmological? It seems that two key elements of a social environment which would support a small group cosmology are lacking: 1) members do not, as Douglas predicts they must in small groups, "gain their whole life support" from the group, and most importantly 2) the group cannot effectively apply levies and constraints on its members.

The kind of social environment the players have constructed for themselves is a somewhat enclosed atmosphere of easy familiarity, boisterousness and verbal repartee, all mediated through the bocce and card games. Participation in the club affirms their vitality at a point in their lives when, as is commonly assumed in American culture, men are beyond their productive and active years. These men can retain a sense of being in control of daily events through manipulation of bocce balls, playing cards, and each other. The most common feature of bocce games is the prediction of the outcome of bocce tosses. Correct judgements give players prestige by validating their knowledge about the future. Players are quick to point out their own predictive successes and they ignore incorrect predictions. Competition is subtle but strong during bocce and card games. Verbal adroitness and the quick one-line "comeback" are highly valued during mock-assaultive interchange. This is entirely consistent with what Gans found to be the principle elements of personal expressiveness in his study of Boston Italian-American "peer group society" (Gans, 1962: 81).

In interviewing the men, I found the predominant view expressed to be one of society being categorized in terms of insiders and outsiders. A consequent fear of outsiders is readily apparent and new members are either actively discouraged from entering the club or uneasily assimilated. Women being outsiders, and therefore potentially disruptive to the relationships established by the men, are excluded. There are effective boundaries that exclude outsiders, particularly the use of Italian. But group boundaries cannot effectively constrain the behavior of the men. Neither is the sense of groupness sufficiently strong to overcome individual apathy. Additionally, interaction among the men is imbedded in an individualist, competitive social fabric. Therefore the group has shifted to the left toward a looser association of subtly competing individuals.

The distance between what the men want the club to be and what it is is a particularly poignant problem for the club and one common to all human groups: how to maintain a view of the world with a way of life that will not sustain it? In so much talk about death and the dying of the group, the men are mourning as well the inability of their way of life to sustain a world view.

Group life is thus fraught with paradox. It is both expressive and sociable within a competitive context. The club is a gregarious, contented association on the one hand and a dying group of survivors, ambivalent about letting new members in, on the other. If the men are dying, why are the dead not being replaced by new members? The men talk about needing "new blood" but they "get nervous" when "new-comers" or "youngsters" join. "Young people and the players don't mix" is one informant's way of expressing a powerful reality about the club: the club's continuation depends on those people (outsiders) who would by their very nature change the sets of meanings the men have constructed for themselves. The easy sociability, good-natured insulting, male camaraderie, the distinction between insider and outsider, the ambiguous equilibrium of social relations — all are major features of an established, satisfying and primarily social group that would be in jeopardy if newcomers were allowed. The club is very important to the men and the social and emotional costs of continuing the club may be too high a price for them to pay.

A further irony is that the manifest function of group life seems to be to provide meaningful social contact among people at the end of their lives, to affirm the vitality of the players through bocce, cards and verbal teasing while the club itself is dying. In associating in a bocce organization, these men avoid isolated deaths, and in effect, partake symbolically in the communal one of the bocce club.

The game of bocce itself, as it's played at the park, serves as a metaphor for social relations within the group. The playing area is marked off with strong external boundary lines which are respected by all spectators. Within these boundaries individual players are not particularly constrained by differentiating lines of play. Just as in the club, the overt nature of the group is gregarious amiability, but the content of interaction is competitive — so, too, with the game. Sociability is maximized through random assortments of teams yet there is individual competition. This competition lies throughout the overtly social nature of the game. One can manipulate the bocce balls only so far, however. If one is too earnest in one's attempts, one's bocce ball is taken out of the game. Likewise, in the interaction of the men, expulsion is the result of attempts to exert too much control on others. The men will accept only a certain amount of manipulation or coercion by individuals or by the president acting in the name of the club. As the president told me, "All these guys want is to be left alone."

Will bocce ball, as it is traditionally played in California by first generation Italian-Americans die out? If this club's experience can be extrapolated to the many other similar clubs in northern California (and preliminary fieldwork in other areas suggests it can), I would conclude probably so. With few or no replacements and an average death rate of two per year, I would estimate this club will survive probably no more than six or seven years. This may be too optimistic since the group's core membership may fall below a certain threshold number and what is left of the group may simply dissolve. Already one of the reasons given by the "bocciatore" for not playing bocce more often is "we can't get four guys to play." Perhaps it is less surprising, given the small numbers of recent Italian immigrants to the area, that traditional bocce ball may be on the way out than the fact that, given the tremendous internal pressures of the small group of individualists with little internal classification, that this bocce ball association has persisted for so long.

REFERENCES

Ciruzzi, Canice G. "India street and beyond: A history of the Italian community of San Diego: 1850-1980." M.A. thesis, Department of History, University of San Diego, 1980.

Douglas, Mary. *Natural symbols—Explorations in cosmology.* Vintage Books 1973.

"Cultural Bias." Occasional paper No. 34 of the Royal Anthropological Institute of Great Britain and Ireland, London, 1978.

Eydoux, Ermanno. Quasi un giallo per le bocce a Rocca D'Arazzo. in *Il Platano.* Somario, Anno V. N. 3, Terzo Quadrimestre. Asti, Piedmonte (Italia), 1980.

Gans, Herbert J. *The urban villagers—Group and class in the life of Italian-Americans.* New York: Macmillan Publishing Co., Inc., 1962.

Gumina, Paolo Deanna. *The Italians of San Francisco/ Gli Italiani di San Francisco 1850-1930.* Center for Migration Studies, New York, New York, 1978.

Radin, Paul, The Italians of San Francisco—Their adjustment and acculturation. R and E Research Associates. (originally published 1935, R and E Associates), 1970.

Scenes from the death of Oakland's Little Italy—Arrivaderci, Temescal. *The Express,* February 27, 1981, pg. 5.

When Italians meet they play bocci—and Mayor joins in game. *The San Francisco Chronicle,* August 31, 1935 H-15.

CONCLUSION

Maynard's account of the history of bicycling brings home forcefully the role of "material" factors in the modern choice of recreation. The "idleness" of our leisure is filled often not by our own free ranging choices, but by what is made available for us by mass commercial forms of leisure. We are remarkably vulnerable to exploitation by the entrepreneurs of leisure. The massive following of all forms of ball sport, of television, of toys for children, of leisure arcades including video games, and of gambling on numbers, horses and casinos is testament to the empirical fact that the bulk of idleness is exploited for money making purposes by large scale organizations of private or state enterprise. Even when we escape these through pursuit of pleasure including games in our own private clubs, as do the Bocce players in the current account, once again we come under the hegemony of the club's norms and traditional way of life. We may be free from work, but the mark of most forms of leisure is some other form of conformity. This is not to deny, of course, that nevertheless many individuals find in these leisure opportunities a contribution to their mental health which is not always obvious to those who do not participate in their particular form of escape, as the article on gambling appears to testify. That middle class anathema of the nineteenth century has now become a middle of the road pursuit for much of the population.

Nor should the normative and conformist character of most leisure pursuits be thought to deny that there still are many who use these opportunities for quite individual forms of differentiation. But these egregious manifestations of freedom must be regarded as in general the exception rather than the norm. Again, we do not know how much of all this is play. There is so much that is pleasurable in leisure without the concept of play being necessarily involved, except in those institutionalized play forms called games, gambling and sports. These latter forms share fundamental characteristics with play, though at the same time add such other public features as commercialism, spectators, and professionalism that place them nearer to the normative economic culture than most nonorganized play forms, but this is a paradox to which we will return.

part *three*

CHILD'S PLAY

INTRODUCTION

This section contains four papers which deal with a variety of aspects of children's activity described as play. Although each case is very different from the others, nevertheless, striking parallels may be drawn amongst the uses to which the authors in each case put their research. In the majority of cases, the focus is upon the functions served by the behavior rather than on the behavior itself. A further similarity lies in the age spans being considered. All but the first paper deal with children from seven years through early adolescence and pertain to children in North America.

The first paper is a review and critique of correlational and experimental studies which have investigated the relationship between play and social cognition during childhood. It carefully suggests problems which arise when play is considered in relation to social and cognitive skills within experimental paradigms and points to the serious limitations of these studies. Its thrust is primarily methodological.

The second paper deals with the organization of play in an elementary school by school personnel on the one hand and by groups of fourth graders on the other. It describes activity in essentially public domain and in particular foregrounds differences in the concerns and structuring of social activity in the adult as opposed to the child world.

The third paper deals with the trance and levitation activities of groups of 9-16 year old girls. In contrast to the second paper these activities are ones that occur in more private spaces and amongst small and select groups of friends. Nevertheless, there are striking parallels in what the participants in both contexts achieve through their game activities.

The fourth paper renders an account of the language and play behavior of a seven year old boy in a psychoanalytic relationship with a male analyst. It is diagnostic and therapeutic in orientation and in that sense, different from the other studies in this section. However, in its claims that the child uses play and language to recreate and construe significant parts of his world, it is similar to what all the child participants described in these papers tend to do at some level when they use their various expressive behaviors described here to negotiate parts of their respective worlds.

chapter 10

PLAY AND SOCIAL COGNITION

E.P. Johnsen and James F. Christie
University of Kansas

Social knowledge represents a psychological reality in the lives of children. It involves knowing about human beings, including ourselves, and knowing about our social relationships. Understanding the intricate inner works of a pocket watch or the meaning of algorithms in mathematics would *not* qualify as social knowledge. Understanding the relationship between man and machine or the motives of the mathematician in pursuing his or her work would.

Social knowledge research in developmental psychology has concerned itself with answering the following types of questions about children's changing conceptualizations of the social perspective of others:

- Visual or perceptual perspective taking — How does another person see the world?
- Cognitive perspective taking — What are other people thinking? What are other people like?
- Affective perspective taking — What kind of emotional experiences is another person having? This is frequently referred to as empathy. (Shantz, 1975)

What is required for a child to grasp the social meaning of other's ideas, feelings, personalities, and motives? According to Flavell (1977), a child must first be aware that others have their own idiosyncratic goals, thoughts, and feelings. Further, a child must have some notion of when and why one might try to diagnose these conditions in other people. Finally, one must have the ability to identify these psychological phenomena, i.e., one must infer what others are experiencing based on adequate information about them.

That children do not, at an early age, acquire the skills or awareness required to accomplish the diagnosis of covert feelings and ideas in social relationships seems fairly well established. There are many parallels between developmental trends in logical thinking and those in social cognition. The limitations a child experiences in making social inferences are referred to by Piaget and others as egocentrism. Generally, this is the difficulty in discriminating between oneself and the object of one's thinking processes, between one's social world. Presumably children begin life completely egocentric, and gradually this egocentrism erodes into what Werner has called perspectivism, the ability to simultaneously be aware of multiple points of view and to infer the relationships between them. One of the significant factors allegedly involved in this evolution of social knowledge is social interaction, which brings us to our topic, play.

Recent authors have shown considerable interest in the role of play, particularly dramatic or pretend play, in the development of social cognition. While engaging in pretend play, children enact a variety of social roles and are required to follow a number of rules (turn alternation, role-appropriate behavior, etc.). Rubin (1980) has suggested that this type of play is "an informal didactic phenomenon that serves to strengthen already formed rule and role conceptualizations through consolidation and practice" (p. 73). Others have argued that the role-taking experiences which occur in pretend play also build empathic skills and hasten the reduction of egocentrism (Smilansky, 1968).

Research

This section reviews correlational and experimental studies which have investigated the relationship between play and social cognition during childhood. Table 1 summarizes the major design features of these investigations.

To our knowledge, only one correlational study has pursued this relationship. In an observational study of preschool children, Rubin and Maioni (1978) found that the frequency with which children engaged in spontaneous dramatic play was positively correlated with visual perspective taking (the ability to take the visual perspective of another) but not with empathy as measured by the Borke (1971) test.

A majority of the studies which have investigated play and social cognition have used experimental procedures. These investigations have all followed the same training study paradigm: (a) children were divided into treatment groups, at least one of which was to receive training in some type of play, (b) the subjects were pretested on a number of dependent variables, including measures of social cognition; (c) the treatment was administered; and (d) the subjects were reassessed on the dependent variables.

Rosen (1974) studied the effects of training groups of low-SES preschoolers in sociodramatic play, a form of symbolic play in which two or more children adopt roles and attempt to recreate a real-life situation, e.g., a family eating dinner. Rosen used a training procedure developed by Smilansky (1968) which involved having an adult take on a role, join in children's play, and model sociodramatic play behaviors which were missing in the children's play. The dependent variables included a measure of visual perspective taking and a cognitive perspective-taking task which involved matching gifts with people (necktie-father). Differences favoring the play training groups over controls were found on these two measures, as well as on several measures of cooperation.

Saltz and Johnson (1974) trained low-SES preschoolers in thematic-fantasy play, a role-playing of familiar fairy tales, e.g. *The Three Pigs.* Results showed that the play group scored higher than controls on Borke's test of empathy. In a series of follow-up studies, Saltz, Dixon, and Johnson (1977) reported that thematic-fantasy play groups performed at higher levels on the Borke test than other groups, including those receiving sociodramatic play training.

Fink (1976) used sociodramatic play training in an attempt to promote the attainment of perspectivism and conservation (the ability to retain a judgment of equivalence or identify across transformations) in middle-class kindergartners. The training group did show significant gains over controls in cognitive perspective taking as measured by a social-role conservation task (a woman can be a lawyer and a mother at the same time). No significant differences were found for either conservatioin of number or conservation of amount.

Iannoti (1978) used two training conditions involving role-playing with middle-class kindergarten and third-grade students. One play condition, called role-taking, involved assigning each child to one role in a skit. The children then acted out their roles and discussed the effects of their actions on others. The other play condition, role-switching, required children to participate in the same skits but also had them change roles within each skit several times. Results revealed that both play conditions, role-taking and role-switching, resulted in higher scores than on Flavell's (1968) cognitive perspective-taking task. Play groups also scored higher on another cognitive perspective-taking task, Selman's social dilemma stories (Selman & Byrne, 1974), but only at one of the two schools involved in the study.

Burns and Brainerd (1979) examined the effects of play training on three types of perspective taking — visual-perceptual, cognitive, and affective (empathy) — with preschool children. Two play conditions were used: (a) constructive play training, which involved building specific objects in a collaborative manner, and (b) dramatic play training, which involved role playing characters in pretend situations. This latter condition was very similar to the sociodramatic play training procedures used in the above studies. Cognitive perspective taking was measured by a task which involved matching gifts to people and by a communication task requiring children to explain a story to a ficticious partner and anticipate their verbal responses. Two emotional matching tasks similar to Borke's procedure were used to assess empathy. Results indicated that both play conditions

TABLE 1
Studies on the Relationship Between Play and Social Cognition: Design Features

Study	Sample and population description	Treatment conditions	Treatment assignment	Duration	Variables[a]
Rosen (1974)	58 low-SES children selected from four kindergarten classes[b]	1. Sociodramatic play training (2 groups) 2. Non-fantasy activities (2 groups)	Intact groups	Ten, 1-hour sessions	Cognitive perspective taking Visual perspective taking
Saltz and Johnson (1974)	75 low-SES children selected from four preschool classrooms in one school[b]	1. Thematic-fantasy training 2. Dimensionality training 3. 1 and 2 4. Listen to stories	Randomized matching	Three, 15-minute sessions per week for 16 weeks	Empathy
Rubin and Maioni (1975)	16 middle- and lower-middle-class children selected from one Canadian preschool[b]	n/a[c]	n/a[c]	n/a[c]	Empathy Visual perspective taking
Fink (1976)	36 middle-class children selected from one kindergarten[b]	1. Sociodramatic play training 2. Play, no training 3. No treatment	Randomized matching	Eight, 25-minute sessions	Cognitive perspective taking

[a]Only social cognition variables are listed. Most of the studies had other dependent variables.
[b]Randomization not indicated.
[c]Correlational study.

TABLE 1
Studies on the Relationship Between Play and Social Cognition: Design Features

Study	Sample and population description	Treatment conditions	Treatment assignment	Duration	Variables[a]
Saltz, Dixon and Johnson (1977)	146 low-SES children selected from one preschool over a 3-year period[b]	1. Sociodramatic play training 2. Thematic-fantasy training 3. Story discussion 4. Non-fantasy tutoring	Random	Daily 15-minute sessions for 7 months	Empathy
Iannoti (1978)	30 kindergarten boys and 30 third-grade boys selected from two middle-class parochial schools[b]	1. Role-taking 2. Role-switching 3. Story discussion	Random	Ten, 25-minute sessions	Cognitive perspective taking Empathy
Smith and Syddall (1978)	14 lower-middle-class children selected from one British playgroup (preschool)[b]	1. Sociodramatic play training 2. Non-fantasy tutoring	Matching	Fifteen, 40-minute sessions	Cognitive perspective taking
Burns and Brainerd (1979)	51 lower-middle-class children selected from three Canadian day-care centers[b]	1. Sociodramatic play training 2. Constructive play training 3. No treatment	Not indicated	Ten, 20-minute sessions	Cognitive perspective taking Empathy Visual perspective taking

resulted in significant and "roughly equivalent" gains in all three (visual, cognitive, and affective) types of perspective taking. In interpreting these results, the authors raise the question of the effect of a confounding variable, the adult guidance or tuition that occurs in all play training procedures.

Smith and Syddall (1978) attempted to separate the effects of adult tuition from play by controlling the amount and type of verbal exchanges in two training conditions. The first condition, play tutoring, involved engaging children in sociodramatic play. The other condition, skills tutoring, entailed producing craft products and "playing" academic games with numbers, colors, and size concepts. a variety of cognitive outcomes were measured, and cognitive perspective taking was assessed by two role-taking preference tasks requiring object or gift matching appropriate to men, women, etc. The outcomes indicated that, in general, both the skills tutoring and play tutoring conditions facilitated many cognitive skills equally well. However, only the play tutoring treatment improved scores on the perspective-taking tasks.

Discussion

A number of problems color the outcomes of the above studies on play and social cognition. First, none of these studies used delayed protests or follow-up assessments to investigate the permanency of the treatment effects. The subjects were simply tested before and immediately after the treatment period. Thus, it is not known if the reported gains in perspective taking were lasting.

The dependent variable measures used in these studies are subject to criticism on two counts: problems in reliability (consistency) and in validity. Many of the cognitive and emotional perspective-taking tasks may be unreliable; the reliability coefficients, when reported, are relatively low, especially for the shorter versions of these scales.

With regard to validity, a variety of perspective-taking scales have been adapted by individual researchers, and many of these tests do not seem to measure the same variables. Accordingly, the inter-correlations between the tests frequently are low. Rubin (1980) has pointed out that many of these criterion measures seem to assess only the most primitive levels of perspective taking and do not include the ability to be aware of the second person perspective, i.e., to think that another is "thinking of me in such a way, or knows that I am feeling happy" (Rubin & Pepler, 1980). In addition, it has been suggested that verbal assessments of social skills may be poor predictors of behavioral performance on the same problem; thus, both types of assessment should be made.

In particular, the validity of the most common emotional perspective-taking task, Borke's Interpersonal Perception Test, has been questioned by many authors. Rubin (1980) has pointed out that the Borke test is considered a measure of egocentric projection rather than empathy. In this test, a series of stories accompanied by pictures are presented. The child listens to each story and selects a facial symbol representing happy, sad, fearful, and angry emotions. The criticism centers on the fact that these stories portray situations which are very familiar in the child's experience. Thus a child may remember his/her own response in such a situation, e.g., struggling with a peer, or recall the response of a playmate. The child's response may therefore reflect a self-description rather than the child's perceptions of another person's emotions.

Many of the cognitive perspective-taking tests also have questionable validity. Those which require subjects to match gifts appropriately with a role model (Rosen, 1974) actually require an association between a physical object and a picture. This process reveals little of what a child infers about others' thoughts or feelings.

The other major issues raised in the literature have to do with the impact of the social interaction which occurs in play, both peer interaction and adult-child interaction.

Smith and Syddal (1978) have raised concerns about adult-child interactions during play activities, suggesting that these interactions may have a didactic character and produce the gains claimed for dramatic play. In their study, they controlled for this variable by observing the quantity of adult-child interaction in the play-tutored and non-play groups and found that there was no difference between the two groups on this variable. The play-tutured group improved their social knowledge skills from pretest to post-test. However, the groups were small with only seven subjects in each, and only a cognitive perspective-taking task, an object-person matching test mentioned above, was used. No measure of emotional role-taking was given.

Rubin (1980) has interpreted the literature to suggest that peer conflict and interaction, rather than pretend play activities, may be the casual component influencing the development of social cognition; thus, play may be reflective rather than productive of change. Rubin states:

> . . . the ability to consider reciprocal role relations may be less a function of nonliteral social play per se and more the outcome of peer interaction and conflict . . . When children beg to differ concerning issues of importance to them, cognitive disequilibria are likely to ensue. Since such mental states are not pleasurable, conflict resolution is necessary . . . (and) compromise results. Suffice it to say that compromise is accommodative and adaptive. In short, given conflict, the child comes to realize that (1) survival in the social world, as well as (2) popularity among peers are marked by compromise and socialized thoughts . . . it is important to note that

peer conflict . . . does not appear to occur during fantasy play itself. Once disagreement between dramaticists has been generated, the actors "break frame": they shift from the nonliteral to literal world vis-a-vis their social encounter. During these "frame breaks" conflicts over dramatized roles, rules, and behaviors are resolved. Once resolved, the boundary of social-fantasy is accessible . . . Thus, while fantasy play serves a consolidating and practice role, and while it demonstrates to the play partner how one thinks about this, that, or the other, the major moving/guiding force is the peer interaction itself and *not* the dramatic activity per se (1980, pp. 80-81).

While we may conclude that increases in pretend play activity are generally accompanied by changes in scores on a variety of tasks measuring some aspect of perspective taking, it is not clear that gains in these scores are lasting or that pretend play is causally responsible for the gains. In the studies reviewed above, there were no follow-up assessments, the tasks themselves were of questionable validity, and social interaction independent of the pretend function itself was a confounding variable.

Future research needs to address the question of the permanency of training effects. Delayed assessments and/or longitudinal research designs would help to determine if play experiences have lasting effects on social cognition. The issue of the confounding effects of adult-child interaction also needs to be addressed. Smith and Syddall's (1978) use of stringent controls over the verbal interaction in treatment conditions is a step in this direction. The effects of peer interaction and conflict also need to be examined. For example, more of the "frame breaks" described by Rubin (1980) are likely to occur in unstructured play situations, in which children have to plan their own story lines cooperatively, than in structured play situations like Saltz and Johnson's (1974) thematic-fantasy training, where children simply follow a ready-made plot. Perhaps future studies can monitor the amount and nature of peer interaction that occurs in different play conditions and can determine the differential effects of these conditions on children's social knowledge.

In addition, the problems of assessment remain. Social knowledge is a broad conceptualization, and debate remains concerning its extension. The measures currently available seem to be measuring phenomena which have a degree of independence to one another. Until these measurement problems are resolved, the process of determining the relationship between play and perspective taking in children will be delayed.

Finally, in the literature reviewed here each author has defined play operationally; in no case has any author dealt with the question ethnographers typically raise about the definitional issue of separating play contexts from play texts (Schwartzman, 1977). We can merely note that this broad issue of definition and theory is beyond the scope of this review.

   Children, as one of our colleagues puts it, continue to play because it is the most enjoyable thing to do (Sutton-Smith, 1981). The fact that adults do not fully understand the role of play in children's developing skill and understanding of the social situation will certainly not detract from play's inherent popularity.

REFERENCES

Borke, H. Interpersonal perception of young children: Egocentrism or empathy? *Developmental Psychology,* 1973, *9,* 102-108.

Burns, S.M., & Brainerd, C. J. Effects of constructive and dramatic play on perspective taking in very young children. *Developmental Psychology,* 1979, *15,* 515-521.

Fink, R. S. Role of imaginative play in cognitive development. *Psychological Reports,* 1976, *39,* 859-906.

Flavell, J. *The development of role-taking and communication skills in Children.* New York: Wiley, 1968.

Flavell, J. *Cognitive development.* Englewood Cliffs, N.J.: Prentice-Hall, 1977.

Iannotti, R. Effect of role-taking experiences on role taking, empathy, altruism, and aggression. *Developmental Psychology,* 1978, *14,* 119-124.

Rosen, C. E. The effects of sociodramatic play on problem-solving behavior among culturally disadvantaged preschool children. *Child Development,* 1974, *45,* 920-927.

Rubin, K. Fantasy play: Its role in the development of social skills and social cognition. *New Directions in Child Development,* 1980, *9,* 69-84.

Rubin, K., & Maioni, T. Play preference and its relationship to egocentrism, popularity and classification skills in preschoolers. *Merrill-Palmer Quarterly,* 1975, *21,* 171-179.

Rubin, K., & Pepler, D. The relationship of child's play to social-cognitive growth and development. In H. Foot, A. Chapman, & J. Smith (Eds.), *Friendship and social relations in children.* London: Wiley, 1980.

Saltz, E., Dixon, D.,& Johnson, J. Training disadvantaged preschoolers on various fantasy activities: Effects on cognitive functioning and impulse control. *Child Development,* 1977, *48,* 367-380.

Saltz, E., & Johnson, J. Training for thematic-fantasy play in culturally disadvantaged children: Preliminary results. *Journal of Educational Psychology,* 1974, *66,* 623-630.

Schwartzman, H. Research on children's play: An overview, and some predictions. In P. Stevens (Ed.), *Studies in the Anthropology of Play*. West Point, N.Y.: Leisure Press, 1977.

Selman, R., & Byrne, D. A structural-developmental analysis of role taking in middle childhood. *Child Development*, 1974, *45*, 803-806.

Shantz, C. The development of social cognition. In E. M. Heterington (Ed.), *Review of child development research* (Vol. 5). Chicago: University of Chicago Press, 1975.

Smilansky, S. *The effects of sociodramatic play on disadvantaged preschool children*. New York: John Wiley, 1968.

Smith, P. K. & Syddall, S. Play and non-play tutoring in preschool children: Is it play or tutoring which matters? *British Journal of Educational Psychology,* 1978, *48*, 315-325.

Sutton-Smith, B. Children at Play. In R. Strom (Ed.), *Growing through play*. Monterey, Calif.: Brooks/Cole, 1981.

chapter 11

PLAY ACTIVITIES AND ELEMENTARY SCHOOL PEER GROUPS

Andrew W. Miracle, Jr.
Texas Christian University
Brian Rowan
Far West Laboratory for Educational Research & Development
David N. Suggs
University of Florida

Classical theories of play have been demarcated by Sutton-Smith (1977) as belonging to two general types. Prophylactic theories imply that play is a subdivision of human adaptation providing some palliative for the human condition. Preparatory theories view children's play as a preparation and practice for adult life. (Sutton-Smith proposes a combination of these in what he defines as preadaptive potentiation.) While the prophylactic theories would primarily concern the psychological variables of the individual, the adaptive theories better account for the socialization/enculturation function of play. This function is often taken to be the primary function of play, or at least the primary social function.

If one examines the organization of play in elementary schools, it can be concluded that play is utilized in a prophylactic fashion, providing alternation with academic work in a play/work cycle. (Play before school, work, play at morning recess, work, play at lunch, work, play at afternoon recess, work, play after school.)

It might be hypothesized that much of the learning of social skills in school settings has to do either with learning authority roles or with learning intragroup relations in an authority-directed task situation. Conversely, it might be hypothesized that play situations emphasize the learning of different social skills. For example, Polgar's (1976) research on peer play and organized sport indicates that 6th grade boys in peer group contexts employ egalitarian consensual models and are concerned with means, whereas the authoritarian and imposed adult situations are concerned with ends. In this sense, at least, peer play may serve a useful preparatory function in elementary schools, providing opportunity to acquire a variety of skills.

As Podilchak (1981) has stated, "In the peer world, socialization consists of adhering to emergent rules and learning to perform adequately in roles which are part of the emergent structure. Unlike the adult supervised world where identities are ascribed, in the world of one's peers identities are achieved."

This paper offers a descriptive case study, utilizing ethno-graphic data. It is intended to provide a platform for exploring the nature of play groups in elementary schools. In this paper, we ask three specific questions about fourth graders in an elementary school. Who plays together? Under what kinds of ecological con-straints imposed by school authority structures do play groups form? How do play groups maintain identity and solidarity?

The research was conducted in an elementary school of a large urban school district in a major southern city. The school's student population numbers 625, of which 53% were black, 41% white, and 6% hispanic. The data were principally collected through participant observation, augmented by the use of informal interviews. Data were collected between October, 1980 and April, 1981.

The Nature of Play Groups

Fourth grade peer groups are, to a large degree, activity oriented. That is, one's friendship group is basically a play group. Each play group is engaged in a unique activity and the particular activity of each is relatively constant over time. This is indicated from the fact that group activities (both male and female) remained stable for the seven-month research period. Observed male activities include kickball, marbles, and a somewhat rough variation of chase. Observed female activities include jump rope, racing, and jump rope-racing.

This implies an important, though not surprising point — the fourth grade peer groups observed were 100% sexually homo-geneous. In no instance was cross-sex grouping observed.

The two classrooms which were under study exhibited four main male peer groups, three subgroups (group-interactive dyads), three floaters and one isolate. The main groups were composed of 3-5 members.

Females in the two classrooms were structured into six main groups, one subgroup, four floaters, and two isolates. Main groups were composed of 3-4 members.

The groups for the most part were racially homogeneous. Among the males of the classroom, 2 of the main groups had one racially distinct member, and one subgroup was a racially mixed pair. Among the females, two of the six main groups had one racially distinct member. The remaining male/female groups and subgroups were racially homogeneous.

Within each of the two classrooms there was a well defined social structure. In fact, there was a pair of parallel structures within each classroom — one male, the other female.

Both males and females recognize athletic ability and academic superiority as prestigious characteristics. Also, all high status indi-viduals displayed middle class dress. Among the males of one classroom "toughness" was accepted as a route to prestige, while in the other class it clearly was not. All females recognized physical attractiveness as a further route to status attainment. Observation indicated that the ranking of prestigious characteristics utilized by the two systems was:

Male
- Athletic superiority
- Academic ability
- Middle class appearance/ toughness

Female
- Physical attractiveness
- Academic ability
- Athletic ability

Ecological Constraints On Groups

Such sex specificity in grouping can hardly be said to be solely the result of ecological factors in the elementary school. Society emphasizes the distinction between the sexes from birth, and the elementary school student brings to school the idea that boys do "boys' things" and girls do "girls' things."

Moreover, Kimball (1974) has demonstrated that schools act as socializing agencies, and the ecological structure of school, in particular the authority structure, emphasizes the distinction of the sexes.

For instance, girls were commonly disciplined for "sitting like boys." Spelling or arithmetic competitions in the classroom were often conducted through classroom division into teams on the basis of sex. One female was observed asking the P.E. teacher if the girls could race against the boys. The response of the teacher was that such a race would be unfair. In general, the girls competed against other girls in P.E. class, and boys against other boys. Finally, when moving from one area of the school to another, the students were invariably made to form lines — one male and one female. Thus, it is clear that the authority structure of the school emphasizes sexual distinction and segregation.

The limitations on time and space usage imposed on students by the authorities kept the possibility of intergrade interaction at a minimum. All 4th grade classrooms were located in one hallway. There were separate lunch periods for each grade and separate recess times. A particular area of the playground was strictly for the 4th grade. Therefore, it is not surprising that peer groups were age-specific as well.

Within the lunchroom each class had its own table at which it had to sit. Classes were, for the most part, self-contained. Even when the two classes went to P.E. together, their activities were almost always separate. Thus, the time and space structuring encouraged intraclass peer groups and discouraged interclass grouping.

The imposition of temporal and spatial restrictions on students in the school had its most noticeable effect on peer group formation and interaction. By and large, the only space and time in which students were allowed to form groups on the basis of free choice was on the playground, after lunch or during recess. It may be that the limiting of natural group formation to activity oriented time and space accounts, to a large degree, for the activity orientation of fourth grade peer groups.

Admittedly, play behavior is a major component in the life of fourth graders outside the school context. Yet it seems highly improbable that friendship formation in extra-school contexts would be based on such a simple selection process as recognition of a common activity orientation.

Given fourth graders' apparent proclivity towards play behavior, it is not surprising that they utilize activity oriented time and space to engage in such behavior. It is therefore suggested that since it is only in such time and space that fourth graders are allowed to group themselves, their peer groups tend to be play oriented.

Boundary Maintenance

There are several factors which contribute to group boundary maintenance. First, and most obvious, is the sex specificity of groups. In the classes observed, personal interactions between children of the opposite sex were extremely limited. In fact, on only 2 of 64 days of observation was any sustained cross-sex interaction observed. This means that the number of probable interactions among students is more limited than it would be if interactions with the *entire* class, males and females, occurred. Thus, one aspect of group identity is obvious; if male they belong to a male group, if female they belong to female group.

Race contributes to group maintenance in a similar fashion. That is, a black student tends to belong to a group composed only of blacks. Thus, race serves as a means of group identity and maintenance.

A common intragroup structure is shared by almost all the groups observed. This structure is basically composed of a group leader, a "second in command" who performs the leader's role in his/her absence, and group members. It is suggested that such a structure contributes to group maintenance. First, a leader is unlikely to leave a group and risk loss of status, that is, one might not be able to become the leader of the new group. This reasoning may be similarly applied to the "second in command." Also, if a second-in-command leaves a higher status group, he or she may lose status outside the group in the overall social structure.

In December a new male student arrived in the school. He was a white male, and openly boasted about his athletic ability. He quickly recognized the status system and began interacting with the highest of the male groups. This group was composed totally of blacks. In the first week he seemed to be conforming to the role of "group member," but was constantly teased, tricked, and picked on by the group leader and group members. Two weeks later he had quit inter-acting with this group and had become, in effect, a new reserve leader (second in command) of the next highest status group.

To some extent, the ecological limitations influence group identity and maintenance. That is, the limitations encourage intra-classroom identity. Thus, only one child was a member of a group composed of students from another classroom (other 4th grade class).

Finally, and perhaps most importantly, is the fact that students impose upon themselves special limitations which isolate each group within a demarcated "territory," and thus limit intergroup inter-actions. For the most part, when recess began the children filed out of the building and went straight to their group's territory on the play-ground. By and large, the groups simply did not invade another group's area. The size of each group's territory was roughly equiva-lent, and the location was typically reflective of the activity of the group. Thus, the "roughhouse" group occupied a long rectangular territory at the back of the grounds. This was suitable for their rough game of chase. Occasionally, the highest status group would invade another group's territory purposely. This was a statement of prestige, and the lower status groups *never* were observed doing this. One other point of interest, however, is that while a "group member" could not enter another group's territory without punitive action occurring (ranging from jeers to physical removal), group "leaders" could enter other groups' territories without such sanctions.

The implication of this is that unless one is a high status individual there is virtually no interaction among members of various groups. In this sense, not being a member of another group and strict terri-toriality combine to express and to reinforce identity with the group to which one belongs.

Conclusion

It is clear from the data reported here that student peer groups do maintain an identity across time and space. Such maintenance of boundaries is indicative of cohesion. Earlier work has pointed clearly to the realization that ecological constraints in terms of time and space allocation by school authorities severely limit the opportunity for peer group formation and interaction (Eddy, 1975; Kimball and Wagley, 1974; and Suggs 1981). This, in turn, means that the opportunities to express and reinforce group motives and goals are likewise limited. After our seven months of observation of elementary school peer groups, it seemed that one basis for identity and soli-darity of peer groups was the expresion and reinforcement of group interests in play activities. While the existing data did not allow the empirical testing of this hypothesis, there were sufficient ethnographic accounts to provide tentative support for this contention.

It is hoped that future research will attempt to gauge the influence of group play interests on the identity and cohesion of peer groups. The current study has been reported with the expectation that it may lead to fuller analysis of the organization and consequences of play in elementary schools.

REFERENCES

Eddy, Elizabeth. Educational innovation and desegregation: A case study of symbolic realignment. *Human Organization*, 1975, 34:2:163-173.

Kimball, Solon T. *Culture and educative process.* New York: Teachers College Press, 1974.

Kimball, Solon T. and Charles Wagley (Eds.). *Race and culture in school and community.* U.S. Department of Health, Education and Welfare, Office of Education. National Institute of Education Project No. 2-0629, 1974.

Podilchak, Walter. "Youth sport involvement: Impact on informal game participation," paper presented for the 2nd annual meeting of the North American Society for the Sociology of Sport, Fort Worth, November 11-15, 1981.

Polgar, Sylvia Knopp. *The social context of games: Or when is play not play?* Sociology of Education, 1976, 49: 256-271.

Suggs, David N. "An ethnographic approach to the ecology of fourth grade peer groups." M.A. thesis, Texas Christian University, 1981.

Sutton-Smith, Brian. Play as an adaptive potentiation: A footnote to the 1976 keynote address. In Phillips Stevens, Jr. (Ed.) *Studies in the Anthropology of Play: Papers in Memory of B. Allen Tindall*, pp., 232-237. West Point, NY: Leisure Press, 1977.

chapter 12

LEVITATION AND TRANCE SESSIONS AT PREADOLESCENT GIRLS' SLUMBER PARTIES

Elizabeth Tucker
S.U.N.Y. Binghamton

Young American girls' slumber parties, within the roughly defined "pre-adolescent" phase from about age eight to twelve, are times of great fun and experimentation. The girls may play all their favorite records, try on make-up, make prank phone-calls, stuff themselves with junk food, and valiantly try to stay up all night: but they are also very likely to experiment with some kind of supernatural game-playing. Levitation and trance sessions, two of the most popular games, are the subject of this paper.

A demonstration of levitation is the clearest way to explain what it entails, but verbal definition will suffice here. The game involves a variable number of people who gather around one person lying on the floor; all of them try to lift that person, using only two fingers on each hand. If the lifting is successful, it is understood that something supernatural has happened. Levitation can be traced back to 1665, to an entry in the diary of Samuel Pepys; more recent inclusions of the game in folklore collections are fairly sparse (Opies, 1959, p. 309).

Trance, another popular practice, consists of inducing — or seeming to induce — a state of hypnotic sleep with involuntary actions suggested by the hypnotizer. Again, there is one central person with an unlimited number of other participants. While the trance behavior of adults has stirred the interest of anthropologists, children's trance phenomena remain virtually unexplored (Knapps, 1976, p. 252).

Data Sample

Within the broad range of possibilities this kind of game-playing offers, I have chosen to focus upon power roles in an all-female group of pre-adolescent age. My data sample, taken between 1976 and 1982, comes from the study of several groups of girls in southern Indiana and New York state. I have found a high degree of cohesiveness in the goals the girls express for these games, either directly or indirectly: a search for excitement, experimentation with "other worldly" events, and submission or dominance within a well-defined peer-group structure.

Before looking at the data itself, we should ask how accurate the term "game" is for girls' experiments with the supernatural. There are certainly some distinctly game like characteristics: levitating a person or putting her into a trance requires following certain rules, according to which *everyone* must participate properly in order to achieve the desired result. In many respects, levitation is a central person game like tag or king of the mountain, where status reversal is of prime importance (Schwartzman, 1978, p. 115; Gump and Sutton-Smith, 1955). As a comparable game, trance shows more differentiation of participants and greater complexity of responses. There is, however, another dimension of both activities that could be more appropriately called "ritual," using this term in the sense of "symbolic action" (Douglas, 1973, p. 21). The persistence of certain symbolic elements, over a wide span of time and space, creates a sense of ritualistic potency. As in many rituals, the order of events must be faithfully maintained, the tone must be solemn, and the outcome is expected to be something almost miraculous; so the word "game" does not quite do justice to the nature of what is happening.

Levitation

Taking the outcome of levitation into consideration first, there *does* seem to be something wondrous about a few girls lifting up a friend of theirs with only two fingers each; that is, if you are looking at the event from a child's perspective. One ten-year-old girl in Indiana described the procedure she knew, adding more details as her excitement grew:

> Well, you lay down, and you get real real real high, and you play that, uh, they step over you, make you real high, and say like if you wanta be a feather, they tell a story what you do, and everything. And you say, "I'd like to be a feather," and you get real real high, people put their two fingers under you and they lift you up like that, like a feather.

The key phrase here is clearly "you get real real high" or "you get real real *real* high," with surprising, almost incredible heights indicated by the speaker. Making one person "get high" is the object of the game, an interesting linguistic parallel to the kind of getting high that adolescents may seek through drugs. This comparison to drug experience may sound far-fetched, but the two kinds of getting high share an important goal: entering another realm of sensation. With levitation, the desired area of experience is the realm of the supernatural.

What is the chain of reasoning that tells children levitation is a supernatural event? It is not very difficult to find the answer to this question: lifting a heavy object is hard to do and always takes the whole hand. Two fingers are not enough to lift something *normally*, so levitation must be extra-normal or supernatural. Empirical evidence, as in so many other areas of children's experience, is of the greatest importance here.

A closer look at this evidence shows that the extra-normal quality of levitation comes from two separate violations of rational sequence. The first is defiance of the law of gravity, a law of falling down and breaking things — and the second is, more subtly, a change in the substance of the person who is being lifted. This change is conveyed by the similes in the name sometimes used instead of "levitation": "light as a feather, heavy as lead" or light as a feather, stiff as a board." By simple analogy, the children who use these terms are indicating that something heavy has been transformed into something light; and, even more amazingly, that something insubstantial has become quite stiff. These transformations can be seen as a kind of rudimentary alchemy, comparable to the medieval quest to change base metal to gold with the philosopher's stone. Anyone who can effect such a change in substance must have significant power and the ability to reverse natural law: hence, the appeal to levitation.

While the physical act of lifting a person with just two fingers remains constant in all the variants of levitation I have collected, the accompanying chant, story, or procession exists in many forms. Ten-year-old Betsy, from a small town in Indiana, gave the following account of a levitation story:

> See, there was these people that get on all sides of you, and you're sposed to lay down, somebody makes up a real spooky story and says that you're dead, and then you say, "Okay, now that you're dead let's rise you from the grave," and it feels like you're floating when they lift you up.

Betsy's version of the game is typical of numerous others in its emphasis upon the story's preparatory role. In order for the liftee to be "dead" she must *feel* as if something dreadful has happened; and a frightening story can evoke such feelings every effectively. The person who tells the story is usually recognized by her peers as a talented narrator of spooky occurrences, so there is some specialization involved. At this point in preparing for levitation, the girls have shifted their focus to a second person rather than just one central figure.

Some levitation stories are very simple, just a few lines about a horrifying death, but others can be quite elaborate. The following example comes from a twelve-year-old girl, Karen, who is certainly one of the more effective storytellers:

> Kristin was riding the school bus home from school one day and all of a sudden, the bus turned over and everyone died except Kristin. She got out of the bus, and nothing looked familiar, so she was scared. Then

she saw a very dark path that led into the very dark
woods. She walked into the woods, and began to hear
eerie noises. Then she thought she knew where she
was and felt better, and more calm. Then, she heard
someone behind her — it was a man with a mutilated
face who jumped out at her. She ran, but he stabbed
her. She kept running, but he stabbed her again and
she died. The next day, her parents found her body.
The body was dead but the soul was still alive. She
was put into a coffin, and she tried to yell but only she
could hear herself, since the body was dead and no
sound came out. The box was closed and lowered
into the ground, and Kristin was still yelling. She saw
dirt being dumped onto her, and that was the tragic
death of Kristin.

The protagonist of Karen's story, Kristin, was the girl about to be lifted
into the air by her friends. Beyond the obviously frightening effect of
the narrative, it is important to note certain details that produce the
right state of mind in the liftee. The initial setting is a school bus, a
familiar and usually safe part of the girls' daily routine; but this
familiarity is exchanged for strangeness with horrifying rapidity. As in
so many children's nightmares, where something well known quickly
becomes threatening (Tucker, 1977, pp. 232-239), Kristin's surroundings become dark and isolated. All of the classic scene-
building elements of horror stories and films are present: a dark forest
(especially potent as a folktale image), odd noises, and finally the
sudden approach of "a man with a mutilated face." The man acts
more like a monster than a human being, and Kristin's death is the
result.

Especially prominent in this narrative is the sequence of
attempted escapes and inevitable recaptures. Kristin thinks she
knows where she is and feels better, but is then attacked; she runs,
but gets stabbed; runs again, but is stabbed some more and then
dies. The need for this feeling of thwarted hope seems clear enough:
powerlessness, compounded by the failure to escape, creates a
strong sense of victimization. For the girl who is about to be lifted,
complete submissiveness to the other girls is necessary. Any sort of
resistance to two-fingered lifting can ruin the desired result. More
than the physical lifting process, though, the need to experiment with
feelings of victimization is significant. Young girls who know something of the world's dangers may worry about being attacked, killed,
or simply left alone in a threatening environment; being symbolically
victimized through levitation stories gives them the chance to act
their worries out.

Scary story-telling may be the only preparation for lifting or it
may occur in combination with chanting, as in this description from a

nineteen-year-old SUNY-Binghamton student:

> One of the lightest girls lied down on the floor and the rest of the group sat around her. The person sitting by her head told a scary story of how the girl lying down had died. There was a series of phrases repeated by every person in the circle: "She is sick, she is dying, she is dead, she is as light as a feather and as stiff as a board, at the count of three we will lift her, one-two-three." Each girl kept two or three fingers underneath the 'corpse.'

The chant in this girl's version "She is sick, she is dying—" not only reinforces the effects of the frightening narrative, but also gives the sense of a formal pronouncement of death. Such a pronouncement seems to be needed, in many instances, before the children are willing to try the act of levitation. In keeping with our society's custom that a person in authority has to confirm someone's demise, the participants in this ritualistic game often turn to a leader. Another variation of the chant just described involves the leader intoning one line, and each person in turn repeating:

She looks sick.
"

She is sick.
"

She looks dead.
"

She is dead.
"

Then the leader says, "At the count of three, she will be light as a feather. One, two, three . . ." and the usual result, either successful or unsuccessful, ensues. During this particular chant, the girls remain stationary, kneeling around the "corpse" they are about to lift, but in other versions there is a circular procession around her. The leader who starts the chant is usually nameless, but in one version — recalled by a nineteen-year-old *boy,* in contrast to the others — the leader bore the imposing name of "The Holy One." All of these elements together — story, chant, responsive intonation, and procession — add up to quite an impressive amount of ritual activity. There is a clear emphasis upon death and dying, sometimes with a finale of resurrection. How can we interpret this ritual, in combination with the act of levitation itself?

If we assume that the concern with supernatural power in the levitation act is likely to be found in the ritual portion, it is possible to identify a significant dimension of authority there. Pronouncing a person dead certainly implies an authoritative role, but actually raising the person from the grave — with the understanding that either renewed life or the afterlife will follow — is a tremendously powerful thing to do. Rather than simply reversing a natural law such as the law of gravity, this event explodes the finality of death and makes it reversible. Such an authoritative act is distinctly godlike, making the name of the chant-leader called "The Holy One" very appropriate.

How much, though, are children really aware of the seriousness of death and resurrection as themes within their ritual? Most of the girls I interviewed or observed doing levitation focussed on the act of lifting, with secondary attention to the ritual. If the attempt *worked*, they were happy, and that was the main thing.

Instead of seeing levitation ritual as a thoroughly serious acting-out of death and resurrection, I find it to be more of a dramatization of changes that all the participants are going through. As they approach adolescence, girls in our society are keenly aware of the need to reach out: to grow, change, and develop new social roles for themselves. Being levitated means, in a symbolic way, being lifted up to a higher level of experience: in other words, rising into a supernatural realm where previously accepted laws are found to be reversible. On a more realistic level, girls of this age-group are beginning to find that their own independence and power can stretch a lot further than they had previously thought possible. They are continuing to discover the importance of cooperating with their peers and sometimes submitting to a demanding peer-group. Being lifted is not just an experiment with victimization, but also a symbolic submission to peer pressure. As a dramatic rendition of social adaptation, then, levitation is an activity that has quite a lot of ritualistic potency.

Trance Sessions

After they have experimented with levitation, many girls go on to the more complex and specialized activity called "trance." In its simpler forms, trance may just mean a kind of mimicry of hypnotic suggestion: for example, one girl recalled "going into a trance" with her friends by imagining different sizes of boxes and counting backwards from 100. When they started to mix up the sequence of numbers, they felt they had gone into a trance. More typical of older girls' (around the fifth and sixth grades) slumber parties, however, is the kind of trance in which one girl is put into a "deep sleep" and influenced by an imaginative teller of scary stories. Three kinds of specialization are necessary for this: one person's storytelling ability; a second's understanding of how to rub the subject's temples to put her into the trance and snap fingers or clap hands to bring her out; and a third person's — the subject's — suggestibility. Mary and Herbert Knapp use the term "trance master" in their brief discussion in *One Potato, Two Potato* (Knapps, 1976, p. 252), but the girls in my sample did not use terms of this sort.

While anyone in a group of girls can be chosen to be levitated, only a few make really satisfying trance subjects. A group of sixth-graders that I visited in 1976 had only one member, Helen, who would go into a trance. She explained, "I'm the only one who can go into them, I guess. But I go into this deep sleep, and they tell me what to do. They tell me a story and I imagine it, and then they tell me what to do and stuff." With this much emphasis upon suggestion and commands, trance seems to be one step up the socialization ladder from levitation: not just submission to lifting by one's peers, but internalization of their suggestions and willingness to respond dramatically to certain orders.

The trance storyteller's art is aimed at making her subject feel upset enough to scream, cry, toss and turn, somersault, or even wet her pants on command. Among these alternatives, my informants assured me, the two most desirable ones are screaming or crying loudly and wetting one's pants. Both responses are linked by a common goal: loss of self-control on the part of the trance subject. While screaming or crying is a good result, pants-wetting is the best of all. Why does this particular hierarchy exist? And why, more generally, is loss of control such an issue for the girls? One answer can be deduced fairly easily: the need for dramatic action to prove to the participants that the trance is really working. If the girls do something they would not normally do, especially something as embarrassing as losing control of their bladders, then their peers can assume the trance is truly a supernatural phenomenon. This explanation of trance expectations is very close to the rationale of levitation as an unnatural and, therefore, supernaturally impressive event.

Going a step further, beyond the girls' direct responses to my questioning, the top status of bladder control suggests another level of meaning. Wetting one's pants is, for a pre-adolescent girl, a kind of regression to early childhood habits. When early elementary school-age children lose control in this way, they are likely to be shamed and taunted, perhaps called "babies" by their peers. But when an older girl wets her pants, the connotations change; since she is more mature and in better command of her body, reversion to past habits is no longer the main issue. Instead, her concern with bladder control indicates a preoccupation with the whole lower portion of her body that is the focus of sexual awareness. Well before entering their teens, girls in our society learn how important it is to protect their genital areas from exposure. Losing bladder control is, for pre-adolescents, analogous to losing control of their sexual organs; it may be called an early acting-out of worries that are not yet fully understood. As Martha Wolfenstein points out, children's joking behavior follows a developmental sequence from the scatological to the erotic (Wolfenstein, 1978, pp. 168-70). In this case, sexual concerns manifest themselves in a familiar, regressively comfortable but still embarrassing wetting of pants.

The trance stories I have collected are designed to provoke

extreme reactions, and the most vivid signs of disturbance come from sexual events within the narratives. A "*real* scary story," one that sounds realistic and frightening enough to be taken seriously by the subject, is the only kind of narrative suitable for trance sessions. Here is the story that Kelly, a self-appointed trance specialist, told Helen:

> One day, when you were walking through the woods, a snake came out and bit you. You started crying. And you ran and ran. Lots of snakes came towards you. They're all *biting* at you. Finally you climbed up a tree. Up there, there was a jagwire. The jagwire *bit* you, and he kept biting you. You fell from the tree. You're bleeding. *Bats* came sprumming down at you. They're eating you, eating, they're trying to eat your *eyeballs.* The snakes are eating you. And they climbed up, and all of a sudden this old, meanish boy, he came out and he raped you, he stepped on you and he almost killed you. The pain! Helen, the pain!

This narrative creates a truly nightmarish situation, where the subject goes through all sorts of horrors but is powerless to save herself. As in the levitation story of Kristin's death, this one goes from threat to threat; each danger, followed by a futile attempt at escape, leads to something even worse. By the end of the story, the protagonist is virtually paralyzed with fright and pain. The feeling of horrified paralysis is a well-known phenomenon of nightmares (Jones, 1951, p. 75). The remarkable thing in this case is not that the storyteller is able to re-create nightmare sensations — many good story-tellers of her age group can do so — but that the trance subject is willing to internalize the teller's nightmare sequence as if it were her own. Such acceptance of another's suggestions is truly impressive in its indication of the need to be guided by one's age group, even through a maze of nightmarish horror.

The sexual symbolism of Kelly's story is particularly interesting. First one snake, and then lots of them — all biting at the frightened girl — give a distinctly sexual tinge to the story, if we can accept the psychoanalytic equation of snakes with the male member (Jones, 1951, p. 94). In some folktales the prince first appears as a snake or another animal and then assumes his true form, capturing the attention of the young heroine with his sexual potency (Riklin, 1908, pp. 41-46). This story is less concerned with happy resolution than with horror, quite a different approach to sexuality, but the sequence from animal to human is the same.

The final and most clearly male figure of the story is an "old, meanish boy": either a vague and paradoxical image or an aptly phrased description. In defense of the second alternative, I would say that boys of early adolescent age seem both "old" and childish to the girls who know them. The boys' sexuality is becoming clearer to pre-adolescent girls, but the threat of violent sexual attack is still rather vague. The rape is the most fearsome event in Kelly's story, last in the chain of horrors; nevertheless, the sexual act itself is described with much less vividness than the bites and kicks are. A definite link emerges and is reinforced in other stories: sex and pain belong together, as a composite nightmare image of the developmental challenges that lie ahead.

From the ritualized raising of levitation to the vivid trance stories of murder and sexual attack, pre-adolescent girls are experimenting with their own power to regulate the intriguing, sometimes threatening awareness of their own development. By manipulating symbolic images and cooperating in a peer-group ritual, they undergo an experience that is frightening or supernaturally inexplicable but still satisfying at the same time. They have *chosen* to pursue this experience, and by doing so they have established limits — at least, within a ritually controlled situation — upon worrisome developmental horrors that they all share.

REFERENCES

Douglas, M. *Natural symbols.* New York: Vintage Books, 1973.

Gump, P. V., and Sutton-Smith, B. The "it" role in children's games. *The Group,* 1955, 17, 3-8.

Jones, E. *On the nightmare.* New York: Liveright Publishing Company, 1951.

Knapp, M. and H. *One potato, two potato: The folklore of American children.* New York: Norton, 1976.

Opie, I. and P. *The lore and language of schoolchildren.* London: Oxford University Press, 1959.

Riklin, F. *Wunscherfullüng und symbolik im märchen.* Vienna: H. Heller, 1908.

Schwartzman, H. *Transformations: The anthropology of children's play.* New York: Plenum Press, 1978.

Tucker, E. *Tradition and creativity in the storytelling of pre-adolescent girls.* Ph.D. dissertation, Indiana University, 1977.

Wolfenstein, M. *Children's humor: A psychological analysis.* Bloomington: Indiana University Press, 1978.

chapter 13

VICISSITUDES OF PLAY IN CHILD ANALYSIS: A SEVEN YEAR OLD TELLS HIS UNIQUE INTRAPSYCHIC STORY

Maurice Apprey
University of Virginia School of Medicine

Child analysis helps a child communicate his concerns. The nature of his problems may be derived by acutely observing his play within analysis. Balkanyi (1964) notes that "verbalization brings about the preconscious quality by which we can think and act purposefully," and follows the emergence of a child's impulse from the unconscious into the preconscious by that means. "By becoming preconscious," she states, "the impulse acquires that quality which we are able to recognize."

Since such verbalization as the child's commentary on his play, and the analyst's spoken interpretations, can facilitate the child's ability to think, visualize, act, and articulate purposefully, the collection of such derivatives which he brings in the early months of analysis is vital. It enables his story to unfold, and the nature of his conflicts and anxieties, etc., to be understood. I agree with Ricouer (1978) that the course of an analysis should take the form of a narrative, and the following case illustrates how mature language can follow action, and also how analysis of the transference ultimately brings resolution of conflict.

A Brief History

Nelson was seven and three-quarters when referred to the Hampstead Clinic for psychoanalytic therapy. He had never been without episodes of soiling and wetting for more than two months at a time, though by then soiling was little more than smears on his underpants from holding back his bowel movements until the last possible moment. His mother, a clerical worker in her early thirties, who had two other children (Leona, 9; and Elizabeth, 6) was also anxious over his "self-destructive tendencies" and the fact that "he couldn't do work at school because he is either too tired or just does not feel like it." His school report noted problems with his work, suggesting that he feared failure, and commenting that he was often sullen and obstinate.

His mother felt that his accident-proneness dated from his having been given his mother's morning-sickness pills by his sister when he was 16 months old. Some months before coming to the clinic he had two head injuries, one scarring his brow and the other requiring stitches. He often dropped or spilled something "accidentally," but his mother thought this was to register resentment over her involvement with friends. He provoked bigger boys to fight, and was often beaten up.

Taking the initiative in the diagnostic interview, he played with his diagnostician and avoided discussing his "toilet troubles." He seemed sensitive and worried. Home and school reports pointed to a wide range of mood and behavior. He was very "mathematical," and well able to use construction toys, measure, and make diagrams; but after expending much energy he would slump in a chair, "too tired to move." He "ran hard and then sat hard." He had trouble with written work at school. Although sometimes objectionably mischievous, he was liked by both teachers and peers.

His mother saw him as "very ugly" but "sunny." His birth had been hard, and he had been breastfed until his sister objected. He had no sleeping or eating problems, walked at one year, and began talking at two. After ingesting the morning-sickness pills, he had disturbances in balance, and probably hallucinations; his condition had been serious enough to keep him in the hospital for several days. He continued having balance problems for a year, and often tripped and cut his head. His sister, Elizabeth, was born when he was 22-months-old, and he was not quite three when he started school; he was not yet properly trained, and did not give up the bottle until after he was three.

His mother had an abortion that year, and spent four days in the hospital. Her marriage to a clerk somewhat younger than she was unstable: she said he often worked late, and was "too tired to talk to the children" when he did get home. Her older daughter, Leona, creative and attractive, competed fiercely with Nelson, and the mother felt she rejected her much as she had been rejected by her own mother. Her younger daughter talked baby talk, and began soiling as Nelson did. Nelson had a good year while four; his mother attributed his occasional smearing then to his being "too tired to go to the toilet."

When he was five he reached special rapport with one teacher; when this failed he would stand beside her, crying. When she left he had a number of other teachers and became unmanageable, having uncontrollable rages. When he ran away from his mother into the street he was hit by a car, and in the same year he had a painful injury to his finger. When he was six and the family's late return from vacation made him late entering school, he rejected his teacher and had to be moved to another class; but he was unhappy, and often soiled himself on the way home. He was beaten up at school, his scooter fell on him, and he hurt himself with an iron bar. At seven, he became calmer, but was still sometimes "goofy," and often got himself smacked by the student who picked him up from school. Five months before he came to treatment his mother had another abortion, which she did not tell her children about.

The Gathering of Derivatives in the First Three Months

One of the first derivatives to emerge from his early enactments was the intensity of his phallic strivings. He made a plasticine candle and asked me to bring matches to our next meeting. I suggested we simply pretend the candle was lit, but he objected — "You are an adult . . . it's safe to light a little fire. Plasticine doesn't burn." When he finally agreed to pretend, the candle became a "bonfire for Jubilee Day." It then consumed a baby and a soldier. This took place in Holy Week, and I told him that the same week marked the crowning of the Queen and a long ago crucifixion. I said nothing about the burning of the baby, since I felt that it might represent the one who mysteriously disappeared with the mother's abortion.

At the preconscious level his phallic strivings included masturbatory impulses and thoughts of copulation, heightened by the pornographic magazines he stole from his father, who, according to Nelson's mother, had taken them from his own father, who had "a need for these sexual things."

Another derivative early displayed was Nelson's need to have things at all cost; his material indicated that his pockets must always be full, whether he had things from home or from me, or had to steal. He was jealous of his time with me; even his father should stay away because "this is not his place!" He noted that this was fair since he could not accompany his father to the races. Still another derivative was his distrust of dependency, and separation anxiety. He saw all adults as unreliable, including me and the police. He built a "batmobile" to protect himself, although he had once heard of a child treated in the clinic who had "escaped" without harm. Wanting not to be "encaged," he wandered widely around the clinic.

In anticipation of the Easter break, he brought extra analytic material. He told of flying kites the previous weekend: "The black kite went away. The yellow one didn't." He knew I came from Ghana but lived in America, and he wished that I were like the yellow kite which did not fly away. His enactment showed a constant desire for things remaining the same, people staying together, and noted that his sisters would assume he was through with analysis when Easter interrupted his schedule with me — projecting his own wish in this.

He asked who else came for treatment in "our" room, and who owned locker four, next to his, which was three, and when that other child saw me. Was it because that other child came on Saturdays that I would not see him then? Did he get more of my time and attention?

He hoped the owner of locker four was a boy, an ally against his sisters, a twin brother, a playmate, and ideal boy-self unafraid of women. "I don't like girls; they tell me what to do," he said. He felt nonetheless pitted against the owner of locker four, and felt the need of a policeman to watch over his belongings — and himself. He indicated feelings of deracination, illustrating this by speaking of flowers uprooted. During this period his mother confided the unhappiness it had caused her to have been reared as an adopted middle child between two children with their natural parents. There was enough preconscious material in all this to suggest that Nelson was unconsciously concerned about the disappearance of younger sibling(s), his mother having never discussed abortion with him.

The Coalescing of Derivatives

He now thought of me as one who should monitor his efforts to control phallic strivings, give him my exclusive attention, and keep his pockets full. I must be trustworthy, and he knew how to ensure this. But first he wanted to work out some confusion: "Americans are brown, and English people are white. When your mother is brown, so are you. My mother is from Canada, where we went last year — no, the year before." He was no doubt concerned over our mixing when he was white and I was black. One notes, too, that *mother determines what the child is* — that what *mother is, is what matters,* father being conspicuously absent. He seemed to assent to our working together when he noted that he had been to Canada, "which is not far from the United States," and concluded, "I feel like I am very near you." There are several preconscious antecedents to his conclusion that although different, we could mix. I was like "Farmer Brown," who owned everything, a policeman, an ambulance man, a farmer, and able to see through a magnifying glass. I was empowered to police his impulses, rescue him from instinctual excess, and foster his maturation. He noted that he could make things with pieces from two different construction sets, and concluded that two different people could build together.

He began to reveal his view of his symptoms, in which there were clearly oral, anal, and phallic determinants. "Television men are taking pictures of food," he told me. "The man whose exhaust fumes got onto the food was jailed." His car, with no exhaust pipe, was safer, he thought, adding, "but this one is sliding in the mud; the brakes are loose." Thus he expressed anxiety about food and the loss of sphincter control, and his reassuring conclusion that one is safe without an anus. He then invented a "control tower." Its original purpose — monitoring space ships — points to concern over the integrity of his phallus, the need of protection from castration. But there was an anal component in his anxiety since he needed to achieve sphincter control. He could gain the upper hand by managing this, and also by managing time. He had warned me that if he were late for school after a session it would be my fault; and I thought this implied that it would also be may fault if he overflowed. Without offering interpretation I noted his idiosyncratic perception of time, which equated being late to anything with being too late to reach the toilet. His time sense depended on his digestion; it was with real anxiety that he warned me not to depend on a battery watch lest if it stopped, and I were in a foreign country, I would have so little idea of time that I would get hungry.

He focused on balance and reciprocity. For example, he must pay for any cookies he got; broken things must be repaired; the front and back bumper of a car should be equally heavy. "My car is more dangerous when the front comes off because the bumper (a phallus-shaped magnet*) is there to hit you," he explained. He asked if the body can be broken, and if so, what parts. He found these questions puzzling, noting that "every time I talk about it I get muddled." He exhibited an odd blend of anxiety and sadness; his castration anxiety required that whatever was broken should be repaired. He was so anxious about lurking danger that he wanted all lights on as we went down the stairs after a session. He noted that *sometimes* one could live after breaking a leg, but the loss of one was more serious. He perceived danger in being a man, since a man whose birthday was a Friday could expect to die like Jesus.

After three months of analysis we were anticipating our first major break, summer vacation. Just before spring break he made up a game in which we rolled coins and a ball between us. When he kept his bottom toward me I understood that he was registering protest about interruption to his sessions, although he seemed to be saying that we were going to keep in touch when he continued rolling things back and forth. But before the summer break he thought I deserved to be crushed by two army tanks, later deciding that only one would do the trick. He consoled himself by preening over having more money than I, who kept very little in my pocket during sessions, and having more interesting things to do than I during the summer.

Two parallel but connected themes were evident: first, Nelson's increasing use of the therapist to help him "become a leader" and manage "adult" activity; and, second, his effort to achieve internal constraints by examination of the situation, internal and external. When I failed to give him a cookie, I was like his bad-tempered father sending him to bed without supper. A teacher should not be too strict with hard lessons, he felt; he was seeking solutions for many obstacles and clearly felt the need of benign and protective external controls.

The first time he went to the toilet before his session was also one in which he focused on animal and human families described in a book he had brought. He explained that there should be children where there is food, and a mother and father where there are

---

*A magnet adheres, stays in place.

children. He wanted things complete, and began to become verbally expressive rather than communicating by such regressive means as soiling. Although he expected me to defend the little men he made in play, he scorned his creative efforts himself, calling the frail "bumper" he made "embarrassing," and his plane, which flew poorly, "silly." He wanted my plane because it not only flew but *returned* to me. He elaborated the theme of how important it is for what goes away to return.

He wanted my exclusive attention, and made something with which to "clonk in the head" any other child I treated; yet he said I should treat more children in order to make more money. He brought three books — *Just William, William the Dictator,* and *William the Rebel.* I interpreted this as showing William's many sides and his wanting me to know that he had many sides — the dictator, the rebel — and "the Nelson who wets and soils." He fell silent.

He rebuked fathers for being poorly protective and actually exposing their children to danger. He played that a father and a grandfather left their children in a tent at the mercy of wolves while they themselves went hunting. He worried about being without provisions, noting that when he went to Canada someone would have to look after his dog. He asked for my watch and a train schedule with which to monitor events. Lost humans, he said, did not have the animal capacity of finding their way home "by the smell of their dung."

He saw growing up as dangerous, involving the loss of other people and of body parts. Since he equated winning with growing up, he felt safer when a game ended with a tie. Analysis of this changed his material; he wanted total control, and was glad to see "the fire engine man" win treasure and emerge as powerful and controlling, able to put out fires (inflammatory sensations). Nelson changed the sign on the door from *Engaged* (in love) to *Free.* Since he had been "bloody forced" by me into our sessions, he felt "enkaged" (sic). Still, he permitted formerly taboo intimacies, and let me bandage his finger. Heretofore, distrusting others, he had wanted to depend on himself.

He related masturbation to conflicts about his body image — particularly feminine and masculine differences. He built a kiosk in which to kill or mutilate criminals, noting that it is worse to lose hands than feet, since without hands "you can't cook, eat, or turn pages." He noted that "men are better cooks than women," and said that when hands are immobilized they cannot do forbidden things.

He converted his kiosk into an engine inside a car. After changing something from outside to inside he would say, "I shouldn't have done that!" Continuing with his preoccupation with "inside and outside," body openings, and bodily occurrences, he said, "You could say there are wheels in the body because the blood goes round in circles . . . and when you go to the toilet the pooh explodes when it comes out . . . When you are having a baby, the baby goes in and out."

His view of time altered somewhat. A watch became an instrument for keeping track of time "if you invite somebody somewhere"; and he no longer believed that his grandfather must die *before* he could hope to obtain for himself his grandfather's valuable stamps. He began calling us "scientists," "producer and productor," "inventors," etc. I was the "producer" who brought things, and he the producer directing our actions. In this postive relationship he was able to relive the accident he had had when he was four. It appeared that this had taken place when he was age-appropriately investigating his body and its functions, and had during that same period in his life been struck by a bumper. He pondered whether a bumper was a protection or a weapon. Equating protrusions like bumpers with penises, he wondered whether girls once had penises and then lost them. The reliving of his accident rekindled anger toward me and other adults, and especially toward his mother, whom, he claimed, had caused his accident by commanding him to cross the street when it was obviously unsafe to do so.

His preoccupation with the body and its workings continued. When he enacted that rockets may take off for distant places but must finally return, he enjoyed the excitement but also felt fear about losing control and body parts. He went on to feel that loving involves dirty and forbidden activity. "It takes four people to fuck," he said. "Two to do it, one to watch, and one to clean up." This remark indicated primal scene fantasies, a scopophilic instinct, and a pointer to reaction formation. Thanks to reaction formation he could now delight in the company of same-sex peers in ways appropriate to the latency phase. He appointed himself field marshal of an "anti-girls" club, but soon began speaking of "a rare little blonde" he liked so much that he wanted me to teach him to impress her.

He began criticizing his mother, whom he mistrusted, saying, "Maurice, you won't believe this: my mum had a baby." This remark revealed his longing for a brother who would be a better playmate than his sisters. His mother might have had babies but "sold them because she didn't have enough money to look after them." He called such baby-selling "blackmail," and said that the woman who bought a baby was a "thief."

Nelson saw me as keeping him in the dark, as his mother did. He dealt with this by turning passive into active — by assuming a position in which I had to guess and work things out by myself. He felt that I should know how it felt to be the one kept in the dark and forever being made to guess. (His mother insisted that he knew nothing about the two abortions she had before the birth of his younger sister.)

By then his desire to grow up and surrender his symptoms

seemed stronger than the regressive pull toward dependence and babyhood he had previously felt. He now wanted to regulate his sphincters; he saw such regulation as a precondition for becoming adult.

Termination: A Brief Note

Toward the end of his treatment he was preoccupied with the anatomy of the digestive system, after watching a fast-moving toy car rush through an entrance and emerge from an exit. He agreed that this entrance and exit looked like mouth and anus, and began to elaborate this notion by telling what different kinds of food go into the mouth and then come out. "Pooh is really undigested food," he said. "Good food stops in the stomach. Bad . . . goes in and out, stops at the exit, and you forget about it. It's harder to show about drinks because then it is the mouth and the willy . . . Salt is between good and bad; sugar is bad food; vegetable is good food. Sweets are bad, but some are good . . . Chocolate has milk, which is in between." Over four sessions he worked away at this, saying such things as "Brown bread is fairly good . . . white is fairly bad," etc.

He then went from following a physiological trip to following a geographical one; he was finding his bearings. His games all required figuring out the way from one spot to another. An indication of how disoriented he was going to be when his treatment ended appeared in his coming to the clinic once when he had no appointment, claiming that he had disagreed with his mother about when it was. He also left his schoolbag in the clinic after a session. He acknowledged the accuracy of my interpretation of this, saying that it would be sad to end our sessions, and that "it will be funny when I don't have to come any more." Sometimes he sounded truly relieved, but at other times he was clearly denying the pain termination meant for him. When he asked for my Christmas gift to be given early, I gave him a geographical compass, which he welcomed warmly. "That's just what we need!" he cried. "Thank you very much." Then he put it to use in his elaborate "obstacle race" play enactment.

Conclusion

We have noted here the importance of the child's interest in words as he worked in analysis, and the shift in interest from outside to inside. Balkanyi's remarks on the anal phase and its relation to verbalization are germane:

> It indicates that developmental moment when symbolization as such acquires its anal imprint. It is then that the child attains the ability to manipulate symbols instead of things and to comprehend values. The word is, like money, another form of currency which can be used instead of the sensual object. Speech development begins before the anal phase and ends long after it. The same applies to the development of

symbolization . . . it is at the passing of the anal phase that words begin gradually to lose their symbolic value and become signs. Simultaneously it is then that it dawns on the child that there is convention in his family safeguarding the meaning of words and the keeping to grammatical rules. (Balkanyi, 1968)

It is no surprise to have Nelson's school report reflect his development in analysis. It noted that Nelson "sees his picture as a whole and the result is therefore quite powerful. He is able to convey weight, strength, or other intangibles in his drawings . . . is capable of thought beyond the obvious. His enthusiasm and ideas and drive make him a good leader. His abilities artistically and physically assist him in achieving high personal satisfaction." When Nelson said, "Maurice, if there were no fossils we would not know that once upon a time there were dinosaurs," he endorsed the comment of Balkanyi that "the fossil is to the archeologist as the swear word is to the analyst." Since the swear word is an index of anal and genital organs and their function, we can see in Nelson's material the shift from concrete anal phase concerns to the higher function of verbalization by which he was able to communicate his needs in word as well as play. With the accompanying shift from outside to inside came the consolidation of the superego, so that reaction formations, sublimations, curiosity in learning, and the stability of an internal aim-giving agency could all together help Nelson move into and negotiate his latency phase with relatively adaptive preparation. Thus his preoccupation with finding his bearings during the termination phase was consistent with the direction and aim-giving function of the superego.

REFERENCES

Balkanyi, C. On verbalization. *Int. J. Psycho-Anal.,* 1964. 45, Pt. 1.

Balkanyi, C. Language, verbalization and superego; Some thoughts on the development of the sense of rules. *Int. J. Psycho-Anal.,* 1968, 49, Pt. 4.

Freud, S. *The interpretation of dreams.* Standard Edition, 4, 5. London: Hogarth Press, 1953.

Ricoeur, P. The question of proof in Freud's psychoanalytic writings. In Charles E. Stewart et al (Eds.) *The philosophy of Paul Ricoeur: An anthology of his writings.* Boston: Beacon Press, 1978, pp. 184-210.

CONCLUSION:

Customarily, adults in our society describe most leisure activity of children as play whether they are jumping rope, racing around the playground, manipulating objects, telling stories, engaging in dramatic rituals like levitation or making believe a range of situations. The authors of the preceding papers have all taken their observations of such behavior to be play. In considering their papers, however, we may ask whether we are given a sense of what in particular makes these behaviors play. Each of these situations is clearly a context for play (as were the festivals and the games in preceding sections), but we are less certain from these articles how much play actually occurs there. For example, even when children are being active with toys, there is no guarantee that they are playing. Much of their activity with toys is a manifestation of intelligent inquiry, but it does not have to be play. It can be analytic (exploration), synthetic (construction), idling or daydreaming, or creative imagining.

Johnson and Christie show that in most experimental studies the situations are so defined by the adults and so affected by them that there is no guarantee that what the children do is play at all — that is, if play is to be regarded as something the children are more likely to pursue by themselves in their own privacy.

It is clear from the Johnson and Christie paper and the one by Miracle that follows, that most of the systematic work on children's play, whether it is called experimental or ethnographic, actually focuses on the functions the play is purported to fulfill rather than on any intensive description of what play is like. The tendency is apparently for adult investigators to be concerned more with the benefits of play than with detailed descriptions of play. We might argue that they have chosen once again to examine a play context (its utilitarian worth) rather than play itself.

The two following papers deal with play in private rather than in public settings and seem to engage themselves to a greater extent in the description of children at play. It is probable that there will be examples of children's play in Tucker's account of a girls' slumber party where the children are in charge. In Apprey's psychoanalytic study again, it is likely that the child will play because he is given the freedom so to do. The problem here, however, is that, like the experiments, this is an adult-provided context, and whatever occurs is perceived through the spectacles of psychoanalytic theory. It is a setting structured by the therapist, no matter how free the child is to play within it.

What we hear from the therapist are his relatively esoteric speculations as he attempts to unmask the significance of what the child is communicating through play. If there is any truth to this analysis, and we imagine, given the history of play therapy and play diagnosis that lies behind it, there is a great deal, then the child is using the opaque language of his play to say a lot of very basic things about his body and about his impulses. It is difficult for adults in this culture to talk about such things in very direct ways. It is not, therefore, surprising that children also must struggle to find ways to communicate about themselves, particularly when they are as troubled as was this child. In both the Aprey and Tucker papers, we again get a glimpse of that most powerful world of impulse and feeling that we saw in the papers on the festivals in the earlier section. We are again reminded that play, among other things, deals with much which society would rather ignore.

part *four*

ANIMAL PLAY

INTRODUCTION

Robert Fagen has been on of the most assiduous pursuers of animal play behavior both in his own studies and in his review of those of others. His book *Animal Play Behavior* is deservedly a classic in its field (1981). He takes a strong position on the role of play in individual and social development — as a strategy of species evolution. The champion players across species are those who have the greatest reason to change their environment. The players are the earth's innovators. "Still they do not play without risk. Venturing novel behaviors can be dangerous. For humans, play may be the arbiter of the shifting balance between tradition and innovation in human culture," he says.

Richard Alford questions the optimism of Fagen about the direct valuable consequences of animal play. He suggests we must know the costs of play before we can so easily assess its credits. It is possible he says that play is not as important as Fagen has argued, but is only one manifestation of the general flexibility of organisms that develop to higher level. Such organisms maintain their "immature" (neotonous) characteristics for a longer time period and are thus more open to continued adaptation. Features of the neotonous complex in humans include not only play but upright posture, reduced dominance and aggression, increased social bonding and behavioral flexibility. He might also have added increased linguistic and symbolic flexibility.

chapter 14

THE PERILOUS MAGIC OF ANIMAL PLAY

Robert Fagen
University of Alaska

I understand that TAASP's first Conference was held here in London some eight years ago to discuss playfully serious questions about human behavior, culture and ritual. I hope that my digression into the animal world and away from deep considerations of the human condition will not strike the humanistically oriented as an example of devolution! I firmly believe that the study of animal play can aid in understanding the nature of organic diversity and the forces holding together natural landscapes; and I am further convinced that the comparative study of social behavior, including an emphasis on comparative aspects of play and games across species, is uniquely valuable for understanding human nature. But as today is April Fool's Day and I see from his introduction to this talk that Brian Sutton-Smith remains at the top of his playful form, let me climb down from my sociobiological soapbox and say a few words about how and why animals play.

Simply stated, animal play is extraordinary. Field naturalists have described wild monkeys' antic chasing and leaping games, elaborate gymnastic routines of young ibex in their mountain home, intricate grappling and wrestling encounters among primates, carnivores or birds in which injury is avoided and dominance distinctions are temporarily suspended, and playful interactions between individuals that also involve objects or terrain features. These social interactions incorporating features of the physical environment closely parallel the more formal structures of human games of skill.

My central theme (See also Fagen, 1981) is that play is a creative force in evolution and development. It is a biological necessity for animals whose lifestyle actively modifies their environmental relationships in novel ways, creating environments for survival.

As my photographs of puppies, kittens and foals at play suggest, animal play is a delight to watch and to study. But that's just the beginning. Animal play offers students of human play an unparalleled comparative baseline. The study of other societies gives us perspective on our own society and on ourselves in two important and distinct but independent ways: the comparative method makes us aware of our own cultural preconceptions and blind spots determined by the givens of our own social context, and the results of comparative study allow us to put our own social milieu into a general theoretical frame work. Cultural anthropology may thus be viewed as a structured intellectual exercise yielding new skills for observing and understanding human diversity. The possessor of these skills, by their very nature, is compelled to train them on his or her own society and ultimately on herself or on himself. But this is exactly the case for a broader comparative perspective embracing other species. Just as perspectives on culture-specific patterns enhance our consciousness of the arbitrariness of our own cultural preconceptions, perception of other species' worlds irreversibly shapes our perception of our own. It is in this sense that animals — not only gorillas, chimpanzees and orangs, although these species are uniquely important for sociobiology, but also elephants, wolves, ravens, and ants — offer perspectives on human nature.

The study of animal play also offers a relatively unpoliticized context for creating new ideas about play in general. For example, Gregory Bateson's ideas on thinking and communication grew in part from Bateson's observations of river otters playing in the San Francisco Zoo. Sutton-Smith (1972, pp. 508-510) has additionally indicated the importance of studies of nonhuman play in supporting the view that play is a separate behavioral system whose essence may lie in its radical character. Moreover, animal play research is close enough in its spirit and goals to field research in cultural anthropology and comparative sociology so that it can benefit from the philosophy and methods of these disciplines. For example, anthropologists' game categories prompt us to ask why games of chance and strategy appear to be absent from animal play, and the centrality of the idea of negotiation in theories of children's play suggests the possibility of such negotiation occurring nonverbally in the play of at least the more intelligent animals.

Young and adult animals put their time and energy into acts that seem unproductive and even dangerous — aimless running in circles, harmless wrestling with a partner, and idle fooling with objects. What makes these "useless" actions so important that animals may literally risk life and limb to perform them?

Play is important because play experience helps make the player versatile, developing skills used in creating new environments and adapting to them. It offers practice of physical skill and develops strength and endurance. In humans, and possibly in a few other species, it leads to innovation and cultural novelty. Finally, play heals, aiding stressed individuals to recover from certain forms of trauma, particularly social deprivation, stimulus deprivation, and protein-calorie malnutrition. In animals and humans play is a recognized sign of clinical well-being. I suppose there is a natural tendency to over-romanticize these scientific results, but play as a format for self-liberation and growth can't be such a bad idea. The program is self-limiting, after all; play played other than for play's sake ceases to be play.

What is play? How do animals play? What forms does play take in animals and how do these compare with the diverse forms of human play?

Let's consider any activity of an animal that fulfills some biological function and must be learned in order to be effective. Some examples of these skills in animal species include catching large, difficult prey; escaping from a predator; using space effectively through navigation, orientation and reference to landmarks and routes; or fighting with another animal. We find that the young of such species will often perform skilled versions of those skilled behaviors. These rehearsals of skilled activity occur under circumstances in which the activity's normal function cannot possibly be achieved. Instead, rehearsal and simulation serve to preserve or increase the effectiveness and flexibility of the behaviors performed and of the cognitive mechanism that organize skilled action. We call these performances play.

Three main forms of play are recognized by biologists. The first is solo exercise, typified by leaps (gambols and the like) and other rapid, graceful movements of the body or of its parts. Locomotor and rotational movements are generally seen. Playfighting (wrestling and chasing) is the second widespread form of play. Animals, like human athletes, seem to prefer scrimmages to calisthenics as training! But some species like the house mouse are not known to play fight at all. Play may be abstractly classified on a scale of body contact, from behavior involving no contact at all (chasing) to a high-contact behavior (wrestling). The point that a given species, population or individual occupies on this scale may be predicted from a consideration of the amount of social interaction between individuals in these groups. Among orangs, for example, interpopulation differences in the amount and physical closeness of social play, as well as the involvement of the father in play, have been documented: in Sumatra, where families are more closely-knit and stay together longer, social play occurs and often involves the male when he is present, but play is rarer, less interactive and physically less contact-oriented among Borneo orangs, whose groups virtually never include the father for more than the brief periods and whose families do not remain together long enough (the older sibling disperses) to allow repeated interaction between infant and older sibling.

A third form of play is the manipulation of an object in a nonfunctional context following mastery of the skilled use of that object, or following thorough sensory investigation. Object play is not as widespread in nature as the two preceding forms of play, but it does occur with considerable frequency in certain groups, particularly carnivores, primates, some marine mammals, birds of prey, and large parrots and corvids.

Play is risky behavior. Animals spend time, burn up energy, and risk physical injury in their play. Though magic, it is also perilous — a grand gambol by nature. Is play so important that it evolved and continues to exist in ever more elaborate form despite these risks? The costs of play must be outweighed by biological benefits if play is to be maintained by natural selection. Play is not simply an epiphenomenon attendant on developing behavior or a large brain, for it occurs only in certain environments (generally, stimulus- and resource-rich habitats) and disappears rather abruptly under resource stress or disturbance.

Play is not a simple behavioral response to certain stimuli. It is active, motivated behavior and even has evolved to incorporate specific communicative signals that serve to elicit and maintain play interactions. The play-face evolved independently three times in higher vertebrates. Birds, marsupials, and placental mammals all evolved play-faces that accompany social play — a striking case of evolutionary convergence in social communication.

Play can be surprisingly elaborate. Animal games — structured social play interactions in which chasing or wrestling is woven into the physical environment — are celebrated features of the most complex animal societies. Tag, peek-a-boo, king of the mountain, hide and seek, and many other culturally widespread human games of physical skill have their animal counterparts. The use of objects, terrain, and other features of the physical environment contributes to the impression of complexity. Play in snow, in water and in trees is noteworthy. Otters and ravens, as well as other species, have social sliding parties in snow. Rhesus macaques have been described playing water games that involve jumping from mangroves into shallow water. The monkeys actually line up at the base of the mangrove tree as if waiting their turn, and monkeys appear to aim their leaps at playmates below them in the water. Films and descriptions of these aquatic revels leave no doubt about the reality of the behaviors cited. Carl Koford, Carol Berman, Donald Symons and John Bishop observed rhesus water games on small islands off Puerto Rico, where the monkeys were introduced from their native Old World habitat. A pinnacle of animal play, social play involving objects and terrain, is presented, not surprisingly, by the chimpanzee. At Gombe Stream, researchers described and filmed a chimpanzee family chasing around the base of a tree, one youngster dragging a palm flower in front of another apparently as a lure.

Interspecific play is another case in which animal play approaches unexpected limits of behavioral complexity. Play between species is a problem, first of all, in communication: how do members of two different species comprehend each other's play signals? And how do they adjust to each other's species-specific style of play? Finally, can members of one species be selected to share the benefits of play with another?

Millions of animal species exist today; only a few exhibit play as we understand the term. Which animals have evolved the capability to play?

Nearly all mammals and birds play under the right circumstances. Invertebrates are not known to play, and reports of play are rare from fishes, reptiles and amphibians. Evidently being a player has something to do with having a large, highly developed cerebral cortex. In this sense the evolution of play may be understood in the light of the evolution of the brain. To this end, we may contrast three adaptive strategies in nature. Bacteria are like plants and many invertebrates in that they survive by allowing their environments to modify them physiologically and morphologically. The brain as we know it developed in vertebrates as a component of their environmental buffering system. Fishes, reptiles and amphibians, and the earliest and most primitive birds evolved a simple brain that allowed them to interact with fixed environmental contingencies through use of stereotyped behavior patterns, thus deriving a degree of buffering from environmental change (for example, behavioral thermoregulation in reptiles or migration in fishes). The third strategy was that elaborated by the rest of the birds and virtually all mammals. They actually change their environments and define their ecological niche by their activities. They construct new environments for themselves, reconstructing the elements of the outer world into a new environment that is sufficient for survival.

Of course, environmental engineering is not restricted to vertebrates. The social insects also modify their environments behaviorally and form complex societies marked by role diversification. Yet social insects do not play. Their blueprint for creating environments is genetically specified, so that they have been creating essentially the same universe for their entire evolutionary history (and, as any termite-beset property owner will recognize, with great sucess). Mammals and birds, on the other hand, create new environments based on individual experience, using flexible behavior and intelligence under considerably more schematic constraints imposed by their genes. Ants are craftspeople, birds and mammals artists.

Within the mammals and the birds, we may recognize certain champion players. These species occur in certain kinds of environments — a regularity which need not have been expected. Tropical fruit-eaters such as chimpanzees and some of the large parrots seem to be unusually playful compared with their close relatives.

Periglacial mammals and birds — those inhabiting the rich, constantly changing environments in the neighborhood of glaciers — are great players: otters, lynx, ravens, mountain sheep, goats, New Zealand's kea, and perhaps the polar bear. Plainsdwelling social hunters and their marine counterparts are champion players. Finally, it seems to be the case that species whose environment is defined by social groups of highly intelligent conspecifics are marvelously diverse and inventive in their play. Many primates, elephants, and man's domestic animals fall into this category.

With this rich lore of natural history to guide us and some very general theoretical guidelines about the evolution of intelligent sociality as an additional aid, we may proceed to examine human play from a comparative perspective. On first impression it is overwhelming. Nothing in animal play quite prepares the earnest sociobiologist for jumprope, hot-air balloons, baseball, pinwheels, or Lake Mendota skate sail tag (for this last-named form of human play, see Carter, 1980). Human play does indeed seem to exhibit many unique features. Manufactured toys, infant babbling and language play, games with explicit rules that can become objects of discourse, play between teams, games of chance (dice) and strategy (chess), the intentional synthesis of play-stimulating drugs, domestication of other species as supernormal playmates, and instrumental music are human play specialties (although one wonders a bit about the manufacture of toys, e.g. in canids and the great apes). Does one general factor, which we may confidently term "human nature," underlie all these seemingly-unrelated facets of human uniqueness? Or, as sociobiologists have long speculated, are they indicators of separate, specific capabilities that developed at different stages of human evolution for unrelated reasons?

The big question about human nature from a sociobiologist's point of view, however, is the possible existence of biological constraints on human playfulness and creativity. With the work of Blaffer Hrdy (1981), Axelrod and Hamilton (1981), Konner (1977), McClintock (1978), and other social scientists trained in population biology, sociobiology promises an increasingly humane biology of human behavior. Sociobiological analyses like these, based on structured approaches to human gene-culture interaction (Lumsden and Wilson, 1981) may well offer powerful insights into the vexing question of human innovative flexibility, and ultimately practical tools for enhancing innovative potential through play.

Play both creates biological and cultural constraints and liberates us from them. Dually, paradoxically, it thus serves as an arbiter of the shifting balance between tradition and innovation in human culture. There is much to be said for the suggestion that play is a kind of radical experience. The essence and functional significance of play cannot be expressed except perhaps metacommunicatively. In a sense, play is more important than anything we can possibly say about it. We are forced to adopt literary and humanistic analogies; the study of play forces us to be human.

We define play recursively: play plays.

We define reality playfully: leaps break earth's grasp.

We define change playfully: the play-face, a parodic, animated death's-head, taunts time.

Play is perilous magic. Like all magic, it calls for appropriate ceremony. So here's to the members of TAASP, and our own appropriate ceremonies; and most of all, to the richly patterned meta-life that we call play.

REFERENCES

Axelrod, R., & Hamilton, W. D. The evolution of cooperation. *Science,* 1981, *211*, 1390-1396.

Blaffer Hrdy, S. *The woman that never evolved.* Cambridge, Mass.: Harvard University Press, 1981.

Carter, L. J. The Leopolds: A family of naturalists. *Science,* 1980, *207,* 1051-1055.

Fagen, R. *Animal play behavior.* New York, Oxford, and London: Oxford University Press, 1981.

Konner, M. J. Infancy among the Kalahari Desert San. In P. H. Leiderman and S. Tulkin (Eds.), *Culture and infancy: Variations in the human experience.* New York: Academic Press, 1977.

Lumsden, C. J., & Wilson, E. O. *Genes, mind, and culture: The co-evolutionary process.* Cambridge, Mass.: Harvard University Press 1981.

McClintock, M. Estrous synchrony and its meditation by airborne chemical communication (*Rattus norvegicus). Hormones and Behavior,* 1978, *10*, 264-276.

Sutton-Smith, B. *The folkgames of children.* Austin: University of Texas Press, 1972.

chapter 15

THE CHILD IS FATHER TO THE MAN: NEOTENY AND PLAY IN HUMAN EVOLUTION

Richard D. Alford
East Central Oklahoma State University

Typically, both natural and social scientists attempt to explain the existence of animal play behavior by suggesting various adaptive functions which it fulfills or is hypothesized to fulfill. The paradigm of this type of explanation is something like the following: 1) Among animals which do exhibit play behavior, it is often costly (in terms of the physical dangers which may be involved, time expended, energy expended, and attention diverted). 2) Considering these costs, for play behavior to have evolved it must be offering the organism tangible benefits (and not all animals exhibit identifiable play behavior; in fact, while most mammals and birds play, 90% of all animals lack play [Fagen, 1982]). 3) By demonstrating that tangible benefits are resulting from animal play behavior, support is marshalled for the hypothesis that a particular variety of animal play evolved because of the adaptive advantage it provides.

Most explanations of animal play behavior take the above form. An exemplar of this explanatory strategy is Fagen's (1976) analysis of the evolution of innovative play. Many play researchers have suggested that play can facilitate experimentation and, at least occasionally, generate significant discoveries. Fagen presents a mathematical model of the costs and benefits of such innovative play. According to Fagen, "The benefits of discovery must outweigh the cost of play if innovative play is to evolve" (1976, p. 103). He concludes, "Behavior formally resembling animal play can be shown mathematically to be optimal for generic learning by experimentation in a relaxed field, while innovative play can evolve even in a population of animals capable of observational learning" (1976, p. 110).

Fagen's analysis, however, suffers from a common deficiency. While he demonstrates that play may well provide significant benefits (in this case, optimal generic learning), he makes no attempt to measure or quantify these benefits, and he entirely neglects the variable of cost. This is typical of contemporary explanations of animal play; the analysis stops when significant advantages of play behavior have been demonstrated. A more satisfactory explanation ought to include at least an estimate of costs as well as benefits.

Explanations of Human Play Behavior

Human play behavior exhibits both enormous similarities with animal play behavior and a number of special characteristics. Some of these special characteristics include:

- enormous amounts of time and energy devoted to play behavior,
- an extension of play into adulthood,
- organized and culturally institutionalized forms of play (games, sports, team play, etc.), and
- the elaboration of varieties of play (while animal play usually involves solo exercise, play fighting, and occasionally play with objects, human play forms include: linguistic play, humor, socializing as play, etc.).

The majority of attempts to explain human play behavior and its special characteristics are quite similar to the paradigm of animal play explanations described above. The benefits of human play are hypothesized and perhaps demonstrated, and it is assumed that these benefits explain the existence of the play behavior or special characteristic of human play (it might be noted that this cost-benefit approach is as appropriate to arguments of biological evolution as to arguments of cultural evolution). Again, the costs of play are usually ignored.

Biologists, however, warn us that selection for a single character is rare. According to Fuller, "Selection for a single character is. . . an abstraction which does not correspond to biological reality. Selection modifies a total genotype and the total genotype controls constellations of characters, not single traits" (1962, p. 76). As the experience of animal breeders has demonstrated: "The relationship between behavioral and physiological phenotypic changes under selection works both ways. Selection for physical characters has been shown to affect behavioral traits, and behavioral consequences are certainly possible in any selection program whatever may be its major objective" (Fuller, 1962, p. 77).

It may be that contemporary explanations of human play behavior have erred in viewing human playfulness as an isolated trait, subject directly to selective pressures (whether biological or cultural). It is possible that human play might be more productively viewed as an element in a complex and its evolution considered in relation to the evolution of that complex.

Play as a Juvenile Characteristic

Returning to a consideration of mammalian play, it can be observed that play behavior is typically a characteristic of a juvenile phase of development and not a characteristic of the entire life cycle. In most mammalian species play behavior is entirely confined to a period of immaturity (Lorenz, 1976), while in some species interest in play is markedly reduced in adulthood (Bruner, 1976). The question arises, why should juveniles play and adults lose interest in play?

Of course, different functional pressures operate in each developmental period or stage. Juveniles are adapted to their environmental niches (both physical and social) just as adults are adapted to their environmental niches. Presumably, for many species play is functional for the juvenile, but not for the adult. In other words, the cost/benefit ratio of play behavior shifts from benefit-dominance to cost-dominance as the individual reaches adulthood. Since mammalian juveniles are, to some extent, protected and fed by adults, they exist in what has been called a 'protected context' or a 'relaxed field.' In this context the costs of play are reduced. The adult, forced out of this protected context, cannot afford the costs of play.

Neoteny

In humans, what is typically a juvenile characteristic in primates, that is, playfulness, is extended into adulthood. The persistence of juvenile characteristics into adulthood is known to biologists as 'neoteny.' Neoteny can occur when there is a retardation of the rate of development of the rest of the body as compared with that of the reproductive organs (Hardy, 1954, p. 126). This results in the retention of juvenile characteristics into adulthood.

Beginning in the 1920s with the observations of Garstang (1922) and Bolk (1926), neotenization has been recognized as one of the major avenues of evolutionary adaption. In a changing environment adult forms of an organism may, through natural selection, undergo gradual and incremental change to adapt to the changed requirements of that environment. On the other hand, some species appear to have adapted to new environments by the simpler and speedier process of retaining juvenile characteristics into adulthood. Since the rates of different developmental processes are genetically controlled, a simple alteration of the timing of developmental processes can sometimes drastically alter the adult phenotype.

The North American salamander *Amblystoma tigrinum,* for example, breathes with gills in its larval condition, but by adulthood, loses its gills and breathes by lungs. In Mexico, however, the same species is found in aquatic environments. Here it retains its gills and becomes sexually mature while its body is in a larval condition. Neoteny allowed the *Amblystoma tigrinum* to adapt to a changed environment (Hardy, 1954).

According to Hardy, "The ostrich and other flightless birds which have miniature wings and retain into adult life the down plumage characteristic of the nestlings of other species may perhaps be regarded in these respects as gigantic neotenous chickens" (1954, p. 136). In other words, birds without the need for flight can occasionally evolve in a new direction through neotenization, acquiring new capacities through the retention of juvenile characteristics.

Neotenization has also been a goal of many animal breeders and domesticators. According to Fox, "With fixed paedomorphic features in certain domestic livestock, the time span from birth to maturity, in some cases, has been reduced, resulting in earlier physical and sexual maturity. This acceleration of growth, coupled with paedomorphic reduction of mature characteristics of the wild animal (e.g., proportion of bone to muscle, reduction of skin thickness) is of great economic importance. . . . Castration is practiced as a standard method, often coupled with synthetic estrogen treatment . . . animals so treated naturally are deficient in sexual activities and also lack dominance, aggressiveness and territoriality" (1968, p. 66). In other words, neotenization, whether naturally emergent or artificially induced, can affect behavioral, as well as physical, characteristics.

A wide variety of domesticated animals exhibit neotenous characteristics. According to Lorenz, "In many extensively domesticated animals, the fighting drive of the adult male is greatly reduced, as is the full manifestation of sexual dimorphism seen in the wild form" (1976, p. 93). Neoteny has been implicated in the dog (Hardy, 1954), the pig (Dechambre, 1949), and the duck (Lorenz, 1976).

That humans exhibit neotenous characteristics has been recognized since Bolk (1926). According to de Beer,

Bolk has shown that many of the features of the adult structure of man show resemblances to those of the embryonic structure of the anthropoid apes . . . These features include the relatively high brain-weight, the position of the foramen magnum and the cranial flexure, the retarded closure of the sutures between the bones of the skull, the dentition, the flatness of the face (orthognathy), the hairlessness of the body, the light colour of the skin, and a number of other features . . . man's erect attitude is associated with the retention during ontegeny of a condition which in other mammals is embryonic and temporary, as it must have been in man's ancestors. The erect posture of man is, in Bolk's view, a consequence of neoteny of the shape of the head (1940, p. 28).

Additional human features which have been identified as neotenous include: the proportions of the head and body, the curvature of the vertebral column (Lorenz, 1976), and the unrotated position of the big toe (Gould, 1981).

Beyond these neotenous physical characteristics, humans also exhibit a variety of neotenous behavioral characteristics. These include an adult interest in exploration and play (Gould, 1981) and a general openness to surroundings (Lorenz, 1976). It is evident that humans display a wide variety of neotenous characteristics.

Presumably, what is common to each of the above cases of

neotenization in evolution is a changing environment which alters the costs and benefits of the characteristics of the adult of the species. In each case, the retention of juvenile or larval characteristics in the adult presumably improves the adaptation of the organism. In many, and perhaps most of these cases of neotenization, neotenous characteristics appear to have developed as a complex, rather than as single, isolated traits. In each case, while some neotenous characteristics are clearly adaptively beneficial, other characteristics provide no obvious adaptive advantages (the down plumage of the ostrich or the reduced brow ridges of humans).

In any case of neotenization it is not necessary that every retained juvenile characteristic should facilitate the adaptation of the organism. What *is* required is that the net benefits should outweigh the net costs of the entire complex of juvenile characteristics. Thus, any particular element in a neoteny complex need not, itself, facilitate adaptation, if the net benefits of the complex outweigh the net costs.

If human play behavior can be considered as an element in a more general neoteny complex, it may be that explanations of human play
- focus almost exclusively on the hypothesized benefits of such behavior (and many benefits *have* been convincingly demonstrated),
- neglect the costs of such play behavior, and
- fail to identify play as an element in the neoteny complex. In this way the positive value of human play may be overestimated.

Advantages of the Neoteny Complex

There are a variety of reasons why the human neoteny complex may have evolved. The benefits of intensified and elaborated play behavior constitute just one of these reasons. Following are six more or less distinguishable advantages which may account (singly or in combination) for the development of the human neoteny complex.
- *Upright Posture* — As Bolk (1926) has suggested, human upright posture would be impossible were it not for the positioning of the foramen magnum in what in primates is a fetal position. Great significance has been attributed to the advantages of upright posture by numerous scientists in many fields. Upright posture also appears to be a very early feature of the hominid line.
- *Reduced Aggressiveness and Dominance Behavior* — In many mammals dominance and aggressive behavior are associated with the adult stage of the male life cycle. In both animals which are artificially induced to retain juvenile characteristics (castrated farm animals), and in animals which have gradually become neotenous (the dog), aggressiveness and dominance behavior are greatly reduced. It may be that human neotenization entailed a similar reduction in aggressive and dominance behavior. As most scenarios of human evolution suggest a gradual reduction of

intra-species competitive and aggressive behavior and an accompanying increase in cooperative behavior, any reduction in male aggressiveness might be adaptively beneficial.

• *Facilitation of Social Bonding and Nurturant Behavior* — Mammals typically invest a significant amount of parental effort in the nurturance of their young. Parental behavior is often elicited by the visual characteristics of juveniles (what has become known as the "cute response"), coupled with some mechanism for identifying the relevant juvenile (that is, the parent's specific child). Not only do infants often exhibit innate tendencies to respond to parents (whether via the rather fixed "imprinting" process [Klopfer, 1971] or, as in humans, with the help of an innate interest in the adult face [Freedman, 1961]), but parents often exhibit innate tendencies to produce nurturant behavior in response to creatures with juvenile characteristics (head-dominant body proportions, hairlessness, short limbs, clumsy style of movement, etc.). The possibility that one neotenous characteristic, relative hairlessnes, has evolved to increase nurturant behavior has been hinted at recently by Alexander and Noonan,

> A possible relationship exists between the relative hairlessness of humans and their emphasis on parental care. In the several published arguments on this question it seems to have been overlooked that the least hairy of all humans are their juveniles. Hairlessness in young mammals otherwise seems to correlate with multiple births and a helpless period in the nest . . . We suggest that the selective value of being a juvenile, or giving that impression, should be investigated in efforts to explain the gradual evolution of hairlessness in humans, and its present distribution among humans of different ages and sexes (1979, p. 451).

Evidence from a number of lines suggests that juvenile features have the capacity to elicit nurturant behavior. In the relatively rare disorder known as "infantile dwarfism" children who suffer severe emotional stress may cease growing altogether and further, retain infantile physical features and bodily proportions. Further, in several cases of children raised in total social isolation, the same retention of infantile features has been reported. Although it is merely a hypothesis, it may be that the retention of infantile features in these cases is an attempt to elicit nurturant behavior. Certainly the conscious exhibition of juvenile characteristics as a method of eliciting care is within the behavioral repertoire of many women and not a few men (Goffman, 1976). In any case, the retention of juvenile characteristics may well serve to increase nurturant behavior and encourage social bonding. Since it has been suggested that enormous parental investments are central to the evolution of the human mode of adaptation (Alexander and Noonan, 1979), any elicitor of parental behavior might be of great adaptive significance.

- *Behavioral Flexibility and Neophilia* — It has often been suggested that two of the most important human qualities are an interest in the novel and an ability to adapt to novel circumstances. Numerous researchers have suggested that these abilities are juvenile characteristics which, in humans, are retained into adulthood (Lorenz, 1976; Reynolds, 1972; Gould, 1981). Their evolutionary advantageousness is too well documented to demand further comment.
- *Playfulness* — As mentioned before, in most mammals playfulness is a decidedly juvenile characteristic. The playfulness of both human adults and adults of other highly neotenous species (the dog) may well offer significant adaptive advantages (innovative play, tension release, socialization to the group, etc.).
- *Particular and Local Advantages* — Certain extremes of neoteny may have developed in certain human populations as a response to the particular demands of a local environment. The short stature of African pygmies may be an instance of this. Pygmies reach puberty at an extremely young age (seven to nine years old), and hence their growth is terminated early. Their short stature, then, is a product of what in non-pygmies is termed "precocious puberty." Short stature is highly adaptive in the pygmies' environment since it allows an individual to move through dense brush with greater ease than taller people (Turnbull, 1961). The hypothesis that the pygmies' short stature is a neoteny-induced trait is lent additional support by the fact that pygmies exhibit other pronounced neotenous characteristics, like juvenile facial features.

It is likely that human neoteny evolved because of a combination of the above adaptive advantages. It is also possible that human neoteny evolved in response to some subset of the above advantages, and that some of these consequences are epiphenomenal. Since neotenous features may well develop in complexes, certain of the consequences of increasing neotenization may have been adaptively neutral or even negative. As Gould has warned, we must guard against attempting to explain every human trait in terms of direct natural selection (1981, p. 333).

While there is no doubt that human playfulness has important and often positive consequences, it seems wisest to consider the evolution of human playfulness and its special characteristics in relation to the evolution of the neoteny complex. This approach, of course, leaves open the question of play's overall adaptive significance.

REFERENCES

Alexander, R.D., and Noonan, K.M. Concealment of ovulation, parental care, and human social evolution. In N.A. Chagnon and W. Irons, (Eds.) *Evolutionary biology and human social behavior.* North Scituate, Massachusetts: Duxbury Press, 1979.

Bolk, L. Vergleichende untersuchengun an einem fetus, eines gorilla und eines schimpansen. *Z. fur Anat.*, 1926, No. 81.

de Beer, G.R. *Embryos and ancestors.* Oxford: Oxford University Press, 1940.

Dechambre, E. La theorie de feotalization et la formation des races de chiens et de porc. *Mammalie*, 1949, 5, 129-137.

Fagen, R. Modelling how and why play works. In J.S. Bruner, A. Jolly, and K. Sylva (Eds.), *Play: Its role in development and evolution.* New York: Basic Books, 1976.

Fagen, R. "The Perilous Magic of Animal Play," paper presented at The Association for the Anthropological Study of Play, Annual Conference, London, Ontario, 1982.

Fox, M.W. The Influence of domestication upon behavior of animals. In M.W. Fox (Ed.) *Abnormal behavior in animals.* Philadelphia: W.B. Saunders Company, 1968.

Freedman, D.G. The infant's fear of strangers and the flight response. *Journal of Child Psychology and Psychiatry,* 1961, 2, 242-248.

Fuller, J.L. The genetics of behavior. In E.S.E. Hafez (Ed.), *The behavior of domestic animals.* Baltimore: The Williams and Wilkins Company, 1962.

Garstang, W. The theory of recapitulation: A critical restatement of the biogenetic law. *Journal of the Linnean Society of London, Zoology,* 1922, 35, 81-88.

Goffman, E. *Gender advertisements.* New York: Harper Colophon Books, 1976.

Gould, S.F. *The mismeasure of man.* New York: W.W. Norton, 1981.

Hardy, A.C. Escape from specialization. In J. Huxley, A.C. Hardy, and E.B. Ford (Eds.), *Evolution as a process.* London: Allen and Unwin, 1954.

Klopfer, P.H. Mother love: What turns it on? In T.E. McGill, (Ed.), *Readings in animal behavior.* New York: Holt, Rinehart and Winston, 1971.

Lorenz, K. Psychology and Phylogeny. In J.S. Bruner, A. Jolly, and K. Sylva (Eds.), *Play: Its role in development and evolution.* New York: Basic Books, 1976.

Reynolds, P.C. "Play, language and human evolution," paper presented at the Annual Meeting of the American Association for the Advancement of Science, Washington, D.C., 1972.

Turnbull, C. *The forest people.* New York: Simon and Schuster, 1961.

CONCLUSION

In this section the debate over functionality increases to a fever pitch. In some sense the book has proceeded from discussing the pleasures of festivals and adult recreation, which we can all directly understand, to discussions of the functionality of children's and animal play which we don't properly understand and for which we do not have too much vicarious empathy. When we can share the experience, we can apparently describe it. When we cannot, we are more inclined to discuss its utility.

Despite their apparent differences, the one focusing more on animal play, the other more on human flexibility, both Fagen and Alford are concerned with the costs as well as the benefit of their subject matter. Both wish to separate out that which is dysfunctional from that which is functional in play or in flexibility.

Alford's position at least has the intuitive virtue of reconciling much of play's apparent "triviality" with its apparent functionality. Perhaps it may contribute to flexibility in general, if in many specific instances it does not.

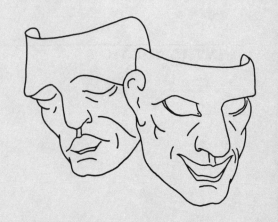

part *five*

_____

THEORY OF HUMAN PLAY

INTRODUCTION

To this point we have touched on whether play is characterized like festivals, by license, or like leisure by voluntariness; whether it is functional or dysfunctional, whether conservative or innovative, or whether public or private, and we have arrived at the conclusion that it may either include or exclude any of these features. Similarly it may or may not function in many of the ways suggested: to socialize, bring mental health, affirm community, allow expression of impulses (like sexual interests) or simply be one of the many characteritics of neotony.

In the following two papers we take up the issue of why child's play seems on the public level to be considered so trivial and yet every modern play theorist (Freud, Piaget, Berlyne, Bateson) insists that it is of great importance in child development. And in the second paper we ask why there seems to be a general public desire to assume that children play but that adults do not, thus continuing the very prejudice that play is "childish" matter. In both of these papers we seek to show that there is a fundamental ambivalence about play in Western Society, and that despite our modern theorizing and the great increase in play research in the past decade, this ambivalence still remains.

chapter 16

THE MEANING OF PLAY'S TRIVIALITY

Diana Kelly-Byrne
University of Pennsylvania

Relationships between the realm of play and other realms, such as work, are highly ambiguous in our own civilization. Further, ways of conceptualizing the activities of these realms are culturally relative and specific. Not only might other groups not take care to make such distinctions, but if they do, do so differently. For example, Turner (1978) has suggested that in many societies the major distinction that demarcates realms of behavior is the sacred/profane dichotomy. Further, Adams (1978) has seen the major distinction in activities among the Basotho Africans as being that of equilibrial and disequilibrial. However, the work/leisure distinction, in which play is taken to be a subset of the latter, does operate in western society and subsumes several modes of behavior as well as a range of values that are attached to them.

During the last century, one of the implications of the work/play dichotomy in industrial western civilization was that the work was serious business while play was a trivial matter. Given the marriage of this bipolar relationship in one way or another in so many societies of which we have knowledge, we might well suspect that whether one term or the other is inflected with cultural value, their apparent opposition may conceal more than it reveals. That is to say, whether seriousness or triviality be stressed, it is always possible that the very opposite is covertly harbored. For example, play, which in time past has been regarded as nothing but trivial, may indeed harbor an ambivalent attitude which covertly functions to defend its importance. What the nature of this importance might be is the focus of the paper.

The Study

This paper is based on a study which investigated a 7 year old female child's play and story relationship with an adult who was the researcher. It is an intensive ethnographic study of a single case. The stance assumed is a phenomenological one in that the event is described from the viewpoint of the participants and is itself taken to be contingent on the meaning making performance of its members. Thus meaning is not taken to be static or *a priori* but seen as emergent and constituted in interaction.

The study took place over a year during which there were 14 visits to the home, each lasting 3 to 4 hours. I believe what occured over that period of time has something to say about play and triviality. I shall relate the story of the relationship and while doing so, propose the meaning of play's ambivalence, at least as it manifested and resolved itself in this case.

The Relationship: A Brief Synopsis of the Seasons

The play relationship had an initial, middle and final phase. The intitial phase consisted of the first five sessions which were crucial to laying the groundwork for what was to come. The first session, as discussed elsewhere, (Kelly-Byrne,1982), was characterized by a great deal of negotiation as is often the case in early play encounters as the work of Garvey (1977), Corsaro (1980) and Schwartzman (1973, 1976) has shown. The investigator came to the child as a babysitter and one whom she had not previously met. The child entered the relationship wearing her public face which in this case was aloof, competent and controlling. The child's goal was to make a relationship with the adult and in particular to do so by luring her into her own private world. The currency used by the child for operating in her own private world was fantasy, and it was crucial to her purposes that she should negotiate a play frame for this relationship. When the child abruptly refused the adult's offer to read her a story in the first session and instead reminded her that "perhaps they had better get to know each other first," she also included two important conditions for doing so. On the one hand she said "You have to come to my room," and then, as they proceeded up the stairs to her room, she stopped short on the landing and said "I tell no one my dreams, secrets, secret languages or about my superheroes, so don't ask me about them." This complex interdiction signalled a negation of that order of behavior which deals directly with those things close to the personal self but by implication asserted the very opposite. What the child implied is that her adult partner and she would share a ludic relationship in her bedroom, a partnership which by its very paradoxical nature would deal with a play upon these worldly phenomena of her fantasy life, her secrets, etc., but not deal with them in everyday "realistic" terms (Bateson, 1956, 1972). This first session was characterized by numerous negotiations for this ludic frame. All of which is to say that play was not only the currency or medium by which the adult and she get to know each other better, but also that it was a *mask* for her most personal concerns.

After the preliminary politics of these negotiations which dominated most of this first session, there was some play enactment that occurred, although during that playful interaction the adult was mainly an onlooker or follower of the child's instructions. However, this play of child and adult led the child to share her fantasy biography with the adult which, although indirectly expressed, was nevertheless a part of her personal self, which was far less public than any she had shown earlier. In addition, at the end of the play enactment, and almost as a coda to it, the child stated her liking for the adult and said: "I like teenagers like you." This event might suggest that a certain level of bonding had occurred. Two other kinds of behavior followed. First, the child engaged in festival play (she sang, danced, laughed and was regressed), and then she formed a collusive pact with her adult play partner against her parents. She locked them out by communicating with the investigator in a secret play language which they had developed earlier in the session.

So this first session ended very differently from the way in which it had begun. It had moved from negotiations to collusions.

In the *second session* only a minimum of negotiation occurred, and once again it was at the very beginning of the encounter. Here, also, even prior to the play, there was an exchange of statements of a personal order. There were questions about what each had been doing, and the child wondered if the adult played with anyone else in this way. In the first session such personal relating occurred, only *after* the play session, not before it. In this second session, also, the play enactments lasted for a much longer time and the investigator was allowed more participation. After the play was over, there was a long period of closely shared television viewing with the child snuggling beside the adult on the bed as they watched.

In the *third session* the child's very first gestures were directly from the play world. Sneaking up behind the investigator, she threw a rope over her head and captured her in terms of her fantasy characters. This was in marked contrast to the more public initial gestures of negotiations in sessions 1 and 2. The early play gestures on this occasion were followed immediately by a personal sharing which pertained to their everyday concerns and opinions about the last television show they had seen together. Referring to them, the child said, "You'll make a good Wonder Woman, cause you look like her." The rest of the evening of several hours was spent in staging and enacting a variety of dramatic plots about heroines and mythic figures initiated and directed by the child. Many of these performances were made for the tape recorder which had been introduced during Session 2. These enactments for the recorder also required negotiations, but they were on a different level from the former negotiation and had to do mainly with plot structure and characterization rather than everyday behavior. Thus, the element of negotiation did not fade from these sessions, but it shifted its domain of application to the play world itself.

In the remainder of the sessions of Phase I (Sessions 1 to 5) and those of the middle phase (Sessions 6 to 9), the behavior of staging plots assumed a central role, and much of the negotiations as well as the child's personal communications about her feelings for the adult were couched in the dramatic enactment of the stories.

In Sessions 4 and 5, there were again lengthy dramatic enactments. Most importantly, the adult was allowed a much more active role in the dramas (which was not true of the earlier sessions). Nevertheless, the child still remained largely dominant and controlling of the flow in this dramatic realm. By contrast, in the child's everyday behavior with the investigator, she had become much more flexible. In this study, it was the child's everyday relationships and behavior which showed flexibility well before that was shown in the play realm. Since play is supposed to be the realm of flexibility, this was surprising (Lieberman, 1979; Fagen, 1981). The present case argues that the play realm when active increases flexibility elsewhere, but maintains with some tenacity its own grip on the player's basic metaphors or emotional concerns. In addition, what is also striking is that as the adult's participation became more active, the child's thematic content also became more explicit. For instance, in Session 5 she controlled the adult by assuming the language of a dog, thus making herself virtually incomprehensible to the adult most of the time. What is notable about this particular strategy on the child's part is that her very powerful parents, who speak several languages, may use at times the same technique of incomprehensible language for controlling and excluding the child as well as others.

In Sessions 6-9 important changes occurred both in the character of the drama as well as in the role given the adult by the child. Instead of being cast in relatively inferior and powerless roles, the adult was given a powerful and attractive mother role where she represented Wisdom, Beauty, Power and Courage. The stories themselves decreasingly dealt with good and bad mothers and forces of good and evil in general, and increasingly dealt with a veiled sexual interest in men's relationships to women and their relationships to children. The parts adult and child played now mirrored, as well as reversed, the relationships of her parents to herself. She and the investigator had become the desired parent figures.

Sessions 10-14 were devoted, almost entirely, to direct conversations. What had been interdicted in the first session was now possible: the direct discussion of intimate interests. Many play dramas were still plotted, but none were ever carried through in contrast to their importance in the prior sessions. In addition, she now asked for intimate details from the adult's personal life. Conversation and intimacy have taken the place of play and indirection.

Conclusion

Always admitting that this is only one case study and at that with a 7 year old girl, what occurred in this play relationship confirms previous views that play with others is not easily undertaken without some prior negotiations. Indeed, not only are the politics of negotiation central in the early stages of establishing ludic relationships, but they continue to operate in different domains and take forms intrinsic to the popular genres used. In this case, the negotiations shift from the everyday domain to the play domain and take the form of staging which is particular to the genre of dramatic enactment. However, what is most dramatic about this particular study is that while all kinds of the play (sociodramatic, galumphing, language and nonsense play, festival play and so on) dealt with in the relationship seem to have various but temporary functions to fulfill, the part of the relationship which is most temporary at first and overtly dismissed in Session 1, increases linearly throughout the course of the sessions. That is to say, the sharing of the self that is most within and which was most heavily masked, at least in the sequence of events, appears to be what is most desperately sought and achieved through the course of the relationship.

We now return to the question of why play seems trivial. The judgement of this single study is that play's apparent triviality guards the most intimate motives which are almost too sacred for this child to share with any other. One does not enter into play lightly with those with whom one cannot trust one's personal secrets. (Note that collusion and secrecy were important aspects of the child's negotiations and her bid to establish a spirit of 'communitas' in Session 1. See Kelly-Byrne, 1982.) When such trust can be established, there evolves within the play a dramatized and indirect symbolization of the ambivalences she feels about the most important relationships in life. However, if play evolves beyond this to a point at which the partners can give very direct expression to their symbolic concerns, then the present case suggests an enormous leap is possible beyond the masks of play into "real" talk and outright sharing of self.

To sum the implications of this, if play was seen as trivial or unserious by our nineteenth century ancestors, it was probably because it was indeed a passage or stepping stone to the most serious of matters which it serves public life to obscure. In fact, we may surmise that the triviality of play pertains not so much to play, which is a serious and significant mode of communication, but to those personal and private matters which may be brought to the public arena if play were allowed its sway. In an industrial civilization which requires an increasingly impersonal and public face, personal and private matters need to be trivialized and passageways to these foreclosed.

REFERENCES

Adams, Charles R. Distinctive features of play and games: A folk model from South Africa. In Helen B. Schwartzman (Ed.), *Play and culture proceedings of the Association for the Anthropological*

Study of Play, 1978. West Point, N.Y.: Leisure Press, 1980.

Bateson, Gregory A. The message "this is play." In B. Schaffner (Ed.),*Group process: Transactions of the second conference.* New York: Josiah Macy Foundation, 1956, 145-246.

Bateson, Gregory A. *Steps to an ecology of mind.* Ballantine,1972.

Corsaro, William. Role-play and peer culture. *TAASP Newsletter,* 1980, *6,* (4), 9-13.

Fagen, Robert. *Animal play behavior.* New York, Oxford, London: Oxford University Press, 1981.

Garvey, Catherine, & Berndt, R. Organization of pretend play. *Catalogue of Selected Documents in Psychology,* 1977 (1589), American Psychological Association.

Kelly-Byrne, Diana. "A narrative of play and intimacy: A seven year old's play and story relationship with an adult." Ph.D. dissertation, University of Pennsylvania, 1982.

Kelly-Byrne, Diana. A narrative of play and intimacy. In Frank Manning (Ed.), *The world of play. Proceedings of the Association for the Anthropological Study of Play.* West Point, N.Y.: Leisure Press, 1982.

Lieberman, J.N. *Playfulness: Its relationship to imagination and creativity.* New York: Academic Press, 1979.

Schwartzman, Helen B. "An ethnographic study of make-believe in a nursery school." Ph.D. dissertation, University of Chicago, 1973.

Schwartzman, Helen B. Children's play: A sideways glance at make-believe. In D.F. Lancy and B. Allan Tindall (Eds.), *The anthropological study of play: Problems and prospects.* New York: Leisure Press, 1976.

Turner, Victor. Comments and conclusions. In Barbara Babcock (Ed.), *The reversible world.* Ithaca, N.Y: Cornell Univerity Press, 1978.

chapter 17

CONTINUITY AND DISCONTINUITY IN PLAY CONDITIONING*: THE ADULT-CHILD CONNECTION

Diana Kelly-Byrne
University of Pennsylvania

It was Ruth Benedict who, almost fifty years ago, alerted us to the many contrary patterns of conditioning in our culture as she exposed the very different values and behaviours emphasized in childhood as opposed to adulthood. Her prime example is centered on the contrasts between the individual's role as a child first and later as a father. She writes that as a child, the emphasis is on docility, sexlessness and non-responsibility or carefreeness, whereas as an adult, it is on dominance, sexuality and responsibility. Such discontinuities are a matter of cultural accretions. They affect our attitudes to behaviour in childhood as well as adulthood and the play/work discontinuity in the life cycle is related to such social dogma. In fact, Benedict insists that our view of the child as wanting to play and of the adult as having to work is more a matter of dicontinuous cultural institutions and beliefs than of physiological contrasts, although she adds that it is physiological schema which are characteristically invoked to account for them.

Although Benedict did not deal specifically with play, it can be shown that play is a behaviour that is treated as a distinctly different phenomenon in childhood as opposed to adulthood. The cultural institutions which publicly support the play of the child are different from those which provide for adult play (for example, education centres versus sports clubs or casinos). They are based on divergent premises and no continuous patterning of the behaviour is encouraged. In fact, a survey of the literature suggests that characteristically, the concept of play is relegated to the state of childhood and when applied to adulthood, is used to refer to sport, games and other recreational activities like various art-and-craft-making endeavours or games of chance. Further, not only is the literature filled with distinctions between the "play" of the two groups, but it also reveals an imbalance in the studies undertaken in the area. That is to say, there is an abundance of material on child play and a relative lack of it on

---

*This notion of "continuity and discontinuity" was used by Ruth Benedict in 1938. See Bibliography.

adult play* which indeed reflects the schism that exists in the culture regarding play in relation to childhood and adulthood. Doyens of play like Erik Erikson have described the discontinuity as follows:

> ... the comparison of adult and child's play [is] somewhat senseless; for the adult is a commodity-producing and a commodity-exchanging being, whereas the child is only preparing to become one. To the working adult, play is recreation. It permits a periodical stepping out from those forms of defined limitation which are his social reality (213) ... The playing adult steps sideward into another reality: the playing child advances forward to new stages of mastery (222), (1963).

Erikson's statement reflects the familiar cultural view of the child as wanting to play and the adult as having to work. However, in addition to the work/play distinction, the statement also implies other issues such as the relationship of play to leisure; of the "playfulness" or otherwise of sport and games and the relationship of play to reality. Such issues have been carefully explicated by many scholars such as Sutton-Smith (1981), Schwartzman (1978), Gruneau (1980), Bateson (1955;1972) and Goffman (1974), and need not be addressed here. But what is pertinent to the central concern of this paper is the acknowledgement that views such as the above are premised on the basic *ideological stances* which people have implicitly towards play. Furthermore, these views have a long history in Western Civilization (Frappier, 1976), the details of which have been noted by many (Dodds, 1951; Frappier, 1976). Therefore, I shall simply mention some of the more consequential accretions which have influenced our attitudes to play and hence its patterning as we know it today. They are as follows:

- The emergence of the view that childhood is a separate state; that its members are immature, innocent, vulnerable and to be moulded and protected (Aries, 1962); that play is a primary means of growth and mastery in childhood.
- That although valued, childhood and play are both to be outgrown and hurriedly discarded. For example, both Freud and Piaget implicitly held the prevailing attitude of 19th Century and early 20th Century Europe toward play, seeing it as a short-lived "interesting'" behaviour that has to make way for a more serious encounter with what they termed "reality" (Freud, 1905; Piaget, 1945). According to Freud, the energies devoted to play become recycled into phantasy activities or according to Piaget, into increasingly socialized purposeful activities.

  The implication of these views for play is that the behaviour is

---

*Although this has been increasingly noticed in recent years resulting in much more attention being given to adult play. See Frappier 1976; Betcher 1981; and Cheifetz 1982.

given meaning in relation to adult concerns and mores, rather than in its own terms and from the child's perspective. Hence, not only is play seen as "immature" and therefore not worthy of "mature" adults, but it is also seen as a phenomenon which must be viewed usefully. The many functionalist analyses of children's play in the literature bear witness to the liberal and utilitarian doctrines which *enshroud* childhood and its play (Hogan, in press; deLone, 1979; and Wishey,1972). While the issue of what function play serves is not an irrelevant question, it is an adultcentric orientation and a preoccupation of those of us who have been tainted by the work ethic. Our concern has been to justify positively the occurrence of play and its encouragement by making it the handmaiden to more respectable behaviour such as problem solving, flexibility, role play, etc. Having framed it as such, we have then proceeded to idealize the behaviour in childhood (Sutton-Smith, 1981). In addition, such views have specific implications for our attitudes toward adult play. For instance, as if being associated with immaturity were not enough to relegate play to secondary status, its historical association with pleasure and with "usefulness" has further contributed to evoking suspicion towards it, especially in adulthood. In cultures where the value of self-denial and practical purpose are steadfastly upheld, any activity that is not ennobled with a self-evident, obvious goal-directedness, is downgraded. Thus, in a work-oriented society, play in adulthood in particular becomes contaminated by the work ethic and is both valued and perceived through this lens alone. Within such parameters, the focus is upon adult play as diversion, as temporary, as different from and also less significant than purposeful activity. However, even prior to the influence of the work ethic, the negative valuation of play may be traced back to the philosopher, Plato, who long presided over the intellectual and religious consensus in Western civilization. Plato chose to imprison human playful activity within constricting dualities, stifling it with the stricture of moderateness and "reason at all costs." It was this moralistic, anti-pleasure orientation to play that had and still has a controlling influence on Western religious and intellectual establishment. The historian and philosopher, Dodds (1951), suggests that this orientation was able to maintain such predominance due to its conditioning of human fears; fear of the irrational, abetted by the radical rationalist and pragmatic outlooks which foster shame for doing something useless, or non-serious; fear of trespassing moral strictures which fosters guilt for "indulging" in and enjoying a sensuous, unproductive and unelevating activity; and the fear of freedom itself with its opportunities and elements of risk. Fear, guilt and shame, when elevated into vastly propagated ideologies as is the case in the West, stand in the way of uninhibited playfulness in adults as well as children. Such ideologies help to explain the attitudes as well as the contingent descriptions of both adult and child play with which we are familiar. In essence, they give rise to descriptions that are publicly acceptable and show a socially redeemable context. That is to say, they are descriptions which imply a need for justifying the phenomenon in relation to some other valued behaviour or commodity and serve our public ends. Further, they are descriptions which are produced by locating the behaviour in particular settings. (See Mead's point about the relationship of settings to behaviour in Mead and Wolfstein, 1955, chapter 1.) Accordingly, our descriptions of play are generally located in contexts such as schoolyards, public playgrounds, parish and youth halls, recreation clubs and sports fields. As public descriptions, our views of play in childhood and adulthood are those which produce a discontinuous pattern of the behaviour. However, we must also note that as publicly acceptable accounts, these renditions of play are purified and idealized. What I wish to suggest is that such translations of the behaviour are but one type of description of reality. And as with all reality, play, too, consists of multiple descriptions, many of which are utterly ignored and denied.

Therefore, let us consider some non-public descriptions. These examples of play may not so easily serve our public ideals. The behaviour is found to occur in such contexts as: private bedrooms, cubby-houses, hide-outs, fraternity houses, in secluded corners of kindergartens, on street corners, in cars, and in general, in spaces that both children and adults make their own and away from the watchful intrusion of outsiders. They are contexts of privacy which support dyadic relationships or those of closely knit groups.

My examples are based on a selection of material which include my own and others' observations of children's play; adult informants' personal diary accounts of play; interview material from both children and adults; on secondary accounts contained in the literature and on references to adult play in verse and dramatic literature. I shall begin with accounts of children's play. These are drawn from the work of the Opies', Knapps', of Sluckin, Sarett and my own.

Children's Play

Amongst elementary school children, *giving a boy titties* is a common game. In this activity, girls are known to twist a boy's T shirt so it looks as if he posesses breasts that are tiny or giant nipples. But since the boy's are not to be beat, they in turn play *Radio*. They invite girls to play *Radio* and when their offer is accepted, they put on imaginary sets of earphones, bend over a girl's chest with an air of supreme seriousness and chant, "Come in Tokyo, come in Tokyo," meanwhile twisting her breasts, pretending they are dials and then ducking. Further, "snapping bras" is also an ambush game and boys creep up on girls and do this to the accompaniment of "Pop goes the weasel" or "Pearl Harbor sneak attack." *Playing the Bases* is another sexual game played by 9-13 year olds. Here one is dared to go through a series of increasingly daring phases of sexual activity such as kissing, flashing and making it. The group spares no pain in taunting those who are intimidated. They are teased for being "greenies" until they relent.

Even in nursery schools there is a great deal of play that would fail to meet the criteria demanded by public descriptions of the behaviour. For example, Sarett reports that girls stuff their T shirts, wiggle their hips suggestively and pretend at sexual activity, boasting that "they did it." She adds that they engage in erotic fantasies of men raping them and often pretend to peek through imaginary windows and see a couple making love. As they envisage this scene, they whisper: "They gettin' down." Another game kindergarteners have been observed playing is called "Fathers." This involves girls setting up house away from the watchful eye of adults and getting down on one another "at night time." In addition, all manner of sexual exploration goes on in the name of the popular game of "Doctors and Nurses."

Besides being sexual as the above examples suggest, much of childhood play is aggressive and flaunting of social taboo. Sarett's study of nursery school play of working and middle class children in Philadelphia and New Jersey confirms the view that much children's play is aggressive. Working class children are found to express this in physical actions and middle class kids are said to express their aggression in more veiled and verbal forms. Sarett explained this difference by suggesting that in the case of the middle class children, their play was carefully monitored by adults (1981). My own informant, Helen and her peers who come from middle class backgrounds and are in elementary school, played a game called *Darlene*. This game was about teasing. The girl who made up the game said: "You see, it's about teasing kids who are kinda stupid and sorta different. I mean, kids who are slow and dumb especially at reading." After some thought she confided: "In a way it's a real game. It happened to me when I was little. You know, my sister's friends used ter make up secrets about me and even pull down my pants. They used ter whisper to each other,'Santa Claus is bringing Ann MS for Christmas,' and then all laugh. I really felt terrible. So but anyway that gave me the idea for Darlene, but, but *Darlene*'s about a girl who's dumb and I'm really smart at reading. I *read* a hundred books for the MS readerthon." When I observed the game, I found it to be filled with taunts and teasing of the verbal kind. The game was made up of a series of social situations based on school and peer life where certain skills like reading or levels of social awareness about sexual dangers in the community or sex education were valued and if not possessed, seen to be cause for embarassment and for being seen as inferior (Kelly-Byrne, 1982).

Other pieces of play commonly observed are of a scatological nature. The work of Sarett, Sluckin and some of my students all report examples of such play. For example, Sluckin writes that children will call out SBD to the accompanying gesture of bringing their palms to their noses in the presence of unsuspecting peers. Since SBD means "silent but deadly farts," this results in much hilarity and red faced-ness on the part of the victims (1981).

To date, investigators have largely failed to foreground these negative and counter-active play patterns in culture. (See Babcock, 1976 for a discussion of counter-active play patterns.) It is hardly that these patterns cannot be described in functionalist terms or legitim-ized, if that indeed is our cultural preoccupation, but rather that they deviate from the generally idealized view of childhood play and the attendant concept of childhood. They are the darker, less public descriptions of play but which, unless considered, distort the face of this behaviour in the life of children.

Further, and quite significantly, this may also be the kind of play to be looked for in the lives of adults if we are to reconsider the popu-larly held belief of discontinuity in the play of childhood and adulthood.

Adult Play

To this end, recent work in psychiatry looks at intimate play and suggests the importance of such play in marriage. This play occurs in a private context in which usually, the members share a relationship of some duration and familiarity at least. William Betcher writes:

> . . . Little attention has been given to the contribution of spon-taneous play to marital adjustment. I am referring here not to a formalized recreational play such as tennis and dancing, but rather to the more idiosyncratic forms of playfulness that evolve over time in an intimate dyad such as private nick-names, shared jokes and fantasies and mock fighting (1981, 13).

Such play is surely real and worthy of attention. Here are some examples: Many couples who were interviewed in Betcher's study reported their play consisted in making up names for their sex organs, personifying them and role playing less inhibited characteris-tics, such as "the Marlboro Man" and a stripper. Further, some spouses reported that they would lie awake at night making up humorous but insulting names for one another. Another reported goosing his partner as part of their play relationship. Interestingly, many of these informants revealed that their particular playful pat-terns were prevalent in their childhoods and seem to have persisted as part of their stored relational potential to be reactivated in the con-text of an intimate relationship. Such information clearly suggests dif-ferences in play behaviour depending on ecological variables, as well as the relationship of the participants to each other (Kelly-Byrne, 1982). More importantly, it suggests some pattern of continuity in the play behaviour of childhood and adulthood.

Similar reports of play come from other groups who are bound by a sense of community or intimacy such as room-mates, members of a fraternity, or a dormitory. All the dormitory members from colleges in the Philadelphia area who were interviewed about their play admitted that they played and stressed the spontaneity of their endeavours. "Goofing-off" was a repetitive term they used to describe their play. One described "goofing-off" as "fun that is spontaneous in contrast to organized fun like tennis." Their accounts contained phrases like "spur of the moment," "spontaneous verbal and physical activity," "utter lawlessness," "going completely nuts," "going bananas," "there's no inhibition at all," and so forth. They reported using private codes or secret languages in their play to exclude the outside world, using nicknames, sharing jokes, fantasies, and engaging in mock fights. Further, their activities commonly consisted of bursting in on each other and throwing themselves one upon another in a pile of bodies on a bed and watching television; of sticking pennies in people's doors so they could not get out; having water fights and shaving cream fights; and of playing hide-and-seek at midnight amongst public buildings like the Philadelphia Art Museum and the Rodin Museum. These avowed lovers of aesthetic surroundings were all male but for one female.

What was also striking about this dormitory play was that the informants described themselves as a clan with a leader, and as assuming roles and having routines in which they regularly engaged. They also used secret codes, had secret venues and distinct rules which were all part of their informal play. Such examples, of which there is no shortage, are strikingly similar to descriptions one reads of child's play.

Finally, we should note that many examples of adult play may be drawn from the depiction of intimate relationships and their interactive behaviour in art. (I shall only use examples from literature here.) For instance, the poems of the 17th Century metaphysical poets, Donne and Marvel, are replete with verbal play of high conceit suggesting the imaginative play and posturing that occurs between lovers; then again the description of the antics of the four lovers in Shakespeare's "A Midsummer's Night Dream" reveal revelry, sexual aggression, madness, horse-play, topsy-turvy and dream enactment of much fantasy; the characters Richard and Sara in Pinter's play "The Lover" depict a couple who live a double life. They form a play alliance in order to be intimate and role play being each other's lovers in which Richard becomes Max and Sara a series of other women. In Albee's "Who's Afraid of Virginia Woolf," George and Martha engage in a great deal of sadistic and pretend play. In fact, Fun and Games is the title of Act I of the play. Many more examples depicting the private play of adults who share a close relationship may be produced by running through instances of a variety of art forms which deal with intimate relationships. However, the point is that adults *do* play and thay do so in contexts that are quite different from those of sport and recreation which are the domains commonly associated with their play. In fact, Schwartzman (1978) and others have pertinently commented that sports and games may be the last places to look if we are to discover the nature of play in adulthood.

Conclusion: The Adult-Child Play Connection

Having shared descriptions of adult play which differ from those commonly held by the culture, I wish to emphasize that these renditions of the behaviour are strikingly similar to the description of child's play behaviour especially amongst friends who regularly play together. In fact, whatever its motivation, clinical and research observations suggest that the play of children is clearly associated with interpersonal interactions. Since intimacy is an important aspect of interpersonal relationships, if one considered play as a relational activity which occurred in a dyad or small group, then the description one would get would be different from those which commonly occur through the literature. As I have noted elsewhere, most play with which the literature deals does not describe the relationship of those who regularly play together in more private settings. (See Kelly-Byrne, 1982, for a discussion of this and also as a counter example.)

Thus, although it is true that observationally, there is a diminished frequency of play in adults which parallels other primate creatures and a concentration or channelling of this pattern into organized and recreational pursuits, if we look at the more spontaneous play of children, and particularly the more informal idiosyncratic forms of playfulness that evolve over time in play partnerships, and compare them with adult play partnerships of a like nature, then one is forced to talk also of similarities in the play of the two age groups. Thus, not only is play *consonant* with the public patterns of enculturation about which we know a great deal, it is also covert, cruel, inversive and sexual at all stages in life, making it dissonant with our other ideals and expectations.

The question we have to ask ourselves is not so much why is child play idealized or why do or don't adults play, but rather, why do we act as if children are innocent and as if adults don't play intimately? In fact even further, I wonder what would happen if we were to value the "darker" and private side of play positively?

In sum, we need to think of child-adult play as a continuous as well as discontinuous behavior. In a final analysis, what might be discontinuity in the culture is not so much the behavior we call play, but rather our attitudes to the play of childhood and that of the adult community.

NOTE

1. For example, the spouse who used humorous insults reported doing this for hours at night with his brother with whom he shared a room. Apparently not only did this verbal play create a benign outlet for their sibling rivalry, but it also was one of their rare moments of intimacy. The man who goosed his partner recalled a cherished childhood atecedent: his grandfather had engaged in very similar coarse joking and touching with him (Betcher, p. 17).

REFERENCES

Aries, P. *Centuries of childhood.* Middlesex, England: Penguin Books Ltd., 1962.
Babcock, B. (Ed.) *The reversible world.* Ithaca, New York: Cornell University Press, 1978.
Bateson, G. *Steps to an ecology of mind.* New York: Ballantine, 1972.
Benedict, R. Continuity and discontinuity in cultural conditioning. *Psychiatry,* 1938, *1,* 161-167.
Betcher, R.W. Intimate play and marital adaptation, *Psychiatry,* 1981, *44,* 13-33.
Cheifetz, D. "Grown-up play: An integrative concept of play and its expressions in adult life." Ph.D. dissertation, Union Graduate School, Union of Experimenting Colleges and Universities, 1982.
Dodds, E. R. *The Greeks and the irrational.* Berkeley: University of California Press, 1971. (Originally published 1951).
Erikson, E. *Childhood and society.* New York: Norton, 1963. (Originally published 1950).
Frappier, P. "The playing phenomenon in adults: A theoretical study." Ph.D. dissertation, The California School of Professional Psychology, 1976.
Freud, S. *Jokes and their relation to the unconscious, Standard Edition,* Vol 8. London: Hogarth, 1955. (Originally published 1905).
Goffman, E. *Frame analysis.* Cambridge, Massachusetts: Harvard University Press, 1974.
Gruneau, R. Freedom and constraint: The paradoxes of play, games, and sports. *Journal of Sport History,* 7 (Winter, 1980) 68-86.
Kelly-Byrne, D. A narrative of play and intimacy: A seven year old's play and story relationship with an adult. Ph.D. dissertation, University of Pennsylvania, 1982.
Knapp, M & H. *One potato, two potato . . .* New York: Norton, 1976.
de Lone, R. *Small futures.* New York: Harcourt, Brace and Janovich, 1979.
Mead, M. & Wolfenstein, M. *Childhood in contemporary cultures.* Chicago: The University of Chicago Press, 1955.
Opie, P. & I. *The lore and language of school children.* London:

Oxford University Press, 1959.

Ottenstein, N. Personal communication.

Piaget, J. *La formation du symbole chez l'enfant.* Paris: Delachaux et Niestle, 1959. (Originally published, 1945).

Sarett, C. *Socialization patterns and childrens television and film related play.* Ph.D. dissertation, Annenberg School of Communications, University of Pennsylvania, 1981.

Schwartzman, H. *Transformations: The anthropology of children's play.* New York: Plenum Press, 1978.

Sluckin, A. *Growing up in the playground.* London, Boston & Henley: Routledge & Kegan Paul, 1981.

Sutton-Smith, B. "The family, leisure and sport: Some antitheses." Keynote address to the IX International Seminar on Sport Leisure and the the Family, a Multi-disciplinary approach. The International Council of Sport and Physical Education. Brugge, Belgium, 9-13 September, 1981.

Wishy, B. *The child and the republic.* Philadelphia: University of Pennsylvania Press. 1972.

CONCLUSION

We have seen in these two papers ample demonstration that both in childhood and adulthood in Western Society play is some kind of communication for hidden or non-admissable feelings and actions. Calling it trivial or confining it to childhood are just two of many cultural masks by which we prevent ourselves from seeing that play is really a kind of communication other than language and that it has to do with bringing into the social arena or the private consciousness those many other aspects of human nature which are not usually an explicit part of public discourse.

REFERENCES FOR INTRODUCTORY AND CONCLUDING SEGMENTS

Babcock, B.S. *The reversible world: Symbolic inversion in art and society.* Ithaca, New York: Cornell University Press, 1978.

Baldwin, J. D. The nature-nurture error again. *The Behavioral and Brain Sciences,* 1982, 5 #1, pp. 155-156.

Cherfas, J. & Lewin, R. *Not work alone: A cross-cultural view of activities superfluous to survival.* Beverly Hills: Sage, 1980.

Diamond, S. *In search of the primitive.* New Brunswick, New Jersey: Transaction, 1974.

Fagen, R. *Animal play behavior.* New York: Oxford University Press, 1981.

Geertz,.*The interpretation of cultures.* New York: Basic Books, 1973.

Kelly, J. R. Leisure and sport. In G. R. F. Luschen & G. H. Sage (Eds.), *Handbook of social science of sport.* Champaign, Illinois: Stipes, 1981, pp. 181-196.

Turner, V. *From ritual to theater.* New York: Performing Arts Journal Publications, 1982.

Turner, V. *Celebration.* Washington, D.C.: Smithsonian, 1983.

part *six*

CONCLUSION

THE MASKS OF PLAY

The title of this book, *The Masks of Play,* takes us into territory already well travelled by those who have labelled play as a form of paradox, beginning with Bateson but including those many members of our own association who have spoken on the subject. See in particular, Volume 6 edited by John Loy and titled *The Paradoxes of Play* (1982). What is written here will be footnotes to their work.

We want to discuss a number of kinds of phenomena. First, there are those many phenomena which we often study as if we are studying play, but seldom actually get to study what is play about them. We mean things like festivals, rituals, and even games and sports. Secondly, there are those phenomena conventionally called play or playful, which are used as a mask or a disguise for other forms of expression which are not play. In these cases the name of play is used but the expression is abused. Thirdly, there is the way play can be masked as if it is something else. Here the name of play is used in order to ignore it. Finally, given these various benign or exploitive fabrications of the phenomen as Goffman would have called them (1974), we want to ask whether there is something about playing that lends itself to this deceptive state of affairs. Are these machinations fundamental to the state of play? Is play in essence a masking or masked phenomenon? Our data for this paper is based on our own research, the student play biographies we regularly collect, and from the literature of play itself.

Masking Contexts

We don't want to argue with the general probability that play is more likely in leisure contexts than it is in other contexts, even though it has been the virtue of Mihaly Csikszentmihalyi (1977) and others to show that play is by no means confined to such places; and particularly of Helen Schwartzman (1978) to argue that games and sports might well be the last places to look if we are to discover play. We do want to point out that the main function of leisure in modern society is to be free of work activity and work temporal obligations, and that empirically we know that the bulk of leisure time is given to idling kinds of activity including talking, visiting, watching television, eating, drinking, smoking and having sex. In short, you can be at leisure without being at play, and that is the more typical state of affairs, or so Kelly (1981) and Ken Roberts (1978) and the others tell us.

As we have noted in Section I, what was remarkable about the papers on festivals in this work was their clear exemplification of human license but very little attention to human play. Thus, in Finnegan Alford's paper we found the Tamahurara, that lonely mountain Indian people of Mexico, gathering together occasionally to get drunk, to be violent, to quarrel and to engage in illicit sex, as a result of which there would be occasional deaths, accidents, falling down steep cliffs, getting pneumonia lying out drunkenly in the cold, or stepping on and smothering babies. In her paper also there was a description of the Santal of India's annual festival of sexual license in which the members of the tribe were permitted a once-a-year sexual binge with the erstwhile loves of their youthful years, now displaced by the arranged marriages which had taken their place.

In Jean Cannizo's study of two childhood groups in Sierra Leone, we were told of their costumed masquerades in which there were displays of immaturity, the evocation of dirtiness, of shit, of degeneracy and trickery and of the behavior of devils. One of the figures, for example, represented the adult male as in an advanced state of degeneracy, palsied, incontinent, inebriated and effeminate, where the progress of maturation was seen as one of progressive decay. In Frank Manning's account of the Toronto Carabana, we were given a picture of erotic dances, or revelling until sun-up the day before the parade and of the last day being a time for unbridled abandon. Even in Robert Lavenda's relatively sober account of two Minnesota town's festivals, there was still considerable attention to the drinking and vandalism that they occasioned and even to the permitted drinking on the streets in one of these towns. Roberta Park told us of the historical violence of Spring Rushes at Berkeley between the classes of the different years, struggle over the symbolic axe, the chasing and horseplay and the resultant injuries. Finally, Smadar Lavie reported on how the Bedouin of the southern Sinai try to deal with the fact that their economy has become dependent on the hippies who use their beaches for parading naked and for fornication, both of which were violations of their traditional mores. One tribesman says, "Today I was praying the noon prayer, and two guys, whose penises were hanging, and whose only clothes were cameras, took pictures of me." Subsequently a leading figure in the village acted out some of the doings of these invaders, playing a fool for his own group and temporarily exorcising their annoyance.

Now, all of this is very interesting and, if licentiousness is also intrinsic to play, then indeed we may be learning something about play. But it is not obvious to us that in any of these papers the play elements were the particular focus of attention. It is not that through-out the history of this TAASP group we have not had excellent papers attempting to disentangle the play elements from the other elements in various festival and ritual occasions (one thinks in particular of Handleman's 1977 "Play and ritual, complementary frames of meta-communication"). But such efforts have been a rarity. We are raising the issue of why there is so much scholarly effort on such play con-texts with so little attention to what is truly playful within those con-texts. The seriousness of our point is we think strengthened if we refer to that other better-known case where psychologists study the topic of children's play, sometimes without ever studying children playing, as Johnsen and Christie make clear in Section III. They test them, they experiment with them, they categorize their interactions, they classifiy their solitariness and their cooperativeness but seldom ever seem to get anywhere near their play. The most general strategy for *not* studying child play seems to be to write articles on their functions and pretty much to ignore the detailed moment by moment descrip-tion of the experience itself as if we already know what that expe-rience is. The Kelly-Byrne data suggests we do not. Is the studying of the ritual and festival contexts of play then also merely a kind of macro avoidance comparable to the psychologist's micro avoidance of the subject?

We believe a very similar case can be made against those who study the relationships between ritual and play, or art and play. In most cases, and again there are some brilliant exceptions (Handel-man, 1977; Adams, 1980), the nearest one comes to play is the cit-ation of some very general structural correspondences between the two realms, as if these family resemblances constituted some kind of explanation. As the critical differences are *not* dealt with, we are left with a vague feeling of global undifferentiation and the sense that someone has attempted once more to make play important by asso-ciating it with something else thought to be *more* important, but has not specifically described play at all, not indicated either its character nor function.

On two occasions now it has been our privilege to debate the position that sport is a form of play. At TAASP in 1981 and at the Sport Conference preceding the British Commonwealth games in Bris-bane in 1982. In both cases it seemed to us that despite our own heroic and playful efforts on behalf of the proposition, the predomi-nant feeling amongst the audience was that sports are not play. So strong, apparently, is the feeling against professional sports amongst those who make their living from studying them (the sports sociol-ogists), they are most reluctant to see sports as play. Although none of them buys Huizinga's elitist presuppositions of *Homo Ludens*, everyone seems to have agreed over-eagerly with his conclusion that play and professional sports can't mix. In short, they, too, on their own account are not studying play — whatever else it is they are studying as sports sociologists.

So our question is, why must it be that after all of us have spoken so well in recent years about the importance of studying the context of play, we seldom actually examine the play within the context we study, whether that context be named ritual, festival, games or sport? We hope we are not just making a peevish case as egregious editors of an esoteric little publication who think that everybody should study *play* and nothing else. On the contrary, we think we are all entitled to study whatever we wish . Most of us still suppose we are studying play anyway, but somehow it keeps escaping us because there are more "important" things to do. Either the subject is still too trivial to study or there is something else about it that inhibits direct examination. We believe the charge could be levelled at our association that we have failed to study play. We are the association perhaps for the Anthropological Non Study of Play, (TANSOP).

Masking Texts

If the study of play contexts is often the means for ignoring play, another kind of case is that in which play is the ostensible text but what occurs under that label is actually something else. We want to discuss play as an excuse for cruelty, for sex or intimacy, for sexism, for power, for marginality, for danger and finally most paradoxical of all, for work. It is important to state clearly that we do not mean to talk of those cases where cruelty, sex, power, etc. are incorporated in the play itself and accepted by the players as a part of the prescribed rules. In those cases we can certainly say that the play expresses cruelty but not rightly that it masks it. We are concerned here with masking alone although there is clearly a continuum between expression and masking and much ambiguity surely results when we try to make these distinctions.

(a) Masks for cruelty and violence

The case with which we are most familiar is that within the family, when the older sibling, while playing with the younger one, is recurrently hurtful to that younger one. When the younger runs in protest to the mother, the older cries legitimately that "he was only playing." Under the guise of play, the elder's jealousy and anger at the younger is played out in a variety of hostile ways. Sometimes, however, the cause lies more in the younger sibling's over eagerness to be a member of the play group when he or she is not wanted by the elders. Despite continual punishments, the younger child persists with its efforts to gain membership in the play group so as not be left out of the play. The price of play in these cases is often punishment or mockery, scapegoatery, etc. In short, there are two sources for sibling use of play as a mask for cruelty; one in the older's hostility and the other in the younger's persistence in seeking membership in the play group.

Our first awareness of this kind of case occurred many years ago when working on a research project out of Wayne University with Paul Gump and others (Gump, Schoggen & Redl, 1963). One of our projects was a day study of Wally at home and at camp. Wally was the eldest member of his family and was not very well adjusted at school. As we watched him playing in his home throughout a very long day, it was depressingly clear that while playing with his younger brother, he was constantly, if incidentally, hurting or torturing him in some way or other, but at the same time always calling him back into the lucid realm by promises of further play. One of us who had been a younger brother with a black and blue arm from the constant punches of an older male sibling, is perhaps particularly sensitive to this kind of deception.

In a recent biography, one of our students talked of the way she "got her own back" on an annoying younger sibling by pretending she was going to give her a most special hair do, a permanent wave. She used glue as her mixture, reassuring her sibling throughout that all was well. Ultimately this led to a situation in which the younger sibling required most of her hair cut off for remediation.

Slukin, in his work *Growing up in the playground* (1981), talks of aggression specialists in games . . . "who are normally friendly but go in for bouts of very violent aggression during games . . . Although normally little trouble, these children have periods of wild excitement usually in a game of some sort, when they appear to become out of control and almost invariably manage to hurt someone . . . One four year old, for instance, found that when he was a robber, there was one little girl who was particularly frightened by his frequent invasions of the Wendy house. Soon he took to singling her out and became even more frightening and intimidating on each successive robbery. Eventually she had to be rescued by a teacher" (1981, p. 81).

Slukin refers also to another kind of play mask of reverse import. He says: "What impression does nine year old Ivan leave when he rushes in and shouts, 'You asked for it now, you stinking fucker' (p. 39) and then lets his face melt into a smile?" That is typical, he says, of the way some preadolescents terrorize others. There is an incongruity between what they say and what they do. Here we have play masked as cruelty rather than the reverse. Slukin gives numerous examples of such redefinition of the circumstances, sometimes using the play as a mask for hostility and sometimes hostility as a mask for play. There is great difficulty for adults in separating pretend from real fighting, and the alternations of the boys between what they themselves say is real and what is pretend on a momentary basis can make observations of play extremely deceptive.

A comparison of 19th century children's games from A.B. Gomme's classic 1964 work with modern games shows many more formalized examples of victimization and penalties for the losers written into the game forms themselves (Gomme, 1964). In an era of more everyday physical combat, and everyday physical discipline and violence to children, it is not surprising that games should contain such codicils of cruelty. Nor would we be surprised if there was in general more violent ambiguities with play assuming its mask like rationalizations.

(b) Masks for Sex and Intimacy

Play texts can be masks for sex also, as is most obviously the case in the universal game of doctors. In these games to which adults contribute with occupational nurse and doctor toys, the important point is sometimes to discover something about sexual organs, and perhaps something about how sexual organs feel, even perhaps about the act of sex itself. As long as the activity is labelled as the text called "playing doctors," there is relative safety both from some of the players who may protest at the happenings, such as the taking off of clothes and the probing with sticks into orifices. But even more important, if parents intervene and become angry, it is possible to use the text as a mask of innocence. In this respect some parents are more gullible than the children who use the text both as a mask for sexual investigation and as a mask of rationalization for the innocence of their own activities.

Kissing games, which we wrote about at length many years ago (1959), were also a game text which allowed for the expression of intimacy on a variety of levels of maturity. One could avoid one's chosen kisser or could kiss (in Spin the Bottle), one could keep kissing (in Flashlight) or could give it up and be ousted by another; one could keep it up in kissing without breathing or one could claim being out of breath. The child could legitimately make use of the game text as an expression for a variety of levels of response. One doesn't doubt, however, that there were sometimes cases where the game was but a mask for a heavier dosage of eroticism than would usually be countenanced.

In Kelly-Byrne's inquiry, she played permissively with a seven year old female subject for a year, keeping careful taped documentation throughout (1982). Reviewing her material, it is possible to argue that the child used the play sessions for about six months to play with the investigator in which many different plots involving power, wisdom, beauty, morality, maturity and strength were dramatized. In the third quarter of the year, however, the child dealt with these anticipated play themes mainly in narrative terms, telling stories rather than enacting them. And in the final quarter of the year she virtually gave up these dramas for a discussion of "intimate" matters with which she was concerned, such as boyfriends, pubertal issues, sexuality, etc. It is possible to conclude that all of the early playing was an unwitting mask for her underlying concerns about power and sex, and that the play represented her earliest attempts to state these problems enactively, the narrative her attempts to state them verbally, and that by the end of the year her relationship (her transference) to the investigator was sufficiently strong, and her symbolic envisagement sufficiently explicated, that she was able to get directly to her actual concerns. Perhaps it is wrong to think of play as a mask for intimacy in this case, though it might have been that. It was certainly a passage way to intimacy.

(c) Masks for Power

Since Bateson, many have studied the importance of negotiations in instigating and maintaining play, particularly that of the very young. It has even been shown that for some children, the negotiation is the better part of the bargain. Children would rather argue the game than play it. The joy is the power of control rather than the play (Farrer, 1981). It has often been thought that children must spend so much time arguing because it is difficult to coordinate their ideas, and that is undoubtedly true. But for some that process may become an end in itself and we might argue that the play is a mask for the display of power. We are all acquainted with adults who similarly use their necessary businesses, if not their play, as a mask for power assertion.

As Von Glascoe (1980) and Hughes (1983) have shown so well, the manipulation of the rules is a primary concern in some girls' games (in their cases, Redlight and Four Square). The gaming takes priority over the game, if we mean by the first the manipulation of the rule situation and by the second the customary expectations for action.

Less normative examples of the use of a play text to exercise dominance-subordination hierarchies would be childhood *initiation rites*. These seldom have the conventionalized and institutionalized character that they do in the adult community, and would probably again be excused by the children as a form of play. If they are thought of as play (and not as embryonic forms of initiation, an equally valid position), then again we can see that they are masks for exercises in dominance, exercises in putting the initiate or the gullible in their places. And, of course, again sometimes masks for cruelty. Here are some examples from the *History of Children's Play* (1981), referring to New Zealand of the 1880s and 1890s.

Ducking under the tap was the most widespread of initiation customs. But there were others with a more unique flavor. Of these, "King of the golden sword" was probably the most interesting. "The new boy was made to face the fence with his hands behind his back.

There was a long ceremony about his crowning and entry into the school and then finally the golden sword (which had been dipped into the latrine) was pulled through his fingers" (Mount Cook, 1890; Taita, 1900; Clyde Quay, 1900). "Another initiation rite was 'Pee wee some more yet'. The initiate was blindfolded and ordered to pee-wee some more yet into another boy's cap. The cap turned out to be his own" (Mount Cook, 1890). One cannot help but be struck by the number of times the forbidden parts of the body were involved in these ceremonies. For example: "We would take the boys' and sometimes the girls' trousers down and then spit on their privates" (Hott, 1900). "One very interesting initiation ceremony was to take the new boys down to the stables and wait till a horse was urinating and then spin him under the stream" (Petone, 1900). "He had to eat half a tin of pipis" (Rangitoto, 1900). "We peed in his cap" (Thomas, 1900). "He was invited to a tug of war with his cap. The cap was held in the teeth of the initiate and the teeth of one of the big boys. Hands were supposed to be behind backs. While the struggle was in progress, the big boy urinated over the initiate who could not see the operation because of the hat, but learned about it only gradually and with surprise" (Takaka, 1870).

(d) Masks for Danger

A great deal of play has risk in it. Probably all play requires some uncertainty at least to raise its levels of excitement and challenge. There is clearly risk in physical games; there is risk of loss in gambling games, there is risk of stupidity in strategic games. At what point do we pass beyond reasonable risk into risk which is no longer sensible? Clifford Geertz recently (1973) termed this kind of non-sensible play *deep play,* quoting Bentham at his point of origin. "By it he means playing in which the stakes are so high that it is, from his utilitarian standpoint, irrational for men to engage in it at all . . . men do engage in such play, both passionately and often, and even in face of the law's revenge . . . (in deep play) much more is at stake than material gain: namely, esteem, honor, dignity and respect" (1971, pp. 432-433).

Whether we should speak of such dangerous play as deep play, or as the use of play as a mask for other extremes of conduct becomes a fine point, perhaps not easily disentangled in the participant's mind as he moves through different phases of an activity, some parts of which are done with a spirit of play and others with the cool chill of desperation. Suffice to say that deep play as dangerous activity masked by play is alive and well amongst our own students as the following examples indicate:

- From a 19 year old female:
  "For me my most exciting play was going to Las Vegas with a

middle-aged stranger whom I had met two hours previously in a bar in Philadelphia. He could have killed me, raped me, or left me stranded there with no money. I didn't know anything about his character. However, none of this happened and it was tremendously exciting. Who knows when I'd get another chance to go to Las Vegas. It was dangerous and degrading and I'd never do it again. But I don't regret having done it once. Being a 'gold digger' is one option for a life style and it was interesting to try it on for myself for a day. We went without luggage and only stayed about ten hours. By going with someone I didn't care about I was able to gamble with his money and truly not care when I lost at the tables."

- From a 23 year old male:
"As an active brother in my fraternity there is one weekend each year in which I am required to forego my activities at school and go away with all of my brothers to an isolated campsite miles from Philadelphia. Traditionally we have made it a point to make this travel and the rest of the evening an unforgettable experience of drinking and pleasure (until we pass out). In order not to continually stop for beer we took with us a keg in the backseat. After all we were seniors and decided to do it in the right way. By the time we arrived we had a soaking wet car full of six drunken, stoned, thoroughly wasted guys ready to hit some bars. Never mind that it is illegal to have a single open beer can in a moving vehicle, let alone a tapped keg and a multitude of empty cups and mugs. Never mind that it is illegal to smoke pot alone in a private home, let alone in a moving car filled with incredibly intoxicated fraternity brothers shrieking obscenities out the window in a 'Can you top this' fashion. Never mind speeding and passing on the wrong side, over solid lines on single lane roadways, all illegal. And never mind that road signs depicting curves and intersections are meant to remain on their metal posts and not in the trunks of passing cars. These are all a part of our play."

- From a 21 year old male:
"My favorite play is climbing buildings, water towers and rock faces after a night at the bar. The risk involved is obvious and not lessened by the effect of alcohol. This is an occupation in which a few of us compete to be first to get to the highest point, such as a church steeple. For example, the one at 42nd Street and Spruce is particularly difficult and takes complete concentration particularly after a night at the tavern. Drinking as a precursor to this kind of play is extremely important, not

only to decrease inhibitions about being shot down by the police but also to increase concentration. While this would seem to be a paradox, knowing that you have been drinking creates a counter response that makes one even more careful than usual. Before any step which seems precarious there is a mechanism which hesitates and causes you to evaluate whether the step is really practical or seems practical only because you are drunk. A re-evaluation takes place and only when you are satisfied that it really is a prudent maneuver do you take the step."

By our count from studies of several hundred students, the largest category of deep play volunteered by males involves physical danger often in speeding cars or in sports play and often with drinking added to deepen the risks. Given that 50,000 are killed in motor accidents each year and a quarter of a million are injured, and that over half of these are said to be due to driving under the influence of alcohol, we must also conclude that some of those were only playing. In our survey sports dangers and risks were also important for females. We especially noted the young woman who went mountain climbing in the last stages of her pregnancy and the girl evangelist who liked the excitement of seeking to save souls amongst motor cycle gangs. The largest category for females, however, involved various forms of blind dating, flirting with strangers, provoking jealous boyfriends and rough sexual activity. Quite surprising in these days of the pill, the diaphragm and the vasectomy, the most widely reported instance of deep play (puns apart) was sex without contraception.

(e) Masks for Work

Just as the activities of play, the conventions of games and sports, etc., can be used as masks for other kinds of impulse and action, so also can the *ideas* of play be used as a mask for other things. In adult life play may be used on a metaphoric level more extensively than on an active level. One often hears workers of one kind or another tossing off their activities as "only play." Creative persons as well as routine workers give themselves distinction by pretending that what they have done was but child's play. It is an elitist mark of distinction and of style to act like you are elevated beyond the oppressions that bind most of us. The metaphor of play is a major piece of armament in the competition which makes our lives seem superior to those of our fellows. While it is possible to see the context of such play metaphors as itself a kind of competitive game (and it can be that); mostly it may be the use of play as a mask for one's own dreariness, or even for the not quite excusable passion one has for one's own work, and one's own preference over it beyond other supposedly more human things. In addition, since play has accrued an ideologically positive character, to contemplate that one is playing while working may well improve one's mood even if not into play!

But we can only make this kind of metemorphic and positive usage of play because it is itself seen to be a kind of leisure, and because it is itself romanticised, a point to which we now turn.

Meta Masks

Most of the prior examples of play masked and unmasked depend very much on more general cultural attitudes about play. One cannot use play as a mask for innocence or sex or cruelty unless play itself has about it the air of some virtuous kind. One would suppose that in those societies in which play is an abomination, this kind of positive masking would not work. It is one of the anomalies of the twentieth century that we have reversed earlier puritan ideology on this matter and have come to idealize play superficially and thus make it possible to use it as a cover. The history of this idealization has been detailed elsewhere (Sutton-Smith, 1981). Put briefly, play theory has picked up the attributes of leisure in modern industrial society, i.e. that play must be optional, freed and have intrinsic motivation. This labelling has occurred whether or not play is best described in these terms, and we have contended elsewhere that it is not. Play has also picked up some of the romanticism of elitist doctrines of play as a noble and creative undertaking (Huizinga, 1955). Its greatest cover, however, has been the theory of evolution which has purportedly shown play to be an essential part of both evolution and human development. Most psychological theories of play are but footnotes to the notion of play as a preparation for life. The psychological theories have focused on whether play prepares by mental adjustment by cognitive consolidation, by exploratory arousal, by problem solving, by the potentiation of novel responses, by creativity, etc. In all of this, very little attention has been given to the kind of cruel, scurrilous, obscene, sexual, absurd examples we have given you, nor to the contention of Fagen above (and 1981) that play is often dysfunctional leading to injury and separation from parents and to death, and to Alford's view above that play itself is only one of a number of ways in which more flexible creatures carry out useful preparatory behavior. It is linked in a conglomerate of adaptive forms rather than being the linear link to better development.

As well as idealization, however, play is masked by confusing it with a variety of other functions of intelligent activity. It is constantly confused with the analytic and synthetic functions of intelligence, with exploration and construction, with creative imagination, with practice activity, with reveries and daydreams. It need be none of these, even though it is possible to be playful with any of these as with anything else.

This means that it is possible to avoid or ignore play on this theoretical level as well as on the empirical level. Just as children may use play masks to excuse their abominable behavior, so can play theorists use play to mask their irrelevant studies. We are suggesting that the apparent idealization of play in our era may be only a more sophisticated mask for its neglect.

But the greatest paradox of all in this metamasking activity is that the most outstanding theorist of modern play has also presented us unwittingly with a metamask of play. We refer to Bateson and his theory of play as paradox. Of course it can be argued, on the contrary, that it is he who has shown so clearly the ambiguity and duplicity of play. It is he after all who says play is a kind of paradox; that it is the animal's nip that connotes a bite and not what a bite connotes; that the player says the opposite of what he means in order to mean the opposite of what he says; that play is not only paradox, it is double paradox. The nip not only does not connote what a bite connotes, it is not even a nip in the first place, it is some kind of a galumph, some kind of exaggeration of a nip. Given all this material in Bateson, it would seem that his is a theory which gives due attention to the ambiguity and the potentiality for multiple meanings or multiple maskings in play. How can he be accused therefore of providing us with a theory which is itself a mask?

Simply, we believe that because Bateson was interested to show that relationships as framed in play take on a logical character and therefore generate paradoxes of membership, he was intent on perceiving play as an evolutionary step in metacommunication. This led him to picture children's play as the learning of metacommunication, an emphasis taken up in a major way by subsequent researchers such as Garvey (1977) and Schwartzman (1978). As a result of this emphasis, he did less to explicate his suggestions about the dynamics of play. For example, it is Bateson who says: "The psychological validity of the paradoxical play frame depends on . . . the continual operation of the primary process part of the mind" (1972, p. 184). He goes on to argue that the reason you can believe in these play realms, which are not real in secondary process terms, is that they continue to be real in primary process terms. The peculiarity of play, he says, is that it is a mixture of primary and secondary processes and as such is an archaic language somewhere between the mood signs of animals and regular human language. Play is like therapy in allowing intensive communication between people about love and hate and other relentless human emotions, but framed in such a way as to make the relationship more like a transference phenomenon than an ordinary relationship. The players say to each other, let us communicate "in this particular sort of partly unconscious way."

There is no masking here. Bateson is saying play's paradoxes depend upon play's psychodynamics, or if you will, upon play's disguises of unconscious material. Throughout *Steps to an Ecology of Mind* (1972), however, it is the first part of the message about paradoxes that he emphasizes, not the second part about psychodynamics. And it is this first part that has been taken up so powerfully in much recent play theorizing. Oddly, both parts appear to have been heard in the work of the symbolic anthropologists (Turner, 1982, 1983). Nevertheless, Bateson has contributed to the one-sidedness of most of those who have followed in his footsteps. Because his own concern was largely with communication and metacommunication, he has made it easier to talk about the logic of play than about its illogic. Unwittingly, he has contributed to that idealization and bowdlerization of play which has been a part of the twentieth century's "scientific" approach to play.

　　Is there any way out of this state of affairs? Can we take off the mask of idealization if it is so deeply a part of Western Culture in its relationships with children? Certainly a first step must be to insist on both of Bateson's fundamentals about play, namely that it is both a *metacommunicative* form and that it is a *psychodynamic* manifestation. To do this is to add Bateson's paradox to Freudian disguise and to recognize that we are dealing with a phenomenon of incredible slipperiness. In these terms, play is like dreams in being evasive as to its meanings, but it is like dreams also in bringing to the realm of experience those matters that are of profound importance to the players. But play is unlike dreams insofar as it deals with the real world and with real others. It defends its dreamlike self and attempts to make relationships grow through use of communicational paradoxes which allow the players to deny or defend themselves against those things they want deeply to express. At any time also, impulse can break through this mask into cruelty and danger as we have seen. Play exists constantly on this boundary between acceptable and overt culture and the unacceptable and covert culture. It is like festivals in wishing to deal with the licentious. It is like ritual in trying to make its antithetical impulse life safely boundaried. It is like games and sports in easily falling into conventionalization and cultural institutionalization as limited forms and therefore compromises of play expression. The culture constantly attempts to take hold of the phenomenon and convert it to its normative purposes. In our society this is the tendency to idealization; in others, it can be the use of games for sacred ends; in others, it can be suppression. But play, so readily idealized, just as readily can fall away from normative goals, maintaining a labile edge and assisting the individual and the group in their personal and social integration, whether these be regarded positively or with anxiety by the other members of the society.

　　In sum, the particular evasions which this culture applies to play may have little universality to them, but the readiness with which this labile phenomenon can lend itself to the expression and disguise of conflict of a personal and cultural sort may mean that the masks of play are no accident.

Conclusion

It has been suggested that if we combine the Freudian view of ambivalence with the Batesonian attitude to paradox, we begin to approach the subtleties of the way play functions. Both are masking functions, the one psychogenic, the other sociogenic. The psychogenic disguises our hidden ambivalences, our conflicts with society and within ourselves in symbolic ways but also seeks expression for these. The paradoxical function finds expression for them in subtle worlds where the boundaries can be changed easily and where we can as well deny as express what is revealed there, thus safeguarding ourselves and others from unpleasant revelation. Play in these terms is a devious kind of expression and communication.

This, then, has been a book on the masks of play, on the way in which with our attention to everything but play — to contexts, to experiments, to functional theories — we avoid the subject; on the way in which play itself is used as a mask for other impulses; on the way in which play is masked by identifying it with a variety of functions that are not play or by idealizing it; and finally on the way in which play itself is a paradoxical and disguising phenomenon, lending itself through its various subtleties to the masks, masking and masquerades which we have so readily used to hide it or elevate it and have used to look the other way while looking at ourselves in the only way we can. Play is that paradoxical language of communication and that disguised expression of human feeling which allows us to live as masked while in polite company. In order to register our belief in the importance of this way of considering the devious play phenomenon, and in order to pay adequate homage to the two greatest modern theorists of play, Bateson and Freud, and their play theories of paradox and disguise, we suggest that our own combination of their concepts be known as the *theory of play as PARAGUISE,* which is a neologism we create from their two key terms, paradox and disguise. We hope that by keeping both phenomena clearly in view in this way we can begin at last the scientific unidealized study of play.

BIBLIOGRAPHY

Adams, C.R. Distinctive features in play and games; A folk model from Southern Africa. In Helen B. Schwartzman (Ed.), *Play and culture*. West Point, New York: Leisure Press, 1980. pp 150-162.

Bateson, G. *Steps to an ecology of mind*. New York: Ballantine, 1972.

Csikszentmihalyi, M. *Beyond boredom and anxiety*. San Francisco, California: Jossey Bass, 1977.

Fagen, R. *Animal play behavior*. New York: Oxford University Press, 1980.

Farrer, C. Contesting. In Alyce T. Cheska (Ed.), *Play as context*. New York: Leisure Press, 1981. pp. 195-209.

Garvey, K. *Play*. Cambridge, Massachussetts: Harvard University Press, 1977.

Geertz, C. *The interpretation of cultures*. New York: Basic Books, 1973.

Gomme, A.B. *The traditional games of England, Scotland and Ireland*. New York: Dover, 1964.

Gump, P.V. Schoggen, P., and Redl, F., The behavior of the same child in different milieus. In R.G. Barker (Ed.), *The steam of behavior*. New York: Appleton-Century Crofts, 1963, pp. 169-203.

Handelman, D. Play and ritual, complementary frames of meta-communication. In Chapman & Foot (Eds.), *It's a funny thing*. London: Pergamon, 1977.

Hughes, L. Beyond the rules of the games: Why are the Rooie rules nice? In F. Manning (Ed.), *The world of play*. West Point, New York: Leisure Press, 1983.

Huizinga, J. *Homo ludens*. New York: Beacon, 1955.

Kelly, J.R. Leisure and Sport. In R.F.G. Luschen & G.H. Sage (Eds.), *Handbook of social science of sport*. Stipes, Champaign, Illinois, 1981, pp. 181-196.

Kelly-Byrne, D. *A narrative of play and intimacy: a seven year old's play and study relationship with an adult*. Ph.D. dissertation. Philadelphia, University of Pennsylvania, 1982.

Loy, J. (Ed.) *The paradoxes of play.* West Point, New York: Leisure Press, 1982.

McDowell, J. *Children's riddling.* Bloomington, Indiana: University of Indiana Press, 1979.

Roberts, K. *Contemporary society and the growth of leisure.* London: Longman, 1978.

Schwartzman, H. *Transformations: The anthropology of children's play.* New York: Plenum, 1978.

Slukin, A. *Growing up in the playground.* London: Routledge & Kegan Paul, 1981.

Sutton-Smith, B. The kissing games of adolescents in Ohio. *Midwestern Folklore,* 1959. *9,* 189-211.

Sutton-Smith, B. *A history of children's play.* Philadelphia, Pennsylvania: University of Pennsylvania Press, 1981.

Sutton-Smith, B. "The idealization of play," paper presented at the Second Annual Conference of the North American Society of the Sociology of Sport. Fort Worth, Texas: November 12, 1981.

von Glascoe, C.A. The work of playing "Redlight." In H. Schwartzman (Ed.), *Play and culture.* New York: Leisure Press, 1980. 228-230.

TAASP Publications from Leisure Press

THE STUDY OF PLAY: PROBLEMS AND PROSPECTS.
David F. Lancy and B. Allen Tindall (editors), 1977. This is Volume 1 in the series of the Anthropological Association for the Study of Play's annual volumes of scholarly works, invited papers and reviewed papers concerning contemporary developments and research in the area of play.
918438-06-3. paper $14.95.

STUDIES IN THE ANTHROPOLOGY OF PLAY: PAPERS IN MEMORY OF B. ALLEN TINDALL. Phillip Stevens Jr.
(editor), 1978. Volume 2 of the Anthropological Association for the Study of Play series.
918438-09-8. paper $14.95.

PLAY: ANTHROPOLOGICAL PERSPECTIVES. Michael
A. Salter, PhD. (editor), 1979. Volume 3 of the Anthropological Association for the Study of Play series.
918438-16-0. paper $14.95.

PLAY AND CULTURE. Helen B. Schwartzman, PhD. (editor),
1980. Volume 4 of the Anthropological Association for the Study of Play series.
918438-52-7 paper $14.95.

PLAY AS CONTEXT. Alyce Cheska, PhD. (editor), 1981. Volume
5 of the Anthropological Association of the Study of Play series.
918438-66-7. paper $14.95.

THE PARADOXES OF PLAY. John Loy, PhD. (editor), 1982.
Volume 6 of the Anthropological Association for the Study for Play series.
88011-000-5. paper $14.95.

THE WORLD OF PLAY. Frank E. Manning (editor), 1983. Volume
7 in the Anthropological Association for the Study of Play series.
88011-059-7. paper $14.95.

THE MASKS OF PLAY. Brian Sutton-Smith and Diana Kelly-
Byrne (editors), 1984. Volume 8 in the Anthropological Association for the Study of Play series.
88011-208-5. paper $14.95.